CW00498714

SACRED
THE EVERYDAY

COMPARATIVE APPROACHES TO LITERATURE, RELIGIOUS AND SECULAR

STEPHEN MORGAN, ORG.

聖若瑟大學
UNIVERSITY OF SAINT JOSEPH

Macao, 2021

Title
Sacred and the Everyday: Comparative Approaches to Literature, Religious and Secular.

Author
Stephen Morgan, Org.

Book Series
Orientis Aura. Book Series. - Vol. 2

Chief Editor
João Eleutério

Executive Editor
Miguel Rodrigues Lourenço

Editorial Board
Anna Chan, Arnold T. Monera, Fausto Gómez OP, Franz Gassner SVD, Peter Stilwell, Roberto Ceolin

Copy Editor
Judette Gallares RC

Advisory Board
Armindo Vaz OCD, Edgar Javier SVD, Isabel Varanda, Randolf Flores SVD, Sérgio Ribeiro Pinto

Cover Design
Faculty of Creative Industries
Filipa Martins de Abreu

Cover Image
Macao Street Scene, 1840-1845 / George Chinnery (British, 1774–1852)
Watercolor on paper
7 7/8 x 6 7/16 inches (20 x 16.3 cm)
Museum purchase, Augustine Heard Collection, 1931
M3810.84
Courtesy of the Peabody Essex Museum, Salem, MA. Photography by Mark Sexton.

USJ | University Library and Academic Press

Publication Date: July 2021
Publisher: University of Saint Joseph, Macau SAR (China).
ISBN 978-99965-940-8-3

Printed in United States, United Kingdom, Australia by Lightning Source.
Printed in Brazil, South Korea, Poland, Germany, Russia, China, India, Italy and Spain by Lighting Source's associated Global Connect Channel Partners.

USJ Library Website: http://libraryportal.usj.edu.mo
Email: library@usj.edu.mo
Publication Supported by: Fundação Macau

CONTENTS

PART I THE SACRED AND THE EVERYDAY

PART II THE SACRED AND THE EVERYDAY IN WORSHIP

PART III THE SACRED AND THE EVERYDAY IN LITERATURE

PART IV THE SACRED AND THE EVERYDAY IN RELIGIOUS CONSCIOUSNESS

FOREWORD

The International Comparative Literature Association held its XXII Triennial Congress in Macao in July 2019, fulfilling a desire of its President, Professor Zhang Longxi that the congress should take place in China. The University of Saint Joseph ("USJ") and the University of Macao were honoured to be asked to co-host the Congress. For three days at the end of July the round-table sessions of the forum on comparative literature and religion took place in the historic surroundings of the Seminary of Saint Joseph, by kind permission of the Bishop of Macao, the Most Reverend Dr Stephen Lee Bun-sang JCD, as a cooperative event under the sponsorship of Renmin University of China and the USJ. This forum was organised by Professor Rochelle Ge, then Vice Rector of USJ, Dr Cathy Zhang Jing of the Institute for the Promotion of Chinese Language and Culture in the School of Chinese Studies and Cultural Exchange at Renmin University of China and myself—I was then Dean of the Faculty of Religious Studies at USJ, located at the Seminary.

The round-table brought together twenty-four scholars from across the world—several joining online—in the presence of students and academics from institutions in Macao and elsewhere in China, to present and discuss papers on the theme "The Sacred and the Everyday." This volume brings together a selection of the very best of those papers in order that they may be brought to the attention of a wider public.

The first section of the book contains papers written by arguably the three most distinguished scholars of comparative literature and religion in the world: Professors William Franke of Vanderbilt University, David Jasper of Glasgow and Renmin University of China and Yang Huilin of Renmin University of China. They range widely across the field, exploring important issues about what can and cannot be said, what can and cannot be written, within the limits of language and human religious sensibilities.

In the second part, I join with Andrew Wadsworth and James Bradley to consider the role of texts of religious worship in the Catholic tradition in forming identity, creating perspectives from the sacred to the everyday and vice versa, and sanctifying time. Six essays focused on the theme of the sacred and the everyday in particular authors—from François Cheng to Fabrice Hadjadi, by way of Shakespeare, Austen, Shaffer, Legge and Chesterton—make up the third section of the book. Finally, there are three papers considering the round table theme in religious consciousness: Cyril Law exploring how two individuals from widely differing cultural and linguistic backgrounds grapple with the same issues, Andrew Leong considering the evidence of both Ancient Chinese Literature and the Hebrew Bible and Stephan Rothlin considering the specifically Ignatian response to religious consciousness.

On behalf of the General Editorial Board of the Orientis Aura series of the University of Saint Joseph Press, I should like to thank the contributors to this excellent volume. The tireless work of the book's editor, Miguel Lourenço and the determination of the director of the Press and USJ's University Librarian, Francisco Peixoto should also be recognised with gratitude.

For four hundred and twenty-five years the challenge of bringing into fruitful contact thinkers from East and West has been a constant project of Catholic Higher Education in Macao. USJ is the lineal descendant of the College of Saint Paul, founded by Andrea Valignano in Macao in 1594. This establishment, which educated Matteo Ricci, Tomas Pereira, Adam Schall von Bell amongst others, was the western style first degree-awarding body in the East. In 1728 it transferred much of its teaching to the Seminary of St Joseph, to the buildings in which the ICLA round-table was held and where, in its modern incarnation—the University of Saint Joseph, the only Catholic University in China—this endeavour continues to the present day. This volume is merely the latest in a long line of bringing into dialogue thinkers from East and West but, for all that, is an important contribution nonetheless. To say that the expression of human religious feeling in literature is both universal and persistent is to make no specific religious truth claims but is merely to observe something deserving of enquiry and study. I commend this collection of papers to the reader, confident that few who pick up this book will not find within it something that broadens and deepens their understanding of human experience and awareness of the sacred and the everyday.

Stephen Morgan

Rector, University of Saint Joseph

January 2021

Part I
The Sacred and the Everyday

Amphibolies of the Postmodern: Hyper-Secularity or the Return of The Religious?

William Franke
(Vanderbuilt University)

Modern Progress and Questions Concerning Technology

Since the Renaissance, humanity has made its world over again in its own image in ways unprecedented throughout all the preceding millennia of human habitation of the planet. Science and the advance of technology that it fosters have prodigiously empowered human beings' own fashioning of their world beyond their wildest imaginings. This human advance progressively encroaches upon the material grounds or substrate of our existence and over time undermines apparent objectivities such as "nature" or "things themselves" and even "reality." By the time we get to the ultra-urbanized postmodern world that billions of human beings inhabit today, even our physical environment is, at least in crucial respects, culturally produced to a degree that imposes upon and decisively alters consciousness.

This unremitting trend of development reaches a threshold where it changes our whole orientation as human beings to the world in which we live. The world is for us no longer something solid and immoveable, nor even verifiably external, as if it were given in the nature of things. As fabricated by our own activity, what counts as real is produced as an effect of human instruments and industry. Nothing is given independently of human contrivances. Everything we deal with has already been assimilated into the human and cultural sphere as the product (at least indirectly) of one of our own activities and, to this extent, a projection of our collective ideas or desires. When all (at least, all that really counts in our perspective on things) is generated by our own making—by means of the manifold arts and sciences and technologies that have been developed through unbridled human invention and ingenuity—reality itself is no longer distinguishable from its artificial simulations, or from the appearance or "effect" of reality.

A suggestive symbol that celebrates and exploits this predicament might be found in the Opry Land Hotel in Nashville, Tennessee, where Vanderbilt University is located. As guests exit from their hotel rooms, they are enveloped by a vast indoor simulation of luxuriant nature. In a thinly dissimulated guise, nature itself turns out to be technologically concocted.[1] This is true on a larger scale also of the cities in which we live. We are surrounded by humanly generated environments and find ourselves enmeshed in their operations. We are transported everywhere by vehicles and mechanical contraptions within an ambit totally managed by human engineering.

Take, for example, Hong Kong (or Macau, for that matter, at least in its modern facets), with its ubiquitous elevators and escalators, its plastic-encased pedestrian bridges and moving conveyer walkways, its high-tech towers that colonize the sky. Consider, further, its bewilderingly complex transportation and communications networks, its dense commercial ferment and infrastructure, its neon landscape of flashing advertisements and video screenings in the street. Hong Kong is an epitome of this vertiginous modern experience of urban apocalypse.[2] In such cities, we remain mesmerized by phenomena that are electronically synthesized. The propensity to completely supplant the natural by the artificial is what leads modernity to the brink at which it is precipitated into postmodernity. This happens at the point where the very difference between the natural and the artificial becomes itself just another artifice (at least for human consciousness and experience) and is consequently undermined.

The erosion of this categorical difference comes about inevitably through progressive human intervention in and control over the physical space we live in, as well as through the progressive reflectiveness of concepts such as nature and reality. Such concepts eventually hollow out their own intrinsic meaning as deriving from the inherent natures of things, so that they become nothing but reflections of our own thinking. Reality—or things as they really are—is traditionally presumed to be different from how things *appear* or are perceived in our experience of them, not to mention how they are represented in our inevitably biased interpretations. This difference is particularly marked in the modern era, but it collapses if pushed to the extreme, for then it is apprehended as itself just another human construct. We have become irrevocably aware that there are artificial constructions in any perception of reality that we can articulate—our language itself imposes such artifices. As soon as we *reflect* on the difference between the real and the artificially constructed, it becomes to us no

---

[1] The very postmodern impression made by this experience is described by Graham Ward in his introduction to *The Postmodern God: A Theological Reader*, ed. Graham Ward (Oxford: Blackwell, 1997).

[2] I began teaching postmodern theory in 2005 as visiting professor at the University of Hong Kong in the Department of Comparative Literature. I thank Professor Jeremy Tambling for this invitation and for suggesting this subject as most suitable for Hong Kong's students. The Vanderbilt Divinity School subsequently hosted my lectures on "Postmodern Theory in the Wake of the Death of God." Both venues became locuses for the global reflections on postmodernism presented in this essay. My experience teaching intercultural philosophy in Macao came later (2013–15).

longer something simply given in the nature of things, but rather itself yet another conceptually mediated and defined artifice.

This situation may appear at first to be very new, but that is only a matter of perspective. The typical modern, Western nature/culture binary can be shown through anthropological comparison to be itself something of an aberration from incomparably more widespread and long-lasting perceptions—hailing originally from immemorial primordial cultures—of a continuity. The modern Western nature/culture dichotomy is based on a culturally relative reduction to a "single container universe" by abstracting from the specific enactments of cosmology that throughout untold ages were performed locally and endlessly through ritual practices disclosing various and disparate aspects of what might best be called a "fractiverse."[3] Only the distinction and separation of the cultural from the natural world enables the idea of a *universe*, in which all is subject to one law, to be formulated in the first place, since it is otherwise impossible to encompass the "all" with any single formula. Creativity, spontaneity, and miracle always emerge to disrupt any supposedly purely natural order. This type of revisionary perspective is pioneered especially by Bruno Latour's penetrating demonstration of deep-seated fissures in any rigid nature/culture binary even within Western modernity itself.[4]

Nevertheless, the difference between the human and the natural still seemed clear for at least a certain mainstream modernity, and the inexorable advance of the humanization of the world, through forming and elaborating on the materially given, traced out a clear vector of progress. The project of modernity was to shape reality into conformity with human wishes and ambitions—and thereby to make raw nature into a civilized world and eventually even a work of art. Such a humanized world was intended by Bauhaus architects, for example, to be aesthetically pleasing, as well as to satisfy practical needs. But once the underlying substrate that is supposed to be reality has been completely absorbed into this process of production, it is no longer clear what the direction of progress is or who is mastering what or whom. Without anything to resist human subjectivity and industry from outside it—without some independently standing material to be worked on and gradually made to conform to human purposes—the very idea of *homo faber*, the human maker, enters into crisis.

In this traditional conceit, human self-making depends on having a raw material to work with and from, and thus on relations to something external or other. The basic postulates of modernity, including concepts such as freedom

---

[3] John Law, "What's wrong with a one-world world?," *Distinktion: Journal of Social Theory* 16, no. 1 (2015): 126–39. Citations, 134.

[4] Bruno Latour, *Nous n'avons jamais été modernes: Essai d'anthropologie symétrique* (Paris: La Découverte, 1991), trans. Catherine Porter as *We Have Never Been Modern* (Cambridge: Harvard University Press, 1993).

and the subject, presuppose always some kind of distinction between an objectivity, which is given, and an autonomous subject exercising its liberty in relation to the resistance of an objective world. Once this tension gives way, through the total triumph of the subject that no longer meets with any counterweight in the world, or with anything at all outside itself, notions such as freedom and subjectivity collapse or, more precisely, implode. The very success of human freedom in totally mediating the recalcitrant matter of the exterior world eventually results in the liquidation of human subjectivity altogether. With this liquidation—or, in other words, with the self-deconstruction of the subject—modernity flows out unstopped into the amazing shapes and often monstrous contortions that are now recognizable as characterizing the postmodern era. This era is made immediately manifest in, and can even be identified with, its images—its many mascots and idols.

Just as the objectivity of the world is gradually undermined by its appropriation for human uses, so that it ceases to be able to resist and to set unsurpassable limits to human subjectivity, on the other side of the subject-object binary—and symmetrically—subjectivity finds itself invaded from within by objective structures and forces that it cannot control. In a postmodern era, it is no longer man or the human subject that realizes itself in a controlled and conscious fashion by rational activity. That seemed to be the case, for instance, in the statecraft of modern democracy, which was designed for "the pursuit of happiness" as it was conceived during the Enlightenment and enshrined, exemplarily, in the United States Declaration of Independence (1776). Precisely that ethos of human self-fashioning animated likewise the even more radical and world-historically revolutionary formulation of the "Declaration of the Rights of Man and of the Citizen" by the French Republic ("Déclaration des droits de l'homme et du citoyen," 1789).

Today, however, impersonal structures of administration and economics are seen to dominate all deliberative social and human activities. The desires of the subject are themselves exposed as artificially manufactured by manipulations of an advertising industry driven relentlessly by the imperatives of profit. A dehumanization of the subject opens up from within the very self, in its own immanent sphere of total self-determination. The modernist narrative of steady amelioration of the conditions of life through progressively greater mastery of reality by free human agency and rational control reverses, through its own success, into a dystopian scenario of dissolution of the human subject and of subjection rather to impersonal forces that are incalculable, irrational, and unmanageable. New monstrosities such as the urban jungle and the savage world of high finance and venture capital, with its ruthless takeovers and unscrupulous investment banking strategies that can throw whole economies into crisis, erupt onto the scene. On all sides round, new, unmasterable powers emerge as oppressing and intimidating mere human persons, while single individuals are reduced to abject impotence. Powerful systems exercising inhuman control produce servile and cringing conformism.

Nevertheless, technological progress in the wake of the resurgence of humanism since the Renaissance is crucial to the story of modernity as the conquest of ever-greater human autonomy. The supplanting of the natural by the culturally produced world is basic to modern and postmodern realities alike, indeed their common generative matrix. All this is what we might call the culture of reflexivity. The human being finds itself reflected everywhere in the world it has produced through transforming the environment by which it is surrounded. But the clearly positive valence of this progress of reflexiveness for the modern era becomes equivocal in the postmodern era. It is no longer clear who or what is in control of the prodigious transformations of the world that human activity has set in motion. The powers that dominate the world come to dominate humanity itself, and from within, so that they cannot even be resisted. On this basis, new and pressing questions arise.

Is this humanization of all reality to be seen as the unambiguous teleological goal of human evolution, the natural end of the development of life? Or does it not rather entail the exclusion and repression of some necessary otherness to the human? In other words: What are the ethical and value implications of humanity's attempt to found and ground itself? What "others" are impacted by humanity's remaking the world all around it to suit its own purposes? By what right does humanity constrain the circumambient universe to bear the scars of its own transformation of itself and of everything else in its train and wake?

Postmodern thinkers raised these issues, thereby calling into question certain crucial assumptions of modernism, with its ideology and teleology of unlimited progress, of human self-completion through the unrestrained exercise of its own creative, demiurgic, formative powers. Especially post-structuralist forms of postmodern thought elaborated by Derrida, Deleuze, Irigaray, etc., were obsessed with the claim of the Other. Groundbreaking in this regard was Martin Heidegger's 1953 essay *The Question Concerning Technology (Die Frage nach der Technik)* in which the Other appears in the guise of Being as the source of a mysterious summons and as humanly and conceptually ungraspable. Heidegger's *Letter on Humanism* (*Brief über den Humanismus*, 1947) already drove home this latter point. And he rendered it more concrete in *The Origin of the Work of Art* (*Der Ursprung des Kunstwerks*, 1950), with his metaphorical description of the Earth's unsubdued rebellion against the World, the humanly created order of art and civilization, against which Earth, in time, always resurges to destroy and reclaim its own. The ruins of a Greek temple decaying back into the earth serve here as emblematic. This type of poetic thinking further asserted the relativization of all human constructions and artifices by an unmasterable otherness that must remain forever mysterious.

Certainly, ecology and other political and religious movements, too, in postmodern times have raised their strident objections to the unlimited hegemony of the human. Yet, at the same time, there is another postmodernism that tends to be more the continuation of modernism rather than to question it and place it in check. This is a postmodernism that entails affirmation of, or at least acquiescence in, universal human hegemony, and so in the complete erasure of the Other. It, in effect, endorses the effacement of every trace of any otherness to the human. The total system of the World Wide Web and an international consumer capitalism that brooks no boundaries in the expansion of its global markets evince no qualms and practice no piety in the face of "otherness." In this sense, the postmodern situation can be described aptly as one of "Empire."[5]

We should mark still a further split and admit that there are both serene and troubled versions of this latter sort of postmodernism that is intent upon extending the modern project of conquering the world and exploiting it for human purposes. The troubled version has an ambivalent inclination to turn back in the direction of the self-questioning sort of postmodernism that emphasizes the *crisis* brought about by the project of universal appropriation and humanization of all that is. The triumphant version relinquishes the human and eventually jettisons this notion in order to reach beyond it to affirm the "transhuman."

This self-affirmative modernism, and also some related forms of postmodernism, typically celebrate the progress constituted by all-consuming "human development." They conceive of human activity as perfecting the materials given it by nature, as making the environment humanly friendly and serviceable. Postmodern thinkers are known to pursue this triumphant trajectory beyond the human into the transhuman, leveraging cyborgs and artificial intelligence and gene technology to construct new life forms purportedly superior to and transcending the human.[6]

However, many postmodern thinkers are bothered and even obsessed by the backlash of this process and by the contradictions it engenders. Taken to the extreme, the progress of development undermines its own basis, cannibalizing and altogether obliterating nature. The underlying material support for any human activity whatever can be degraded and destroyed by this very activity itself. Rather than displaying steady progress, it seems that the course of history

[5] Antonio Negri and Michael Hart, *Empire* (Cambridge: Harvard University Press, 2000).

[6] Luc Ferry, *La révolution transhumaniste: Comment la technomédicine et l'uberisation du monde vont boulverser nos vies* (Paris: Plon, 2016) considers both opportunities and risks that emerge with the technologies enabling transhuman development. While apparently untranslated as such, much discussion of *The Transhumanist Revolution: How Technomedicine and the Uberization of the World will Upset our Lives* is available also in English online.

outlines a progressive disaster—and not only in the more ethereal, surreal, postmodern sense of *dés-astre* (literally "unstaring") suggested by Blanchot.[7]

In the typical modern perspective, in any case, one tends inexorably to lose touch with any ground and root for our life standing securely outside of human, technological production. If modernism is a movement based on development and mastery of the natural world, then modernist postmodernism goes even further in this direction and projects a world of pure artifice without any reference or basis or grounding in nature at all. Reality is absorbed and transmuted into simulations and becomes just the mirror image of human activity. There are no longer any original presences that are not produced in perfectly transparent ways by representation. Reality disappears into its simulations and becomes purely virtual, in ways provocatively described and analyzed by Jean Baudrillard.[8] This can be seen as the continuation, but also as a collapse, of the project of modernism. Indeed, the idea of shaping the world in the human image is shattered, as impersonal forces of system and chaos supplant human agency and control.

Carried far enough, human conquest of the world ends up by absolutizing certain finite human powers, and at this point the very success and completion of progressive modernism become its own undoing. The positive powers wielded by human activity no longer work to shape and order the world, whether natural or material, in which they are embedded. Unchecked by any external, resistant reality, these finite powers—for example, fascist governments and multinational corporations—are liable to mistake themselves for unlimited and infinite. And then, in order to effectively assume or assert this status, they must vie for hegemony by attempting to efface or absorb all potential competitors for power. They recognize nothing as simply given, as beyond their power (the Nazi eugenics program, for example, aspired to remake humanity as a superior race), and so they must recreate the whole world out of their own intrinsic structures and resources.[9] But this entails inevitable conflict with every other finite, worldly power which could restrict or limit them.

In this situation, the foundations of human cultural production and construction tend to be corroded by their own development *in extremis*. The limits within which the development of human culture made sense and could be shown to be a positive progression are exceeded. Progression appears no

---

[7] Cf. Maurice Blanchot, *L'écriture du désastre* (Paris: Gallimard, 1980), trans. Ann Smock as *The Writing of the Disaster* (Lincoln: University of Nebraska, 1995).

[8] Jean Baudrillard, *La précession des simulacres* (Paris: Minuit, 1978). In English, see Baudrillard, *Simulacra and Simulation*, trans. Sheila Faria Glaser (Ann Arbor, MI: University of Michigan Press 1994).

[9] Cf. Giorgio Agamben's analysis of the logic of sovereignty in *Homo Sacer: Il potere sovrano e la nuda vita*, vol. 1 (Turin: Einaudi, 1995), trans. Daniel Heller-Roazen as *Homo Sacer: Sovereign Power and Bare Life* (Stanford: Stanford University Press, 1998).

longer to be true or real, nor to be clearly distinguishable from regression. It may still be possible to affirm the surpassing of values such as truth and reality as outmoded, so as to reinsert these more complicated developments back into the modernist narrative of continuing progress. Yet such affirmation and optimism, together with the *grand récit* or metanarrative of progress that undergirds them, are also themselves liable to being rejected as outmoded. A mood of peering anxiously into the inscrutable, without any comforting narrative of linear progression at all, is—at least equally, if not more—characteristic of the postmodern age.

Beyond the consternation it likely causes, this loss of a sense of direction and of a vision of the goal of human progress can also be exhilarating. The mystery of existence in and for itself, freed from all human constructions of its purpose, is rediscovered in its sheer miraculousness. The world may again become estranged for us, even as we become "strangers to ourselves" ("étranger à nous mêmes," as Julia Kristeva writes) once there is no positively definable program that precomprehends the world and us.[10]

This suggests how postmodernism follows the development of modernism to its furthest consequences and results in certain reversals and in some respects in a *reductio ad absurdum* of the hopes and program of modernism. Elimination of any alien reality outside of human making and culture results in a wildness appearing unaccountably from within: our world and we ourselves become unknowns. This is the opposite side of the coin from the absolute banalization of human life produced by the rampant technologization that reduces everything, including human beings, to digital systems of 0s and 1s and to meaningless, mechanical activity. Poles of opposition, such as subject versus object, apparent versus real, given versus made, collapse when human creative power and shaping activity makes absolutely everything over again in its own image.

Of course, there is always some sort of a support, some material or perhaps spiritual basis for this activity, and forgetting this substrate sets it up to come back with a vengeance in unexpected, often unconscious ways: we find ourselves facing the return of the repressed. What had been treated as exterior to humanity then turns up as a dark, shadowy, nightmarish underside within its own all-encompassing life and consciousness. This exteriority discovered as arising from within turns out to be, at least for some interpreters, a rediscovery of the religious (or the sacred).

Such a radical otherness to—or of—humanity can be recognized as the continuation of the experience of the sacred or divine as it was known in pre-

[10] Julia Kristeva, *Étrangers à nous-mêmes* (Paris: Fayard, 1988). The implications for a "religious turn" of Kristeva's thought are finely sifted by Arthur Bradley, "'Mystic Atheism': Julia Kristeva's Negative Theology," *Theology & Sexuality* 14, no. 3 (2008): 279–92.

modern times. At that earlier stage, the divine still wore strange faces that had not been made over in the image of man. These faces could be frightening like those of the fiery Cherubim guarding the gates of Paradise against human reentry in Genesis 3:24. Postmodern religion is apt, in this manner, to recover a sense of the numinous as it was experienced before the humanization of God through anthropomorphic, so-called "revealed" religion. The world can become reanimated and subjectified, perhaps even "reenchanted," as is suggested by certain influential exponents of postmodernism.[11]

Genealogies of Two Mutually Opposed Postmodernisms

Mark C. Taylor, in "Postmodern Times" (and elsewhere), distinguishes between a "modernist" postmodernism and an alternative "poststructuralist" postmodernism.[12] Modernism is understood by Taylor as the enactment of the outlook first reached by German idealism and fully articulated in Hegel's system: the subject achieves total consciousness of reality through complete and total representation of it as nothing but an object for a subject. Human activity, as Spirit, finds itself mirrored in everything as the principle of all reality. This is a rigorous and systematic working out on an intellectual level of the postulate of human autonomy—of the human subject as the only maker of its own world. This is the principle that has been realized in Western civilization since the Enlightenment, eminently through technical and technological advances. It is the prolongation of the project inaugurated by Descartes and his program of a science based on the conscious subject ("I think, therefore I am") as Archimedean point for leveraging the whole universe. Heidegger would later designate this historical epoch as "the age of the world picture" ("Das Zeitalter des Weltbildes," 1938) —meaning that reality is equated with a subject's representation of the world. Our making it into a picture enables the world to be totalized and comprehended on the basis of principles totally immanent to the human subject.

Although Hegel himself was not always necessarily a direct influence on the majority of modernist artists and writers, Madam Blavatsky's theosophy and Rudolf Steiner's anthroposophy did achieve wide diffusion in the ambiences of modernist art, and they in effect mediate the idealist view of a universe perfectly knowable as pure form in consciousness. Postmodernity moves in two directions from this point. On the one hand, it can extend the aestheticization of reality turned wholly into an object of representation for a subject. The

---

[11] David Ray Griffin, ed., *The Reenchantment of Science: Postmodern Proposals* (Albany, NY: SUNY Press, 1988) gathers together a selection of such voices.

[12] "Postmodern Times," in *The Otherness of God*, ed. Ollin F. Summerall (Charlottesville, VA: University of Virginia Press, 1998), 175–89. Of Taylor's many writings touching on this subject, the cited essay is perhaps the most concise digest.

historical dimension of temporal development that is so crucial to Hegel's vision is elided in the immediacy of this purely aesthetic version of postmodernism. The simultaneity of all things together in one immediate sensation is experienced in typically postmodern forms of hyperreality such as cyberspace and virtual universes. All grounding in historical reality drops out, but still the total connectedness of all in one is affirmed and indeed appears now enhanced as empowered by new technologies in previously unimaginable ways.

On the other hand, there is the historical consciousness of a radical disconnect, of the ending of the modern project in abject failure. This raw awareness will develop into disconsolate and sometimes at least apparently incoherent forms of postmodern expression. Modernism was already acutely conscious of a brokenness in the world as represented, for example, by T. S. Eliot—in the fragments which he "shored against [his] ruin" in *The Waste Land.* Still, modernism generally sought to transcend this predicament through art. No longer necessarily believing, as some Romantics did, in a seamless organic wholeness between art and reality, nevertheless modernists typically deemed some kind of wholeness to be possible at least in the aesthetic sphere cultivated, for example, by Walter Pater in his essays on the Mona Lisa and other subjects especially in Renaissance art *(Studies in the History of the Renaissance*, 1873). Friedrich Schiller's aesthetic education of humankind (*Briefe über die ästhetische Erziehung des Menschen*, 1793–94) had envisaged using art to reconstruct human wholeness after the initial lesions and dismemberment of the dawning industrial age and the breaking up of the classical pursuit of wisdom into specialized areas of scientific knowledge. This vision of wholeness in the midst of fragmentation leads to the comprehensive aesthetic masterpieces of high modernism, eminently Proust's *À la recherche du temps perdu* and Joyce's *Ulysses*.

The postmodern age, in contrast, does not often produce consummate works of art like *The Waste Land* or Picasso's *Les Demoiselles d'Avignon*. Masterpieces of art with high spiritual aspirations such as the paintings of Kandinsky, Malevich, Mondrian, and Barnett Newman are quintessentially modernist. In postmodernist productions, the high seriousness of modernist art is often exchanged for triviality and irony (although there are certainly notable exceptions like the paintings of Anselm Kiefer). This type of postmodern perspective envisages the total realization of the real here and now in the profane world. The "real" is immediate in the image. Signs no longer have clear external referents, but rather than being discarded in a direct assault upon the absolute, as in modernist abstract expressionist painting, they are themselves absolutized: signs are made into images that are themselves, even as simulations, completely real or rather *hyperreal.*[13]

There is another possibility, however, in this revolution of the sign in relation to the real—the possibility of admitting that the signs are empty and that we are left without any access to reality, which thenceforth is irrevocably lost and an absence for us. This leads to a postmodernity that does not proclaim absolute presence of the real as immediate, aesthetic, and iconic, but rather its infinite absence as absolute difference and deferral. The real is never attainable: it is only a trace of what can never be present as such. This turns postmodernity in the direction of the elusive, unattainable Other—the type of postmodernity pursued by Derrida in the wake of Levinas, or by Kristeva following Lacan.[14] In either type of postmodernism, that of total presence or that of insuperable absence, the relation between sign and referent has been broken, and there is no longer any claim to grasp the deep structure of the universe. There is no key to the essence of reality, such as modernist art seemed to promise. There is no longer even any "reality" that can be intelligibly spoken of or thought about. Precisely "reality," as basis or fundament for thinking and life and language, has proved illusory and been abandoned. It has been dissolved into bottomless simulation.

In either case, the relation of phenomenon to ground and of sign to referent breaks down and becomes a matter of indifference or of an impossibility of relation. No longer concerned with signs as relating to some external reality, postmodernism deals with images that are only themselves, or rather with simulations that usurp the reality of what they represent. When the sign becomes fully identified with reality, there is no longer any otherness to reality beyond or behind what it manifestly is or signifies. Immediacy flips over into infinite mediation that never arrives at any destination. Either this world of images can be proclaimed as the absolute fulfillment of human desire, the overcoming of alienation and need in the state of nature, or else it can be felt as itself empty, in which case desire is directed to something beyond the world as the totality of signs and images that desire fabricates. The first alternative produces a form of postmodernism that is the continuation of the project of modernism and its completion, fulfilling it infinitely by erasing all opposition to human making in the total realization of the real as a work of art (or artifice). The second alternative results in a form of postmodernism that looks beyond this

[13] This process of the implosion of signs producing "simulacra" is described most originally by Jean Baudrillard, for example, in *L'échange symbolique et la mort* (Paris: Gallimard, 1976), especially pp. 110–17 on "L'hyperréalisme de la simulation."

[14] Creston Davis, Marcus Pound, and Clayton Crockett, eds., *Theology After Lacan: The Passion for The Real* (Eugene, OR: Cascade, 2014) emphasize that the Lacanian impossible object, the *objet petit* a, is precisely not "the big Other" of much traditional theology (11).

achievement of the technological world as a total system of human self-realization to what is altogether and irreducibly other than it.

Taylor finds the seeds of both of these forms of postmodernism in Kierkegaard's reaction to the Hegelian system. Kierkegaard's aesthetic stage of existence prefigures the modernist postmodernism, which thinks itself in possession, if not of reality, then at least of its effects and sensations, in the immediacy of the image. But beyond this, Kierkegaard envisages an ethical and, above all, a religious stage of existence that respects the absolute difference and unknowability of what it is attuned to, without ever being able to attain to or possess it. Here, too, there is a notable lack of any foundation in a reality that can be securely grasped: and this predicament leaves human beings in fear and trembling vis-à-vis a numinous presence that they can in no way pin down.

The experience of being suspended within a maze of signs, with no way of getting outside them, has these two very different valences, and both tendencies have produced much postmodern art. The black comedy of Kafka's novels, of never knowing why one is being prosecuted (*The Trial*) or of being perversely obstructed in one's task as land surveyor (*The Castle*), expresses the perplexity of the second attitude, which relates to an inscrutable transcendence, whereas Andy Warhol's pop art brashly exploits the deliberate, unrepentant superficiality of the first attitude, in which the image is apotheosized into reality itself. Taylor's *Disfiguring*, his religious genealogy of postmodern art and architecture, accords Warhol a special place of prominence as realizing the modernist postmodernism that seamlessly coheres and colludes with the world and knows nothing of any Other: "The world that Warhol represents is the world of postindustrial capitalism. The aestheticization of the commodity and the commodification of l'oeuvre d'art join in the 'realized utopia' of the culture industry celebrated in Warhol's art. 'Making money,' Warhol exclaims, 'is art!'"[15]

Taylor suggests that Warhol's art is "a perverse realization of the utopian dreams of modernity, in which art and life become one. Pop art discovers redemption by redeeming appearances" (p. 181). Since signs are no longer taken to signify anything real, they become themselves the only reality that can be known or experienced and are in this sense absolute. Any other reality beyond them is abolished, and we find ourselves under the reign of the simulacrum. Jean Baudrillard explains that "Pop art signifies the end of perspective, the end of evocation, the end of witnessing, the end of the creative gesture and, not least of all, the end of the subversion of the world and of the malediction of art. Not only is its aim the immanence of the 'civilized' world, but its total

---

[15] Mark. C. Taylor, *Disfiguring: Art, Architecture, Religion* (Chicago: University of Chicago Press, 1992), 178.

integration in this world. Here there is an insane ambition: that of abolishing the annals (and the foundations) of a whole culture, that of transcendence."[16]

Along lines similar to those of Baudrillard, Taylor analyzes pop art as idealistic, as "an idealism of the image." There is no other reality than that of the image, so the image is real and the complete realization of the ideal, a utopia of the simulacrum. As Warhol says with disarming simplicity and candor, "Pop art is liking things." Something like this applies also to pop artists such as Roy Lichtenstein, Jasper Johns, and Robert Rauschenberg. For the equivalent in architecture, under the rubric of "logo centrism," Taylor highlights the work of Philip Johnson, James Stirling, Charles Moore, and Michael Graves, with his Walt Disney World hotels. This architecture is supposed to be fun and entertaining. In line with Venturi, and in the spirit of Las Vegas, such building represents the realization of utopia in the modernist vein, but also in a new orgy of superficiality bringing in incongruous content to disrupt the deep structure and formalist purity of high modernism. Their eclecticism and historicism, making a modern skyscraper in a gothic style, for example, mixing traditional and modern building materials, parodying pure forms by suspending and complicating them (Stirling), facilitate an illusory realization of all time and place here and now. This is the pretense also of the ubiquitous Disney World theme-parks and the casino-hotels—"Lisboa," "Venetian," "Parisian," "Greek," "Galaxy," "World of Dreams"—that mushroom all across Macao in Greater China in imitation of Las Vegas, but multiplied times nine.

For Hegel, absolutely everything fits together in a totally organic system. The Logos gives the underlying and centering principle on the basis of which everything is aligned and combined. Aesthetic postmodernism has assimilated the lesson that there is nothing outside the system, but this insight is no longer seen as a logical illumination of the real and a grasp of existence in terms of concepts. The self-enclosure of the system in pure immanence has abandoned this dimension of depth and of connection with reality. All phenomena are taken at face value and not as necessarily connected through any deeper essence, especially not through any underlying logic or principle. This is a world without depth and without transcendence. It absolutizes surface and appearance, for they are now freestanding and autonomous, not the surface and appearance of any underlying reality.

The alternative postmodernism that does not erase difference (the difference between the manifest and the latent, between the same and the other, between the ordinary or worldly and the uncanny or even sacred, etc.), but remains obsessed by it, echoes Kierkegaard's religious stage of existence, which is meant to challenge Hegel's seamless system fundamentally. Taylor finds it

---

[16] Jean Baudrillard, "Pop: An Art of Consumption?," in *Post-Pop Art*, ed. Paul Taylor (Cambridge: MIT Press, 1989), 35, quoted by Taylor, ibid.

in the art and architecture of André Masson, Peter Eisenman, and especially in the work of Michael Heizer, Michelangelo Pistoletto, and Anselm Kiefer. In these artists, the repressed difference of the unrepresentable and unassimilable returns and leaves an open wound that can never be healed, according to Taylor.

In "The Painter and Modern Life," Baudelaire wrote that, "By modernity I mean the ephemeral, the fugitive, the contingent, the half of art whose other half is the eternal and the immutable" ("La modernité, c'est le transitoire, le fugitive, le contingent, la moitié de l'art, dont l'autre moitié est l'éternel et l'immuable").[17] Taylor aligns high modernist postmodernism with the second of these aspects and the more self-critical postmodernism with the first. There are ways in which the modernist postmodernity makes even more exaggerated claims to total or eternal presence than modernism did. This style of postmodernity evidently declares the total presence of God in unprecedented carnality and materialism, extending nineteenth-century "theoesthetics": "the return of repressed figuration, which disfigures the purity of the abstract work of art, coincides with the death of the transcendent God, who reappears as radically incarnate in natural and, more important, cultural processes" (*Disfiguring*, p. 145). For modernism, Taylor remarks, "the goal of theoesthetics is union with the Absolute or the Real, which underlies or dwells within every person and all phenomena" (*Disfiguring*, p. 152). Such a goal is given up and is often mocked in other postmodern circles that are more ascetic and rigorous, less cocky and self-glorifying.

Nonetheless, we should not overlook the important fact that precisely because for postmodernism this presence is no longer real, it can become total: it becomes total simulation because there is nothing real to stand outside of and over against it. Postmodernism implies the removal of the original and of the authentic, but then an ersatz "presence" may very well take on totalizing guises and extend itself all across the global network. With no real basis or foundation in anything outside itself, there is nothing to prevent this total fabrication of presence from turning itself into total presence since there is no longer any way to distinguish between the simulated and the real. "Reality" is itself apprehended as a simulation.

The Foundations Metaphor Discarded: From Modernity to Postmodernity

One of the metaphors most basic to the whole movement of modernism is the metaphor of foundations, and accordingly the passage into the age of postmodernism can be characterized most succinctly as consisting in a shattering of foundations. Descartes, at the inception (or rather one of the inceptions) of

[17] "Le peintre de la vie moderne," in *Œuvres complètes de Charles Baudelaire*, vol. 3: *L'Art Romantique* (Paris: Calmann Lévy, 1885), 69.

modern thought, uses this metaphor in his *Discours de la méthode* (1637) to describe how he is going to build the edifice of knowledge on the unshakeable certainty of self-consciousness expressed in his first principle: "I think, therefore I am." When this foundation falls away, we enter into the uncertain, foundationless dimension of postmodernism. Anticipating and provoking such an event, the certainty and unity of the self are undermined in different ways by Nietzsche (through constitutive metaphors and masks) and by Freud (through unconscious thoughts and desires). Both of these thinkers prepare for the breaking out of radical attacks against the integrity of the subject that characterize the postmodern thought of Deleuze, Lacan, Derrida, Irigaray, Foucault, etc.[18] The self interpreted as subject can no longer serve as foundation for knowledge, or even for consciousness and experience.

Modernism (from Latin *modo* meaning "just now") is obviously conscious of some kind of discontinuity with the past, of being a new and different epoch with respect to what has gone before. Yet the newness is typically a matter of a new beginning on new foundations that restore a ground after loss and devastation left in the wake of preceding history. Whatever foundations past cultures were working from have become dispersed in the course of their evolution. The architects of *modernism* decide that it is *now* time to begin again, and in order to do so they define new principles, axioms, and foundations from which to work. Descartes did this in philosophy. Kandinsky, Mondrian, and Malevich attempted to do it in painting. Le Corbusier, the *Bauhaus* movement, and Mies de van der Rohe pursued such aspirations in architecture. And Stravinsky, Schoenberg, and Berg brought forth something comparable in music, with a new twelve tone or even atonal system.

Even though modernism sought to "make it new," in the slogan so often repeated after Ezra Pound, the refounding was almost invariably a return to something that was already there, to one's own past appropriated and understood and "owned" for the first time. The new, in this sense, is actually a renewal. It is a recovery of one's long lost heritage and ground. Accordingly, modernism was also typically about rediscovering the primitive, as in Picasso's and Braque's fascination with the masks of Africa and Oceania and with the arts of other primordial cultures. Modernism, while making it new, was at the same time a search for origins. Especially alluring in this regard were aboriginal, tribal societies supposed to be living in some kind of unbroken continuity with nature. The desire for foundations can also be a desire to unite with the primitive and original. Since this is a way of *appropriating* such origins, modernist primitivism at the same time expresses a will to be autonomous and without dependence on any outside or Other. *Finnegans Wake* and *The Waste Land* can be placed alongside each other in this category of high modernism. As

[18] Well-selected, representative texts of these and other crucial figures can be found in *From Modernism to Postmodernism*, ed. Lawrence Cahoone (Oxford: Blackwell, 2003).

Eliot states in his notes, he based his manifesto modernist poem on the quest myth of the Holy Grail, as treated most directly by Jessie Weston in *From Ritual to Romance* (1920), but he includes also references to the Upanishads and many other traditions with a view to their source texts. Similarly, primitive religious practices, particularly druidical ones, but also rites deriving from world cultures ranging from Scandinavia to Egypt to Tibet and China, are evoked all through Joyce's culminating text in its promiscuous reshuffling of the universe and of the archives of human consciousness. Pound's *Cantos* likewise embody this fragmenting, and yet also eclectically universalizing, method on an epic scale. They constantly turn their attention to resuscitating, or at least to resurfacing, submerged origins.

Such quests for origins are generally given over in the postmodern age. At least they are not taken earnestly as tendering the keys to any kind of salvation. Interest in them or their residues is more likely to be colored with irony. This can leave the postmodern mind disabused and empty of the pretenses of the great, constructively modernist projects. There may still be a pervasive mood of desolation and of mourning for irrecoverable loss. But the postmodern condition can also generate a much smugger and more sanguine attitude of self-satisfaction on the part of those who have no need to search for anything beyond their own immanent awareness because all such searching is exposed as metaphysical illusion. The consumer society and the culture of the "me generation" also express certain unrepentantly self-serving, Narcissistic aspects of the phenomenon of postmodernism. There is in this type of postmodernism the exhilaration of cutting free from all narratives of the past, even without having any sense of direction for the future. In fact, there is no future for postmodernism. Neither is there any real past. There is only an ever-elusive present. With its dismantling of historical narrative, this fictitiously constructed present has come from nowhere and is going nowhere. Thus, perhaps there is not any real present either—that too is but an illusion, or rather a simulation. Postmodernism of this ilk locates itself in a cyberspace without real time. Unbounded by past or future, the present leaks away into nothing real.

In such postmodernism, none of the tenses can serve as a foundation for time and for building a continuous life or history. The gesture of refounding that characterized modernism is typically rejected by the postmodern sensibility. The feeling is rather that there are no foundations: we begin always in *medias res*. Nor is there any real destination or goal or completion that can be envisaged. Such beginnings and endings, *arche* and *telos*, would be the pivot points for some *grand récit*, some master narrative such as no longer holds sway, according to Lyotard's summary definition of postmodernism as "incredulity towards metanarratives" ("En simplifiant à l'extrême, on tient pour 'postmoderne' l'incrédulité à l'égard des métarécits").[19]

In the modernist vision, art can function as a means to the fulfillment of human potential, to the achievement of total presence of the ideal in the real, or in other words to the realization of the *Parousia*—the divine Presence, or Kingdom Come. Something like this was Schiller's vision for the purpose of art as serving for the aesthetic education of humankind, which laid down important premises for modernism already in the late eighteenth century. The theosophists applied basically the same vision, derived from the German aesthetic and religious thinking of Kant, Schleiermacher, Schelling, Schiller, and Hegel, in ways that had a direct influence, through Madam Blavatsky and Rudolph Steiner, on modernist founding figures from Kandinsky to Mondrian to Malevich. The old alchemical dream of purity and perfection in human identity with the divine is realized as total presence in a variety of modernist projects. *Finnegans Wake* is "the crucial text," as Ihab Hassan puts it,[20] for this realization of presence in the textual present of Joyce's writing, for example, in the last lines of *Finnegans Wake*:

> Lff! So soft this morning, ours, Yes. Carry me along, taddy, like you done through the toy fair! If I seen him bearing down in me now under whitespread wings like he'd come from Arkangels, I sink I'd die down over his feet, humbly dumbly, only to washup. Yes, tid. There's where. First. We pass through grass behush the bush to. Which! A gull. Gulls. Far calls. Coming. far! End here. Us then, Finn, again! Take Bussoftlhee, mememormee! Till thousendtsthee. Lps. The keys to. Given! A way a lone a last a loved a long the

This text, with its explosive phonemic plenitudes, intimates and performs the pure presence of apocalyptic simultaneity of all reality.

Modernity is focused on the present, the time that it distinguishes and privileges by marking it as modern, as "now." According to Taylor, who quotes these lines, "Despite its complexity, the presence of modernism can be understood as, among other things, the conviction that presence is realizable in the present" (*Disfiguring*, p. 12). Everything is enacted in the "now" (again, literally *modo* in Latin) of *modernity*. In postmodernism, not only does the self shatter as a metaphysical postulate and the subject disintegrate as an epistemological first principle; not only does the free agent of ethical action lose its self-mastery and its ability to determine itself and even just its own will: in addition,

---

[19] Jean-François Lyotard, *La condition postmoderne: Rapport sur le savoir* (Paris: Minuit, 1979), 7.

[20] Ihab Hassan, "POSTmodernISM: A Paracritical Bibliography," in *From Modernism to Postmodernism: An Anthology*, ed. Lawrence Cahoone (Oxford: Blackwell, 2003).

all areas and aspects of individual existence and collective social life are affected and are, in fact, shaken to their foundations.

In postmodernity, the identity of self with itself becomes impossible since the inextricably temporal self is constituted by a past that can never actually be re-presented and a future that can never actually arrive. The full self-presence of the subject is thus impossible. "Always hurrying to grasp the fleeting here and now, representation can only re-present a presence/absence that never is and never can be fully realized … representation inevitably opens the gap it seeks to close ... Inasmuch as all presentation is representation, the subject's struggle to secure identity and establish a proper name *inevitably* fails."[21] Any simple sort of self-identity is precluded by Taylor's, as by almost any other, style of postmodern thought, and the unity of the world, too, consequently disintegrates.

In postmodern science, chaos replaces natural law. Chaos and complexity theory reckon with an open universe in which there is ultimately no foundation for the intricate order of things that simply arises inexplicably. Biological developments come to be understood as random. Life processes are open to chance. They are based on exchanges of information that may or may not arrive: only probabilities can be calculated. Life has no concrete foundation, no tangible substance or intrinsic nature. It consists only in a coded reference with content of an abstract nature within a formal system. Biological processes are understood simply as communication of information without substance. Viruses and antibodies dissolve into messages rather than consisting in material bodies as such.[22] This, of course, can also be understood as an emancipation from materialism and as the re-enchantment of the modern world.[23] It has been so construed by certain postmodern interpreters such as David Ray Griffin and also by a flourishing group of theorists writing in Taylor's wake. Collaborators such as Jeffrey Kosky have consecrated themselves especially to the interpretation of modern art.[24]

Following up on Taylor's project, Bradley Onishi and Tyler Roberts develop such a line of interpretation into a vibrant, religiously cultivated and

---

[21] Mark C. Taylor, *Erring: A Postmodern A/theology* (Chicago: University of Chicago Press, 1984), 49.

[22] Taylor extends his interpretation of postmodernism into these arenas of culture especially in *About Religion: Economics of Faith in Virtual Culture* (Chicago: University of Chicago Press, 1999).

[23] Jane Bennett, *The Enchantment of Modern Life: Attachments, Crossings, and Ethics* (Princeton, NJ: Princeton University Press, 2001).

[24] Jeffrey L. Kosky, *Arts of Wonder: Enchanting Secularity—Walter De Maria, Diller + Scofidio, James Turrell, Andy Goldsworthy* (Chicago: University of Chicago Press, 2012).

sensitive form of "non-secularist secularity."[25] Other direct students of Taylor, including Thomas Carlson and Mary-Jane Rubenstein, have been influential in advocating this approach to using continental philosophy to revive a sense of the importance of religion to culture even in a postmodern age after the collapse of the Weberian secularism thesis.[26] In Carlson's terms, the "apophatic analogy" between mystical experience of an ineffable God and the existential experience of death as the impossible (since the experiencing subject would no longer be there to have the experience) opens a field in which religious phenomena and texts interpret the meaning and reveal the significances of our modern, secular life. They reveal our existence at its limits and in its most extreme, but also its most characteristic, forms. There is much emphasis in the wake of Taylor on the visual arts, but literary tradition is just as apt to become the vehicle of a kind of secular form of religious revelation—as my own work in literature and religion over several decades, notably *Secular Scriptures*, has been at pains to demonstrate.[27]

The collapse of foundations can lead in a direction of absolute immanence in which the secular world is all in all, and religion, with its projection of a transcendent divine ground, is definitively banished. Lack of foundations is then synonymous with lack of religion, and postmodern culture can be defined by its emancipation from religion. On the other hand, the collapse of foundations, or of any solid basis, can also be experienced as an intrinsic feature of the system: as such, it can become an excruciating wound that can never be stanched. Literary tradition from ancient to postmodern times offers innumerable compelling illustrations of this constitutive woundedness. Paul Celan's poetry proffers a poignant contemporary case in point.[28] The lack of foundations means that, so far from being unnecessary and irrelevant, the foundations

[25] Bradley B. Onishi, *The Sacrality of the Secular: Postmodern Philosophy of Religion* (New York: Columbia University Press, 2018). Tyler Roberts, *Encountering Religion: Responsibility and Criticism After Secularism* (New York: Columbia University Press, 2013).

[26] Mary-Jane Rubenstein, *Strange Wonder: The Closing of Metaphysics and the Opening of Awe* (New York: Columbia University Press, 2010). Thomas A. Carlson, *The Indiscrete Image: Infinitude and Creation of the Human* (Chicago: University of Chicago Press, 2008).

[27] My first book—*Dante's Interpretive Journey* (1996)—was published in the series on Religion and Postmodernism edited by Taylor at the University of Chicago Press. I have continued this trajectory in several books, including most recently *A Theology of Literature: The Bible as Revelation in the Tradition of the Humanities* (Eugene, OR: Wipf & Stock Publishers, 2017); *Secular Scriptures: Modern Theological Poetics in the Wake of Dante*, Literature, Religion, and Postsecular Studies series, ed. Lori Branch (Columbus, OH: Ohio State University Press: 2016); and *The Revelation of Imagination: From Homer and the Bible through Virgil and Augustine to Dante* (Evanston, IL: Northwestern University Press, 2015).

[28] I pursue this in "Paul Celan, Dante's Manfred, and the Woundedness of Language as our Common Bond," in "Paul Celan Today," ed. Michael Jacob, special issue, *Compar(a)ison: An International Journal of Comparative Literature* 2013/1 (2017): 131–43.

that are lacking *because they are lacking* become the overriding obsession of a culture. Everything is directed towards what *would* found this world but is, in fact, experienced always only as lacking. In this case, pure immanence is not the fulfillment of desire and of the dream of immediacy of access to everything, but the perpetuation of a state of unfulfillment, of being separated from the real, the divine, the Other, which is never encompassed within immanence but is none the less paramount as the missing ground of all that is. Thus, religious modes of experience become paradigmatic rather than indifferent in this second way of interpreting postmodernism. The sphere of pure immanence is an emptiness that implodes and opens us outward in the direction of what the secular world can never comprehend. The loss of foundations can be interpreted thus either as the definitive realization or as the complete undermining of the modern secular world.

Such an ambiguity produces the uncannily disguised ambivalence toward theology of a paradigmatically postmodern thinker such as Gilles Deleuze. Famous for hammering theology at every opportunity, he nevertheless unwittingly lends himself to being construed as an iconoclastic theologian.[29] At one point, Deleuze defines theology as "the science of non-existent entities."[30] Such "entities," nevertheless, condition real experience throughout its whole extent and "animate language." Beyond or before "re-ality" (consisting in signifiable things—*res*), something else is exposed that escapes signs. Consequently, the typical Deleuzian insistence on immanence in the end points to a dimension wholly other than what can be signified.[31] As the currents of thought flowing now over several decades especially from Mark Taylor's work in religion and postmodernism indicate, extreme secularism betrays an instability and readiness to flip over into its opposite and show another face of postmodernism as a religious, or at least a post-secular, turn of thinking.

Postmodernism as Post-Secularism: The Revival of the Religious

Graham Ward writes of an "implosion" of the "secular" world to describe what happens to the system of total immanence inherited from German idealism and become complacently superficial or disturbingly opaque in

[29] This is the central argument of F. LeRon Shults, *Iconoclastic Theology: Gilles Deleuze and the Secretion of Atheism* (Edinburgh: Edinburgh University Press, 2015).

[30] Gilles Deleuze, *Logique du sens* (Paris: Minuit, 1969), 327: "La théologie est maintenant la science des entités non existantes, la manière dont ces entités, divines ou anti-divines, Christ ou antéchrist, animent le langage."

[31] The theological potentials of Deleuze's immanentism have been brought out effectively by Daniel C. Barber, *Deleuze and the Naming of God: Post-secularism and the Future of Immanence* (Edinburgh: Edinburgh University Press, 2014).

postmodern renderings.[32] He thereby gives an account of postmodernism that is parallel to and yet sharply divergent from Taylor's. Ward, like Taylor, pays careful attention to the colorful and intriguing phenomena of emerging popular culture and media, and like Taylor he discerns the all-important difference of the religious dimension that can be exalted or elided by the uncontainably various forms of postmodern expression. For Ward, however, postmodernism allows something of a return to or recovery of pre-modern religious consciousness and practices, for example, as realized in the liturgy of the Church. Taylor, in contrast, erects barricades against any such recovery. Taylor, in this respect, is seen by Ward as a liberal thinker and as still beholden to an outmoded modernist progressivism.[33]

The crucial difference here is that theology comes back in a "post-secular" guise for Ward.[34] He emphasizes that the dogmas declaring secularism and science to be the true story and definitive account of the universe have been undermined by the post-structuralist critique levelled particularly by French philosophy. Foucault and Derrida, among others, have delivered fatal blows to the secular ideal of omnicomprehensive scientific knowledge.[35] Taylor agrees with this critique, but he does not see it as working to the advantage of theology. He refuses as nostalgic the idea of a return to theology. Whereas for Taylor theology is now inauthentic and must finally end, Ward presents theology as timely and peculiarly attuned to the postmodern age. In the postmodern age, indeed, theology can replace philosophy as furnishing the general paradigm of thinking. Philosophy, especially modern philosophy from Descartes to Husserl, seeks to be self-grounding, but theology is by its nature turned towards the Other. "Theology—as discourse, as praxis—proceeds groundlessly. It cannot think its own origin; it seeks and desires among the consequences of that which always remains unthought. But its seeking is not nomadic, for it seeks another city, a heteropolis." There is thus a powerful motivation and even necessity for

[32] See particularly the introduction to Graham Ward, ed., *The Blackwell Companion to Postmodern Theology* (Oxford: Blackwell, 2001).

[33] Such a critique of Taylor is outlined already by Gillian Rose, *The Broken Middle* (Oxford: Blackwell, 1992), in the section: "New Jerusalem, Old Athens: The Holy Middle." Taylor is here analyzed as inadvertently complicit in a "*rearticulation*" of the "totalizing domination of Western metaphysics." Moreover, by accepting the diremption of moral right from actual power, "Taylor's ecstatic affirmation remains exiled in an interior castle."

[34] This is argued in various ways by multiple authors, including Ward, in *Post-secular Philosophy: Between Philosophy and Theology*, ed. Phillip Blond (London: Routledge, 1998).

[35] Johannes Hoff, *Spiritualität und Sprachverlust: Theologie nach Foucault und Derrida* (Munich: Paderhorn, 1999) is especially perspicuous and thorough in demonstrating the potential of French post-structuralist critique, particularly as practiced by Foucault and Derrida, to be exploited for theological insight and reflection.

theology in a post-secular age. For Ward, "only theology can complete the postmodern project."[36]

Theology, unlike philosophy, does not set out to establish its own foundations: theology proceeds groundlessly, since it cannot think its own origin (namely, God). It is, therefore, our guard against idolatry, against the illusions of the self-sufficiency of the subject (in the last analysis, its divinization) and of a purely autonomous, self-enclosed, self-grounded secular space. Against the radical immanentism found, for example, in the British religious thinker Don Cupitt,[37] Ward counterpoises a transcendental empiricism as characteristic of postmodern theological sensibilities (p. xl). The latter idea is developed by thinkers whom Ward characterizes as "theological realists," and he portrays them as taking the more "difficult path," in contrast to the "aesthetics of nihilism" (p. xliii). They are on a relentless quest for "another city, a kingdom of God, founded in diremption" (p. xlii).

In this vein, Ward collaborates with John Milbank and others in the Radical Orthodoxy movement in developing a postmodern theology that powerfully diagnoses the predicament of secular culture. An unlimited reification and commoditization (in traditional theological terms "idolatry") not only of all objects, but also of all values—moral, aesthetic, and spiritual— followed in the wake of the death of God. "We have produced a culture of fetishes or virtual objects. For now, everything is not only measurable and priced, it has an image." Ward goes on to describe this change in terms of a turn from "the Promethean will to power" by rational domination of the real to "a Dionysian diffusion, in which desire is governed by the endless production and dissemination of floating signifiers."[38] In either case, the desire in question is unbounded in its infinity; it enters in this sense into a dimension that I interpret as theological, as turned toward an unspecifiable Other. By focusing on a finite object, however, like the images of money or sex presented by the mass media, such desire becomes idolatrous, perverse, and even demonic.[39]

The endlessness of human desire is inhabited by theology, or at least by the impulse to theologize. If this desire does not find expression in theological discourse that manages to discern and skirt the ever-present risks of idolatry,

---

[36] Ward, *The Postmodern God*, xlii, xxxiv. Ward's *Cities of God* (New York: Routledge, 2000) expands on this motif. Compare also John Milbank, "Only Theology Overcomes Metaphysics," in *The Word Made Strange: Theology, Language, Culture* (Oxford: Blackwell, 1997).

[37] See, for example, Don Cupitt, "Post-Christianity," in *Religion, Modernity and Postmodernity*, ed. Paul Heelas (Oxford: Blackwell, 1998).

[38] Ward, Introduction to *The Blackwell Companion to Postmodern Theology* (Oxford: Blackwell, 2001), xiv.

[39] For Wendy Brown, *Walled States, Waning Sovereignty* (New York: Zone Books, 2010), this is the revelation of what God has meant all along: "as capital, God is not dead, but rather finally deanthropomorphized—finally God" (66).

it will lead to inappropriate strains upon the immanent sphere of finite powers and eventually to implosion. Theology attempts to keep open this dimension of the infinite that is ineradicable in human desire, whereas idolatry fetishistically pretends to realize the end of all desire here and now. Nothing finite can substitute for the infinite, and therefore finite structures vested with the burden of the infinite are destined eventually to implode.

In postmodern times, the infinity of our desire proves to be far from outmoded. What is new is that the postmodern world offers unprecedented possibilities for unification and immanentization of apparently endless fields of objects. The new technologies may even realize something infinite in the sense of being producible and reproducible without end. The world-wide-web is in principle (if not in practice) infinitely extendable. However, identifying it with the Infinite is, nevertheless, idolatrous. Inevitably, our desire will do this: it will deceive itself into finding the Infinite that it desires in some finite object that it can grasp and possess. The world market of capitalism thus produces unprecedented scenes and scenarios of idolatry, as it grants access to and command over previously undreamt-of domains of objects now given up to our possession. As the human conquest of the planet and of the real completes itself and seems to meet no opposition and to find nothing outside itself, there is the illusion of having overcome all resistance and of having to acknowledge nothing outside and beyond us and our system. The system takes itself for unlimited and, in effect, for the Infinite. But just as the dimension of the infinite seems to be totally realized in this way, the infinitely Other has been definitively elided, forsaken, and forgotten. Such an antithesis between the infinitely Other and all totalizing systems is built as a crucial axis into the postmodern thought of Emmanuel Levinas in his landmark book *Totality and Infinity*.[40] Many postmodern thinkers have pursued the consequences for politics and society by recognizing the theological presuppositions of secularity.[41]

Postmodernism, as a form of cultural practice, breaks into the dimension of the infinite. It no longer has any reality outside itself to work on in its dream of realizing a total system or of realizing the world as a work of art. Reality itself has been absorbed into the production of virtual images with no referents

---

[40] Emmanuel Levinas, *Totalité et infini: Essai sur l'extériorité* (Dordrecht: Kluwer, 1992; La Haye: M. Nijhoff, 1961).

[41] A distinguished sampling is gathered by Hent de Vries and Lawrence E. Sullivan, eds., *Political Theologies: Public Religions in a Post-secular World* (New York: Fordham University Press, 2006). Charles Taylor, *A Secular Age* (Cambridge: Harvard Belknap, 2007) has sparked much discussion around this issue, for example, in *Varieties of Secularism in a Secular Age*, ed. Michael Warner, Jonathan VanAntwerpen, and Craig Calhoun (Cambridge: Harvard University Press, 2010). William E. Connolly, *Why I am Not a Secularist* (Minneapolis, MN: University of Minnesota Press, 2001) has also been prolifically generative in critiquing secular society's narrowly rationalist exclusion of religion from public life.

beyond themselves. But this is an idolatrous infinity. Modernism remains in the phase of striving for such total realization, and it has not been fully realized as long as there is still something external to work on. Just this external other is what is abolished in postmodernism. The lack of an external object can lead to full identification of the infinite with the immanent or, alternatively, to full disidentification and thus to the acknowledgment of the wholly Other—the acknowledgement that our desire is driven by what it can neither encompass nor comprehend. A postmodern thinker like Slavoj Žižek manages to embrace both of these contradictory alternatives in an ironic defense of Christianity.[42]

There is thus a deep-seated ambiguity in postmodernism. Do the totalizing systems of the world-wide-web and the global economy turn everything into immanence without remainder, or do they present only formal codes and systems that simply churn the emptiness of their own artificial fabrications and leave totally untouched some more basic and concrete or, in any case, *other* reality? The language of the "real" is typically considered to be metaphysical by postmodern writers, Jacques Lacan's psychoanalytical usage of it notwithstanding. The "real" itself can be seen as just another linguistic production like the virtual, just another homologous production of the same, and thus as not truly *other*. For what is outside the totalizing system of language and culture is not articulable at all. Is it nothing, or is it more real than everything that can be articulated? Is it more than this morass of Maya that consumerism and commerce fabricate all around us? This outside must be a surreality, if it is anything. Is it a hyperreality that is more than just hype? Can this *other* reality be conceived—as it typically is in religions from Hinduism to Daoism to Jewish, Christian, and Islamic monotheisms and New Age spiritualities—as the source of all reality as we know it? Or is any supposed other reality only the virtual reflected image of the empirical reality that is available to investigation by science and subjected to exploitation by industry and commerce? Such is the question that rives postmodernism into flagrantly contradictory expressions by rival factions ranging from the radically secular Death-of-God theology to the deeply religious and liturgical approach of Radical Orthodoxy.

These contradictory postmodernisms strike out in opposite directions from a common crisis.[43] Viewing them together in their contradictory amphibolousness is perhaps the greatest challenge and the most important lesson to be

[42] Slavoj Žižek, *The Puppet and the Dwarf. The Perverse Core of Christianity* (Cambridge: MIT Press, 2003). Žižek extends his defense of theology and particularly of Christianity as salvific for the world in *Less than Nothing: Hegel and the Shadow of Dialectical Materialism* (New York, Verso, 2012), 1010. He develops a "materialist theology" in Chapter 2 of *The Parallax View* (Cambridge: MIT Press, 2006).

[43] I treat this rivalry more extensively in *A Philosophy of the Unsayable* (Notre Dame: University of Notre Dame Press, 2014), chapter 6: "Apophasis as the Missing Mean between Radically Secular and Radically Orthodox Theology," 271–325, where the tension is contemplated in the (non)horizon of apophatic thinking.

learned from postmodernism in its wide array of contradictory and confusing manifestations. We are nudged, or even forced, toward an apophatic vision of the coincidence of opposites, mirroring the bifocal vision of John Scott Eriugena and echoing, in another tonality, the "apophatic analogy" mentioned above. The hyper-secular turns out to enfold a kind of recrudescence of the religious that brings rigorous rational inquiry back into intimate contact with religious mystery. And this artifice furnishes fertile ground for continued, re-doubled critical investigation, along the rich array of trajectories explored above.

Saving the Soul

David Jasper
(Glasgow University | Renmin University of China)

Abstract

In the nineteenth century, George Gordon, Professor of English Literature at Oxford University, announced in his inaugural lecture that "England is sick, and … English literature must save it. The Churches (as I understand) having failed, and social remedies being slow, English literature has now a triple function: still, I suppose, to delight and instruct us, but also, and above all, to *save our souls* and heal the state." In 1906 the Chinese writer Lu Xun famously remarked that it was the task of literature to "touch society and *stir the nation's spirit.*" Later in the earlier twentieth century and in the field of psycho-analysis, Carl Jung was to speak of "*the spiritual problem* of modern man."

This brief paper will address the cross-cultural search in literature for the sacred and the spiritual in the perceived secularity of the modern everyday world.

**

I begin in Northern Europe in the fifteenth century. In about 1445 the Flemish artist Rogier van der Weyden (c. 1397–1461) paints a picture of the Annunciation, now to be seen in the Louvre in Paris. The European northern Renaissance in art tends to emphasize realistic details (though always with symbolic significance) in the setting of devotional art. This painting is not an exception in the countless Renaissance depictions of the Annunciation, and I will limit myself to one comment about it. The setting is an interior of a contemporary Flemish room with bed, furniture, chandelier—and a window that looks out onto the every-day world outside. In this room stands the angel before a kneeling Mary. Two worlds meet, the sacred messenger alights upon the secular at the very conception of Christianity.

As the angel speaks to Mary in human words (Luke 1:28), so the language of religious discourse must begin within the reality of the everyday before anything can be done with it as regards our understanding. "There can," writes Michel de Certeau, "be no textual work until the postulates of the remarks I make on Christianity are unearthed from their silent opacity. It is the relation between these remarks and their site of production which is the real subject here."[1] This site of production for our language, in contrast to the 'silent opacity'—that is, the deep dark religious mystery—of the Word, must be in the here and now. And that which is to be Christologically conjoined, heaven come to earth as the angel and the girl are met for "earth was the only meeting place,"[2] have been all to often cast asunder in our modern oblivion. The sacred and the profane or secular now stand apart in our cultures, or so it seems. Moving now quickly, but deliberately, across literary authorities and disciplines, Carl Jung, writing of our 'psychic evolution', acknowledges this separation and the soul-quest it provokes in his essays published in English as *Modern Man in Search of a Soul* (1933). Jung's translator, Cary F. Baynes, expresses the issue clearly: "between [the] two extremes of traditional faith and militant rationalism, every conceivable shade of opinion about this great problem of humanity's next step in psychic evolution is to be found."[3] In his essays, as a psychiatrist Jung searches for our lost souls, propelled by the wisdom "gained in his many years of practice and analyst" and laying before his readers "a challenge to the spirit."[4]

But why have I begun here, in European culture, shifting rapidly from the certitude of the Christianity of the fifteenth century to Michel de Certeau and then to Jung? The swift sleight of hand is deliberate, moving us rapidly across different anxious fields of human enquiry. The common anxiety is rooted within the biblical culture in the question posed in Matthew 16:26: "For what is a man profited, if he shall gain the whole world, and lose his own soul." (KJV). The Greek word for soul here is ψυχη, rendered less pointedly in the modern NRSV as 'life'. But the concern for the soul, more precious than all worldly allurement, seems ineradicable—and no inhabiting of the everyday or appropriation of earthly power, even to the whole world of it, can maintain a sense of meaning for us—without a soul, without the presence of the angelic other.[5]

Terry Eagleton long ago reminded us of the words of George Stuart Gordon, an otherwise largely forgotten Merton Professor of English Literature at

[1] Michel de Certeau, "The Weakness of Believing," in *The Certeau Reader*, ed. Graham Ward (Oxford: Blackwell, 2000), 215.

[2] See, Edwin Muir, "The Annunciation," in *The New Oxford Book of Christian Verse*, ed. Donald Davie (Oxford: Oxford University Press, 1981), 264.

[3] Carl F. Baynes, "Translator's Preface," in *Carl Jung, Modern Man in Search of a Soul*, trans. W.S. Dell and Cary F. Baynes (London: Routledge & Kegan Paul, 1961), viii.

[4] Ibid., viii–ix.

[5] A recent exhibition on the subject of angels in the Glasgow's St Mungo Museum of Religious Life and Art attracted large and varied crowds. There was clear public curiosity, and more.

Oxford in the early part of the twentieth century, uttered in Gordon's inaugural lecture in 1922:

> England is sick, and … English Literature must save it. The Churches (as I understand) have failed, and social remedies being slow, English literature has now a triple function: still, I suppose, to delight and instruct us, but also and above all, to save our souls and heal the State.[6]

Since the key mid-Victorian figure of Matthew Arnold, and perhaps before him, we have grown accustomed to the Victorian crisis of faith,[7] the nineteenth century decline in the churches and in Christian belief with all its social consequences. Christianity had been the glue of all social well being, and what was now to replace it? There were those who, like George Gordon, put their faith in literature and art which, in a secularized culture, might still perform the salvific activity of the salvation of souls and the making whole of the State. Religious terms are here transferred to the agency of literature which now assumes a function that far exceeds mere entertainment or aesthetic stimulation.

Let us turn now a very different culture, to modern China—or more precisely to a Chinese writer in Japan and words written in 1923 just one year after Professor Gordon's inaugural lecture in Oxford, though under very different circumstances. In 1906, the writer Lu Xun was attending a lecture in a Japanese medical school when he was shown a slide of a moment in the Russo-Japanese War of 1904–5, a conflict which was partly fought on Chinese territory. In the Preface to his first collection of stories entitled *Outcry* (1923),[8] Lu Xun recalls this incident and his reaction to it, changing him from a medical student to a writer:

> I unexpectedly encountered Chinese people, whom I hadn't seen in a long time, in a slide. There were many of them. One was bound in the middle and many others stood to his left and right, all physically strong bodies, yet displaying expressions of apathy. According to the explanatory caption, the one bound had served as a spy for the Russians and was about to be decapitated by a Japanese soldier….
>
> … Citizens of an ignorant and weak nation, no matter how healthy and sturdy their bodies, can serve as nothing more than

[6] Quoted in Terry Eagleton, *Literary Theory: An Introduction*, 2nd ed. (Oxford: Blackwell, 1996), 20. (Emphases added).

[7] See, Anthony Symondson, ed., *The Victorian Crisis of Faith* (London: SPCK, 1970).

[8] The essay was first published in the literary supplement to the *Morning Post* (Chen bao) on August 21st, 1923, shortly before the publication of *Outcry*.

subject matter for or spectators of meaningless public displays. That many of them die of disease is not, necessarily, something unfortunate. Our most important mission lies in transforming their spirits,[9] and at the same time I felt that the best way to transform their spirits was, of course, through literature, and so I wanted to promote a literary movement.[10]

In the wake of this incident, Lu Xun and some of his fellow Chinese students in Japan, founded the short-lived journal *Vita Nova* (New Life) which was dedicated to reviving the classics of Chinese literature, its title echoing Dante's earliest writing on Beatrice which sees the beloved as the instrument of spiritual salvation.

How should literature be the instrument to transform our spirits, the word in Lu Xun looking back into the ancient Chinese tradition in its sense of body and spirit? But one senses that we are not so very far here from the words of Professor Gordon on the task of literature, speaking of a country weakened and demoralized in spirit after the tragedy of the First World War. Here, then, are two men from England and China writing in 1922 and 1923 of literature's capacity to salve the spirit, to offer salvation and healing to the State: people, Jung might say, in search of lost souls or the lost spirit of the people. And it is Jung who hints at the link (it demands a certain cultural creativity, I admit) between this twentieth century search and late Medieval Christian art with its linking of the sacred and the secular, or rather the finding of the sacred in the everyday. Can we say that George Gordon and Lu Xun, in their different ways, seek through literature a "new attitude that is demanded without having on the one hand to regress to what is but a thinly veiled medieval theology, or on the other, to fall victims to the illusions of nineteenth-century ideology."[11]

The sacred theology may be thinly veiled and the secular ideology may be an illusion, but both remain present in the text, haunting and prompting the quest. Let us take two more examples from twentieth century literature, again one Chinese and the other British, or more precisely Irish.

The Nobel prizing winning writer Gao Xingjian began his great 'novel' *Soul Mountain* (Lingshan) in Beijing in 1982 and completed it in Paris in September 1989.[12] Its autobiographical origins lie in a near death experience when Gao Xingjian was wrongly diagnosed with lung cancer, a disease that had

[9] Julia Lovell, in her translation of this passage, suggests, "The first task was to change their spirit...." See *The Real Story of Ah-Q and Other Tales of China: The Complete Fiction of Lu Xun* (Harmondsworth: Penguin, 2009), xvii.

[10] Lu Xun, *Jottings Under Lamplight*, ed. Eileen J. Cheng and Kirk A Denton (Cambridge, MA: Harvard University Press, 2017), 20–21.

[11] Cary F. Baynes, "Translator's Preface," viii.

[12] The French version, published in 1995 is entitled *La Montagne de l'âme*.

killed his father some years previously, after which he spent ten months wandering in the remote forests of Sichuan and tracing the Yangzte river to its source. The critic and translator Mabel Lee describes the book in this way:

> *Soul Mountain* is a literary response to the devastation of the self of the individual by the primitive human urge for the warmth and security of another, or others, in other words by socialized life. The existence of another resolves the problem of loneliness.... Human history abounds with cases of the individual being induced by force or ideological persuasion to submit to the power of the collective; the surrender of the self to the collective eventually becomes a habit, norm convention and tradition, and this phenomenon is not unique to any one culture.[13]

Behind *Soul Mountain* lie isolated, even sometimes eccentric Buddhist monasteries and Daoist retreats suggesting nonconformist religious responses to a soulless world, a world that had embraced the apathy of the Chinese onlookers in Lu Xun's slide in Japan. And are there even echoes in this text of that biblical question, "for what is a man profited, if he shall gain the whole world and lose his own soul?" Into this quotidian world, a phenomenon not unique to any one culture, the radical 'other' enters and speaks like the angel to Mary.

Let us allow texts of literature to find each other across the divisions of culture and, even more radically, religion. Towards the end of *Soul Mountain*, chapter 72 to be precise, the writer suddenly confronts the reader (or perhaps it is the other way around) with an indignant statement: "This isn't a novel!"[14] Literature has a habit of creatively transcending the limits of the genres with which we are comfortable—the novel, the epic, the lyrical poem, and so on. The last two pages of this chapter in a novel that is no novel are a cascade of words and images without grammatical structure or punctuation. Everything seems to find its way in, including religion. Let us break into the middle of this torrent of words, and then step out again:

> ... everyone wanting to be God about the worship of idols by atheists and self worship being dubbed philosophy about self love about indifference to sex transforming into megalomania and schizophrenia and about sitting in Chan contemplation about sitting not in Chan contemplation about meditation about the Way of nurturing the body is not the Way about effability

[13] Mabel Lee, "Introduction to Gao Xingjian," in Gao Xingjian, *Soul Mountain* (London: Harper Collins, 2004), vi.

[14] Gao, *Soul Mountain*, 452.

> or ineffability but the absolute necessity for the effability of the Way about fashion about revolt against vulgarity is a mighty smash with a racquet about a fatal blow with a club and Buddhist enlightenment....[15]

One wonders what Carl Jung might be thinking now. Reading carefully there is a logic here, or perhaps better a narrative which links the everyday with an inescapable presence of something 'religious'—or other. It reminds me of another text in another culture, though there are literary echoes—I mean, of course, James Joyce's *Finnegans Wake.*

But let us link these two far distant 'novels' ("This isn't a novel!") through the wisdom of a French philosopher with otherness and the other: Paul Ricoeur and his masterwork *Soi-même comme un autre* (Oneself as Another) (1990). At the outset of this work Ricoeur admits his theological obsession, yet banishes it, at least in any overt way. But it remains, barely admitted in the agnostic space of the text, though it is the driving force of everything:

> It will be observed that this asceticism of the argument, which marks, I believe, all my philosophical work, leads to a type of philosophy from which the actual mention of God is absent and in which the question of God, as a philosophical question, itself remains in a suspension that could be called agnostic....[16]

As a philosopher Ricoeur admits that his study "consists in an ontological investigation that involves no ontotheological amalgamations."[17] Traversing boundaries of literary genre as well as culture, might not the same be said, in the end, of Gao Xingjian or Lu Xun? Is that not exactly what they are doing, in literary creativity and utterly without ontotheological amalgamation, searching for the soul, for the presence of the 'other' in the everyday, a human quest that emerges also, in one form at least, in the creative art of Christian theology?

But I would not wish to be accused of false conflation, merely pointing out unlikely similarities in literary texts. If all of China seems to be in Gao Xingjian's book, a Dubliner also once cried of Joyce's *Ulysses* (1920): "We're all in the bloody book!" Even more is this the case for Joyce's even greater work *Finnegans Wake* (1939), the oldest part of which—and almost its centre at the conclusion of book 2, chapter 3—is a scatological, yet deeply sensitive, revisiting of the sacramental and Eucharistic centre of Joyce's Catholic, if rebellious, heart. Allow me to add my own literary voice to that of Joyce and Gao Xingjian (a presumption, I am aware) in words that I wrote on this central

[15] Ibid., 454–5.

[16] Paul Ricoeur, *Oneself as Another*, trans. Kathleen Blamey (Chicago: Chicago University Press, 1992), 24.

[17] Ibid.

passage in *Finnegans Wake* some ten years ago in a book entitled *The Sacred Body* (2009):

> The language of these pages lives.... Finally, in the physical reading, the text devoured and devouring, proclaimed and deepening in endless repetition in reflexivities that simultaneously ... undermine coherence—a fraction of language—and re-establish it in shocking celebrations of the necessary evil of writing, a fall into sanctity in the sanctuary of all the bars in all the world.[18]

Of course, I have given myself away. One always does. The betrayal lies in the language one uses—my case scriptural, sacramental: but also in one's cultural context, growing up, as I did, with Humphrey Bogart's character, Rick, in *Casablanca*.

At the very heart of literature is the allusiveness of language, and those cultural foundations that are almost impossible to destroy despite religious inquisition or political oppression. For those foundations, or a better metaphor might be roots, are lodged deeply in the spaces between the sacred and the everyday, acting as a bridge between them. In that space, at least in the Christian biblical tradition, the angel speaks to Mary and heaven is joined with earth. In that space too, it is not the same yet the echo is heard in the words of literature, Lu Xun finds his most important mission to lie in the transforming of the spirits of the Chinese people, words written beyond the claims of church and creed, in silent opacity to "save our souls and heal the State."[19] The search for salvation may be deemed sacred or secular, but in fact at its heart is the sacrality of the secular[20]—known profoundly and equally in their fictional writings, by the exile James Joyce, in Catholic Ireland, and Gao Xingjian, another exile in Paris, in contemporary China.

[18] David Jasper, *The Sacred Body* (Waco: Baylor University Press, 2009), 151–2.

[19] George Gordon, see above note 5.

[20] See, Bradley B. Onishi, *The Sacrality of the Secular: Postmodern Philosophy of Religion* (New York: Columbia University Press, 2018).

在"圣-俗"与"有-无"之间
BETWEEN THE "SACRED/ PROFANE" AND "YOU 有/ WU 无"

Yang Huilin

(Renmin University of China)

The concept of "sacred" is greatly challenged by the interaction between Christianity and Chinese ancient tradition, and the meaning of "Dao" might be the most typical example to show this influence. As Qian Zhongshu (1910–1998) once commented, "Dao is unspeakable. Although there are sayings about Dao all over the world, none of them can tell the truth of Dao."[1] It might be better if we reverse his comments: "Dao is unspeakable! Even so, there are sayings about Dao in every corner."

James Legge traced the history of the western translation of *Dao De Jing* in his "Preface to *Texts of Daoism*." In the earliest Latin translation, "Dao" is used at the sense of "Supreme Reason of the Divine Being," "Creator," and "Governor." Abel Remusat (1788–1832), the first French Professor of Sinology, argued that "Dao" is hard to be translated because it contained three layers of meanings: "de souverain Être," "de raison" and "de parole." His successor Stanislas Julien (1797–1873), in his French translation of the full texts of *Dao De Jing* in 1824, rendered the nature of "Dao" as "devoid of action, of thought, of judgment, and of intelligence," which is neither "the Primordial Reason," nor "the Sublime Intelligence." As a result, he translated the title *Dao De Jing* as *Le Livre de la Voie et de la Vertu* (*The Book of the Way and Virtue*).[2]

In sum, the major terms used to translate "Dao" in later days already appeared in the earlier Western translations, and in Western languages, words such as "Way," "Reason," "Word" also contain multi-layered meanings. For instance, at the beginning of the *Gospel of John*, the Greek "λόγος / logos," the Latin "Verbum" and the English "Word" can refer to the same meanings but also bear nuanced differences. Furthermore, the duplicity of meaning might be a problem any language or concept cannot avoid. Goethe's *Faust* re-translated the first sentence of *Gospel of John* "In the beginning was the logos" as "In the beginning was the word," and even expanded the saying as: "In the beginning was the mind" and "In the beginning was the deed."[3]

---

[1] Qian Zhongshu, *Guan zhui pian*, vol. 2 (Beijing: SDX Joint Publishing House, 2007), 719.

[2] James Legge, *The Sacred Books of China: The Texts of Taoism* (Oxford: Oxford University Press, 1891), 12–13.

[3] Johann Wolfgang von Goethe, *Faust*, trans. Qian Chunyi (Shanghai: Yiwen Press, 1989), 67–68.

Another missionary scholar William Edward Soothill (1861–1935) translated "Dao" as "the Way, the right road," a reference that can easily remind the Christian reader of the Chapter 14 of the *Gospel of John*, in which Jesus was consoling his disciples: "'My Father's house has many rooms; if that were not so, would I have told you that I am going there to prepare a place for you? And if I go and prepare a place for you, I will come back and take you to be with me that you also may be where I am. You know the way to the place where I am going.' Thomas said to him, 'LORD, we don't know where you are going, so how can we know the way?' Jesus answered, 'I am the way and the truth and the life. No one comes to the Father except through me.'"(NIV, Jn 14:2-6) From these verses we can understand why W. E. Soothill and other missionaries translated "Dao" as "the Way" or why they would extend the meaning from "the Way" to "the Truth."

If we keep tracing the origin, however, we find more interesting expressions. In Jerome's Vulgate Bible, "*Ergo sum via et veritas et vita*" carries some extra deeper meanings: the alliteration and assonance of the words "*via et veritas et vita*" link "Way" and "Truth" naturally: *veritas* binds *via* and *vita*, which means "life" connects "I" and "you." In other words, the Latin rhetoric might have implied some deeper meanings that the English or Chinese translation failed to express: "the Way, the Truth and Life" are mutually correlating, mutually defining and mutually fulfilling one another.

The translation work of the missionaries embodied a typical philosophical difference in languages, and contemporary philosophers can help us grasp some deeper meanings in their choice of words. For instance, Alain Badiou repeated quoted Slavoj Žižek's claim: "the way our path towards truth coincides with the truth itself."[4] Badiou uses it to analyze "Ereignis" and "event" through Heidegger's "being as being-on-the-way," and to refer to Wittgenstein's saying: "The world is everything which happens."[5] However, "the eventual statement" he describes is precisely the structural cycle of "event, truth and subject."[6]

[4] Slavoj Žižek, *The Sublime Object of Ideology* (London: Verso, 1989), 64. See also Peter Hallward, *Badiou: A Subject to Truth* (Minneapolis: University of Minnesota Press, 2003), xxvi.

[5] Alain Badiou, "The Event in Deleuze," *Parrhesia* 2 (2007): 37. According to Bardiou, the original words of Wittgenstein in his Tractatus Logico-Philosophicus is "Die welt ist alles, was der Fall ist," which is translated as "The world is all that is the case." Badiou thinks that it should be "The world is everything which happens." See Badiou, "The Event in Deleuze," 43n4.

[6] Detailed discussions please see Yang Huilin, *Yi Yi* (Significance) (Beijing: Peking University Press, 2013).

Similar trinitarian formulae as "the Way, the Truth and the Life" are common in the Bible, such as "who he is, who was and who is to come" in Revelation 1:4. The three kinds of "time" said by St. Augustine is in the same vein (may also needs a further explanation of later generation philosophers): "there are neither times future nor times past. Thus, it is not properly said that there are three times, past, present, and future. Perhaps it might be said rightly that there are three times: a time present of things past; a time present of things present; and a time present of things future."[7] What is important is that such argument focuses not only on the "psychological time" of "memory, sense and expectation," in Alain Badiou's words, "The event is neither past nor future. It makes us present to the present."[8]

In essence, the time that is marked by "event" can only be the "vanishing mediator" and is "an in-temporal instant."[9] Going back to the saying of "who he is, who he was and who is to come" from this point, we can know that the described time is not any specific time but "being" three tenses. If we say the cycle of "Way, Truth and Life" is an inter-argumentation, the saying of "who is, who was and who is to come" is to provide a form for the time that is impossible to be described.

This reminds us of Alain Badiou's stress on the "predicative description" and its nature of being "sufficient."[10] Comparing with François Jullien's retort of "Diue est" and "je suis,"[11] we can discover that Soothill's discussion on "the Way, the Truth and the Life" has ignored the crucial "je suis."

"Je suis" comes out of the important dialogue between God and Moses in the *Book of Exodus*: "God said to Moses, 'I AM WHAT I AM. This is what you are to say to the Israelites: 'I AM has sent me to you.'"(Exod. 3:14) Common scholarly expression tells us that "Yahweh comes from the Hebrew verb 'to be (להיות)', ... In 'I AM WHO I AM,' YHWH (I AM) are consonants, which is a tradition of showing reverence by not calling the name directly. The vowels are omitted and replaced by 'adonai'. If we insert the vowels of 'adonai' into YHWH, it is pronounced as 'Yahweh'."[12]

---

7 Augustine, *Confessions*, trans. Zhou Shiliang (Beijing: The Commercial Press, 1996), 247.

8 Badiou, "The Event in Deleuze," 39.

9 Ibid.

10 Badiou and Žižek, *Philosophy in the Present*, p. 32.

11 François Jullien thinks that in ancient China there was no similar expression of "je suis," nor would there be "Dieu est." As a result, there was no need to discuss whether there exists God. See François Jullien, "A Response to Chung-ying Cheng," in *Ideas and Methods: Possibilities of a Chinese-Western Dialogue in a Globalized Age*, ed. Fang Weigui (Beijing: Peking University Press, 2014), 63.

12 Lin Hong-Hsin, *Xi tong shen xue* (Systematic Theology) (Taipei: Campus Press, 2017), 533.

Connecting the saying "I AM WHAT I AM" with the Hebrew "YHWH," and tracing the fundamental problem of Western philosophy from "YHWH" or "je suis," Martin Heidegger's expression might be the most inspiring:

> We do not know what 'Being' means. But even if we ask, "What is 'Being?', we keep within an understanding of the 'is', though we are unable to fix conceptually what that 'is' signifies.... in what is asked about, there lies that which is to be found out by the asking."[13]

Why the "Being" "we do not know" can only be presented by asking "what is"? It is because "Being" is "the 'is'" and "what that 'is' signified." Heidegger is confident that the "Being" "we do not know" is similar to the God Moses tried to ask "what is his name." It is less important to wonder if this is a "misuse of his name" (Exod. 20:7) than to realize that "je suis," the statement of "Yahweh," has been highlighted as a grammar of ideas.

The question is, why in the Chinese Union version, the "je suis" of "YHWH" can only be replaced by "I AM WHAT I AM"? It is related to the varied Chinese expressions of the "Sacred," which also have left us a meaningful space of ideas.

In ancient Chinese, "je suis" did not have the function of explaining "I AM WHAT I AM." In regard to the question of "what is being," the ancient Chinese would reply, "Why asking this question?" "Being" is not innately connected to the concept of "to be." Modern Chinese "shi 是 (to be)" is used as a linking verb. Although it contains the meaning of expressing "what something is," its key point is not necessarily the "is." As François Jullien discovered when he started to learn Chinese: in the question, "What is this?" [the Chinese are "zhe shi shen me dong xi" (What is this dong-xi? 这是什么东西) the essential point is not the "is" but the extra two characters pointing to two opposite directions: "dong (east, 东)" and "xi (west 西)." When these two opposite directions are put together, their meanings are changed from direction to something, a different meaning category. Therefore, there is a fundamental difference in the Chinese way of asking "what is it," which is a correlational structure established by the "two opposite poles." In Julien's words, "The polar relations of 'dong (east) - xi (west)' has produced a completely different way of understanding," and he then understands "why the history of Western ideas and science cannot cover the Chinese ideas."[14]

Such a meaning structure composed of opposite poles such as "dong (east) - xi (west)" is common in Chinese. Another phrase, "Shi-jie 世界" (meaning

[13] Heidegger, *Being and Time*, 25.

[14] François Jullien, *Penser d'un dehors (La Chine). Entretiens d'Extrême-Occident*, trans. Zhang Fang (Zhengzhou: Elephant Press, 2005), 23–24.

"the world") is a compound word consisting of time and space. In the Buddhist Shurangama Sutra, it is explained: "What is shi-jie? Shi is the changes of time, and Jie is the location and orientation." The ancient Chinese dictionary *Shuo wen jie zi* has a similar definition: "Thirty years may be called one 'Shi', ... Jie, the end and boundaries."[15] We find more phrases in Chinese have the same structure, such as "yu (space 宇) - zhou (time 宙)"[meaning universe], "tian (upper 天) - xia (lower 下)" [meaning universe or the world], "guo (nation 国) - jia (family 家)" [meaning the country], etc. Such an "relational approach" and its "correlation" are telling us the Chinese metaphysical grammar.

The discussions on "present/absent" may help us understand the Chinese metaphysical grammar from another aspect. Some sinologists noticed the differences between Western "Being/Non-being" and Chinese "*you* 有 / *wu* 无" (literally means "having" / "nothing"). In their eyes, "Being" is the parallel of "Non-being" in the Western metaphysical sense, while the Chinese "*you*" is "being present," the parallel of "being absent." Accordingly, "*you*" (having) is not the negative form of "*wu*" (nothing), and "*wu*" is not "nothing" but just an "absence."[16]

Some Chinese scholar share the similar view, arguing that both "you and wu" are "Dao" (the Way), coming from the same origin but with different names. Other Chinese scholars think the contrary and argue that the sayings in *Dao De Jing*, "you wu hun cheng 有物混成" (There was something undefined and complete) and "Dao yin wu ming 道隐无名" (The Dao is hidden, and has no name), can be interpreted through the English terms "Being" and "Non-being," and the author even alluded to an explanation from *Yu pian* 玉篇 (ancient Chinese dictionary), in which "*bu you* 不有" (do not have) is used to explain the meaning of "wu."[17]

If we read James Legge's interpretation and translation of Chinese classics, we may also find a more convincing explanation for this argument. Legge translated the Confucius' saying about spirits and sacrifice in *Analects* Chapter 3 as: "Sacrificed to the dead as if they were present. Sacrificed to the spirits as if the spirits were present.... I consider my not being present at the sacrifice as

---

[15] "Shi 世," in Shuo Wen Jie Zi (Online), http://www.cidianwang.com/shuowenjiezi/shi40.htm (published in 2010; accessed on June 29, 2019) ; "Jie 界," in *Shuo Wen Jie Zi* (Online), http://www.cidianwang.com/shuowenjiezi/jie2417.htm (published in 2010; accessed on June 29, 2019).

[16] Roger Ames and David L. Hall, *Tao Te Ching: A Philosophical Translation*, trans. He Jinli (Bejing: The Academy Press, 2004), 108.

[17] Li Ruohui, ed., *Lao zi ji zhu hui kao* 老子集注汇考 (Collected Commentaries and Annotations of Lao Zi), vol. 1 (Shanghai: Shanghai Lexicographical Publishing Press, 2015), 389-390.

if I did not sacrifice."[18] Legge used "to be present" three times. But the second one is the "presence" of the spirits, and the first and third "presence" are referring to the presence of the "dead" and "I," the self. One then can understand why Zhu Xi, the founder of Neo-Confucianism, always stressed "having sincerity" and "empathy" when interpreting this saying, paying no attention to the word "*zai* (being present)."[19]

The difference between the two Chinese terms "*zai* 在" and "*zai chang* 在场" is not the issue of expression or translation. It is the linguistic structure and meaning of the word that have defined the thought itself. A Spanish scholar Santiago Zabala pointed out two crucial approaches in contemporary Western philosophy.

Firstly, there has been a mode of thinking of "Why are there beings at all instead of nothing?" This not only is "the core of Western ontological thinking, but also shows a fundamental duplicity in Being." Zabala quoted Earns Tugendhat and explained that "Being 'is' only as long as the two parts are joined, creating a relation between two terms where one refers to the other as the predicate and subject." In other words, "the presence of Being" is explained "by duplicating Being."[20] This is in fact a more subtle explanation of Martin Heidegger's *Time and Being*,[21] but the focus is to explore (or demonstrate) the linguistic structure of our thought.

Secondly, contemporary continental philosophy can be connected through the "weak concepts" such as "trace," "event," and "remains." Jacques Derrida's "non-original origin," "a-conceptual concept," "neither all nor nothing"[22] are in the same vein. According to Zabala, the philosophy in this line is

---

[18] James Legge, *The Chinese Classics*, 159. 《论语·八佾》：祭如在，祭神如神在，……吾不与祭如不祭.

[19] Qiu Yexiang, *Zi wo yu ta zhe* 自我与他者：经文辩读视域 中的理雅各论语译解研究 (Self and the Other: Study on James Legge's Translation of Analects from the Perspective of Scriptural Reasoning) (Beijing: Chinese Academy of Social Sciences Press, 2017), 51–52.

[20] "Puzzling over the correspondence between subject and object, we lose sight both of the world within which all things are given and of our own engagement as beings. Truth, whether in Aristotle's, Tarski's, or Husserl's terms, shares the metaphysical structure that is at the origin of all Western logic, where Being is interpreted only as the presence of something present, that is, objectively in this distinction, the subject and predicate -- in other words, the relation between two terms where one refers to the other -- not only represent the logical and verbal structure but also the imposition of this same structure." Quoted from Santiago Zabala's series lectures "Being and Truth" in December of 2018, which are now in his new book, *Being at Large. Freedom in the Age of Alternative Facts* (see fn38).

[21] See Yang Huilin, "The Potentiality of 'Polarity' and 'Mutuality,'" *Social Sciences in Chinese Higher Education Institutions* 6 (2017): 97–101.

[22] Jacques Derrida, *Of Grammatology*, trans. Wang Jiatang (Shanghai: Shanghai Yiwen Press, 1999), 61.

not focusing on "what is" but "what remains" outside or prior to the symbolic system. Therefore, "trace," "event," "remains" are "what is coming" to resist "the present of the presence."

To sum up the above two, "the presence of Being" and "the present of the presence" seem to be related to James Legge's translation of "*ji ru zai*" (to be present when sacrificing). The difficulty is that the predicate and the subject referring to each is to explain the unexplainable "Being," and the "weak concepts" from "trace" to "event," isto free "Being" from the symbolic pitfall of "what is." The effort of sinologists' using "*wu*" to explain the "absence" of "being present" might not be able to convey the deep implications of this Chinese-Western translation activity.

In Legge's translation, "being present" refers to three different subjects, "spirits," "the dead" and "I," in which "the predicate and the subject" are not referring to each other. Accordingly, the "trace" or "remains" that can influence the construction of symbols outside or prior to the symbolic system is the "*wu*" of "not being present." To grasp the questions "remaining" in "*ji ru zai*," and explore the resistant elements that can genuinely fight against the "*zai*" of "*zai chang*," we need to go back to the Chinese debate of "you and wu." Interestingly, generations of interpreters have been repeatedly coming back to these terms, using Buddhist term "*se kong* 色空" to explain "*you* and *wu*" or "*xu jing* 虚静" to explain "*xin xing* 心性."

Furthermore, the Chinese Buddhist sutra, "the Heart Sutra of Prajna Paramita," deals with "*yuan qi you* 缘起有" (being in the sense of dependent origination) and "*zi xing kong* 自性空" (voidness in the sense of its self-nature). In other words, we can define "being" in the sense of "dependent origination," but the "*se* 色" (substance) caused by "origination" is in the end "voidness with no self-nature," which means that "being" is also "voidness." Therefore, "reality 实相" can only be said as "no-empty" and "no-being." As said in the "the Heart Sutra of Prajna Paramita," "the appearances of emptiness of all ways are, [They] do not produce, not extinguish, not become filthy, not become pure, not increase and not decrease." Later Ji Zang uses "Eight Negations" to explain the "middle path": "Neither birth nor extinction, neither cessation nor permanence, neither uniformity nor diversity, neither coming nor going."

In summary, "*zi xing kong*" and "*yuan qi you*" are related, the latter is the counterevidence of the former. As such, the question of "being/presence" and "non-being/absence" is transformed into the question between "*yuan qi*" (dependent origination) and "*xing kong*" (voidness of nature), and into the relation between birth and extinction, cessation and permanence, uniformity and diversity, coming and going.

In other words, when ancient Chinse discussed "*you* and *wu*," they said "*shi er bu you* 实而不有 (entity but not having)," *xu er bu wu* 虚而不无 (void but not empty)," which did not have the "duplicating" of "being/existence," nor any "remains" outside or prior to the symbolic system. In short, the presupposition of "*guan you* 观有 (observe you or being") is "*ju wu* 居无 (in the position of *wu* or non-being)," in other words, *you* or being could be only observed on the basis (or in comparison) of *wu* or non-being. In this way, the "*you*" one observes can "*bu wei you suo ai* 不为有所碍 (not being blocked or biased by *you*/the being)."[23] Comparing with the "Being" of Western metaphysics and Zabala's two "resistances," the epistemological logic of "*ju wu yi guan you*" is more akin to the polysemic "Dao." The essence of this logic is to replace the transcendental entity with the "relational being.

Lacan once offered a brief and clear definition for "Holy Spirit": "The Holy Spirit is the entry of the signifier into the world."[24] If we can use "Sacred Mode of Being," "Theology's Cultural Mode of the Sacred" and "Culture's Theological Mode of the Sacred" to summarize three aspects of David Jasper's thought on the "Sacred," for Chinese interdisciplinary studies, it might exactly be the signifier of the Sacred into the world.

[23] Zheng Cheng, *Dao De Jing ji jie* 道德经集解 (Collected Interpretation of Dao De Jing), in *Lao zi ji cheng*, ed. Xiong Tieji and Chen Hongxing, vol. 7 (Beijing: Religious Culture Press, 2011), 460.

[24] Slavoj Žižek, *The Puppet and the Dwarf: the Perverse Core of Christianity* (Cambridge: The MIT Press, 2003), 9.

Part II
The Sacred and the Everyday in Worship

TEXT – COMMUNITY – IDENTITY: *DIVINE WORSHIP* AS A PROJECT OF LITURGICAL TEXT PRESERVATION

James Bradley JCD
(School of Canon Law at The Catholic University of America, Washington DC)

ABSTRACT

In this short paper I will present an overview of the development of the liturgical provisions of the apostolic constitution *Anglicanorum cœtibus.*[1] The apostolic constitution was promulgated by Pope Benedict XVI in 2009 to provide for personal ordinariates—structures juridically equivalent to dioceses—allowing groups of Anglican faithful to enter into the full communion of the Catholic Church in a corporate manner, whilst preserving certain elements of the liturgical, spiritual, and pastoral traditions of Anglicanism. After a brief introduction I will present the principles that guided the development of these liturgical provisions, given expression in the liturgical books published under the general title, *Divine Worship*. I will offer a number of examples of these principles at work in the process of collating, approving, and promulgating these liturgical texts, and identify ways in which *Divine Worship* can be understood as a project of liturgical text preservation, by which the identity of a specific and existing community is preserved in a new context. At the same time, with the purpose of demonstrating the overall success of the project, I will draw attention to some of the limitations and pitfalls of such a process.

**

On 18 October 1964, in the midst of the Second Vatican Council, Pope Paul VI canonized twenty-two martyrs from Uganda. In recognition of the death of a similar number of Anglicans in the same atrocity, in his homily the Holy Father specifically commemorated those Anglicans who were killed *pro Christi nomine*—for the name of Christ.[2] The Decree on Ecumenism of the Second Vatican Council, *Unitatis redintegratio*, was promulgated the following month, on 21 November 1964. The document speaks of those ecclesial communities which have not enjoyed communion with the Apostolic See since

[1] Benedict XVI, apostolic constitution *Anglicanorum cœtibus*, 4 November 2009: *Acta Apostolicæ Sedis* (=*AAS*) 101 (2009): 985-990. Unless otherwise stated all English translations are taken from Benedict XVI, *Anglicanorum cœtibus. Apostolic Constitution and Complementary Norms* (London: Catholic Truth Society, 2009). (=*AC*).

[2] Paul VI, homily, 18 October 1964: *AAS* 56 (1964): 903–12.

the sixteenth century.[3] In doing so it singles out Anglicanism as a particular example of such a community, designating it "a special place."[4] The reason given for this accolade is the manner in which, within the Anglican tradition, "Catholic traditions and institutions in part continue to exist."[5] In this we might include certain broadly theological and ecclesiological principles, such as the hierarchical ordering of ordained ministers as bishop, priest, and deacon, and the maintenance of the model of the local church in the form of a diocese. We might also include certain aspects of the liturgical, spiritual, and pastoral patrimony of Anglicanism, some of which developed before the secession of full communion, and some of which was a result of the rediscovery of the Catholic heritage of the Church of England in the nineteenth and twentieth centuries.[6]

In October 1970, Pope Paul VI celebrated the canonization of the Forty Martyrs of England and Wales, concluding his otherwise Italian homily in English, and affirming the principles of *Unitatis redintegratio*. With regard to

---

[3] Second Vatican Council, decree *Unitatis redintegratio*, 21 November 1964: *AAS* 57 (1965): 90–107. (=*UR*).

[4] *UR* 13: "… Aliæ dein, post amplius quattuor sæcula, in Occidente ortæ sunt ex eventibus qui sub nomine Reformationis communiter veniunt. Exinde a Sede Romana plures Communiones sive nationales sive confessionales seiunctæ sunt. Inter eas, in quibus traditiones et structuræ catholicæ ex parte subsistere pergunt, locum specialem tenet Communio anglicana…."

[5] Ibid. It cannot be left unsaid that since 1964 the Anglican Communion has further diverged from a common understanding of the nature of ordained ministry between Anglicans and Catholics, and in particular through the ordination of women to the episcopate. In an address to the 2008 Lambeth Conference, the then-President of the Pontifical Council for Promoting Christian Unity, Cardinal Walter Kasper, lamented the decision to proceed to the ordination of women as bishops. Kasper said that this would imply "a turning away from the common position of all churches of the first millennium … the older churches of East and West will recognize therein much less of what they understand to be the character and ministry of the bishop in the sense understood by the early church and continuing through the ages." He went on to say that whilst "dialogue has led to significant agreement on the understanding of ministry, the ordination of women to the episcopate effectively and definitively blocks a possible recognition of Anglican Orders by the Catholic Church. It is our hope that a theological dialogue between the Anglican Communion and the Catholic Church will continue, but this development effects directly the goal and alters the level of what we pursue in dialogue." Following the decision to ordain women as bishops in the Church of England, it has been on the understanding of a changed direction and purpose of ecumenical dialogue between Anglicans and Catholics expressed by Cardinal Kasper, that unity-minded Anglicans sought an alternative path for reconciliation with Rome, of which *Anglicanorum Cœtibus* may be understood to be a fruit. See Walter Kasper, "The Lambeth Conference 2008. Address by Cardinal Walter Kasper," 30 July 2008, *The Pontifical Council for Promoting Christian Unity Information Service* 129 (2008/III): 143–9.

[6] Cf. *UR* 23: "Christiana horum fratrum conversatio fide in Christum alitur, baptismatis gratia et verbo Dei audito fovetur. Manifestatur quidem in oratione privata, in meditatione biblica, in familiæ christianæ vita, in cultu communitatis ad laudem Dei congregatæ. Ceteroquin cultus eorum nonnumquam elementa conspicua communis antiquæ liturgiæ præ se fert…."

the possibility of Anglican reunion, the Pope said: "There will be no seeking to lessen the legitimate prestige and the worthy patrimony of piety and usage proper to the Anglican Church when the Roman Catholic Church—this humble 'Servant of the Servants of God'—is able to embrace her ever beloved Sister in the one authentic communion of the family of Christ."[7] Here is an idea which is of importance to us as we consider *Divine Worship*. The description of a "worthy patrimony of piety and usage proper to the Anglican Church" brings to mind precisely the liturgical texts which have developed within Anglicanism during its years of separation from the Apostolic See.[8]

On 4 November 2009, Pope Benedict XVI responded to repeated and insisted petitions for some means for corporate reunion between Anglicans and the Apostolic See with the apostolic constitution *Anglicanorum cœtibus*.[9] This provided "the general normative structure for regulating the institution and life of personal ordinariates for those Anglican faithful who desire to enter into the full communion of the Catholic Church in a corporate manner."[10] In addition to this a set of Complementary Norms were issued by the Congregation for the Doctrine of the Faith, the responsible dicastery of the Roman curia, to guide and govern the internal life of the future ordinariates. To date, three personal ordinariates have been erected: in England and Wales, the Personal Ordinariate of Our Lady of Walsingham (January 2012); in the United States, the Personal

[7] Paul VI, homily, 25 October 1970: *AAS* 67 (1970): 746–53.

[8] Ibid. The Constitution on the Sacred Liturgy of the Second Vatican Council makes provision for this legitimate diversity in liturgical rites, provided that the substantial unity of the Roman rite is preserved. *See* Second Vatican Council, constitution *Sacrosanctum Concilium*, 4 December 1963: *AAS* 56 (1964): 97–134, nn. 38 and 39 (=*SC*). This is one of the stated goals of the process undertaken by the Interdicasterial Working Group *Anglicanæ traditiones*, regarding its work on the *Ordo Missæ* for use in the personal ordinariates: "to propose an Order of Mass at once distinctively and traditionally Anglican in character, content, and structure, while also being clearly and recognizably an expression of the Roman Rite, in both its ordinary and extraordinary forms." See Steven Lopes, "A Missal for the Ordinariates: The Work of the *Anglicanæ Traditiones* Interdicasterial Commission," *Antiphon* 19, no. 2 (2015): 116–31. Lopes served as the secretary to *Anglicanæ traditiones*, and was appointed as the first Bishop-Ordinary of the Personal Ordinariate of the Chair of Saint Peter in 2015.

[9] *AC* Preamble: "In recent times the Holy Spirit has moved groups of Anglicans to petition repeatedly and insistently to be received into full Catholic communion individually as well as corporately. The Apostolic See has responded favourably to such petitions. Indeed, the successor of Peter, mandated by the Lord Jesus to guarantee the unity of the episcopate and to preside over and safeguard the universal communion of all the Churches, could not fail to make available the means necessary to bring this holy desire to realization."

[10] *AC* Preamble: "… In the light of these ecclesiological principles, this apostolic constitution provides the general normative structure for regulating the institution and life of personal ordinariates for those Anglican faithful who desire to enter into the full communion of the Catholic Church in a corporate manner. This constitution is completed by Complementary Norms issued by the Apostolic See."

Ordinariate of the Chair of Saint Peter (January 2013); in Australia, the Personal Ordinariate of Our Lady of the Southern Cross (June 2013).[11] In addition, the Deanery of Saint John the Baptist was erected in Canada under the jurisdiction of the Personal Ordinariate of the Chair of Saint Peter on 16 November 2012.[12] Groups also operate in Scotland, under the jurisdiction of the Personal Ordinariate of Our Lady of Walsingham, and in Japan and the Torres Strait under the jurisdiction of the Personal Ordinariate of Our Lady of the Southern Cross.

Our focus here is the liturgical text provision made by *Anglicanorum cœtibus* and given expression in the liturgical books of *Divine Worship*. Paragraph III of the apostolic constitution makes the following remarks pertinent to the liturgical life of these personal ordinariates:

> Without excluding liturgical celebrations according to the Roman Rite, the Ordinariate has the faculty to celebrate the Holy Eucharist and the other Sacraments, the Liturgy of the Hours and other liturgical celebrations according to the liturgical books proper to the Anglican tradition, which have been approved by the Holy See, so as to maintain the liturgical, spiritual and pastoral traditions of the Anglican Communion within the Catholic Church, as a precious gift nourishing the faith of the members of the ordinariate and as a treasure to be shared.[13]

On the basis of this provision, since the promulgation of the apostolic constitution in 2009, and the subsequent erection of three personal ordinariates, the Apostolic See has approved a number of liturgical books which draw on the Anglican tradition for use by the clergy and lay faithful of the personal ordinariates. The process for the development of these liturgical texts took place under the auspices of the Congregation for the Doctrine of the Faith, by means of an Interdicasterial Working Group established in partnership with the

---

[11] Congregation for the Doctrine of the Faith, *Decree of Erection of the Personal Ordinariate of Our Lady of Walsingham*, 15 January 2011: *AAS* 103 (2011): 129–33; *Decretum quo erigitur Ordinariatus Personalis Cathedræ Sancti Petri*, 1 January 2012: AAS 105 (2013): 852–5; decree *Ordinariatus Personalis Our Lady of the Southern Cross Australiæ*, 15 June 2012: AAS 104 (2012): 599–603.

[12] Gerhard Müller, Letter to Monsignor Steenson, 16 November 2012, Prot. N. 204/11-41029 [Private].

[13] *AC* III: "Liturgicis haud exclusis celebrationibus secundum Romanum Ritum, Ordinariatui facultas præbetur celebrandi sacram Eucharistiam ceteraque Sacramenta, Horarum Liturgiam aliasque liturgicas actiones iuxta libros liturgicos Anglicanæ traditioni peculiares, ab Apostolica Sede adprobatos, ita ut intra Catholicam Ecclesiam vitales serventur spiritales, liturgicæ pastoralesque Communionis Anglicanæ traditiones, ad instar magni pretii doni, ad sodalium fidem alendam ac participandam."

Congregation for Divine Worship and the Discipline of the Sacraments, and known as *Anglicanæ traditiones.*[14] The working group comprised officials from both dicasteries, as well as experts familiar with the Anglican liturgical tradition. It met on several occasions, in order to prepare both a collection of texts known as *Divine Worship: Occasional Services* (2014)—containing rites for baptism, marriage, and funerals—and *Divine Worship: The Missal.*[15] In addition the Congregation for Divine Worship and the Discipline of the Sacraments made provisions for each of the three personal ordinariates by means of the authorisation of a lectionary, according to the Revised Standard Version (Second Catholic Edition) translation of scripture, and particular liturgical calendars for each ordinariate.[16]

The work of *Anglicanæ traditiones* was governed by a set of statutes issued jointly by the Congregation for the Doctrine of the Faith and the Congregation for Divine Worship and the Discipline of the Sacraments on 3 October 2011.[17]

---

[14] Congregation for the Doctrine of the Faith, decree, 8 October 2011, Prot. N. 217/08-36793.

[15] The Order of Funerals: Congregation for Divine Worship and the Discipline of the Sacraments, decree, 22 June 2012, Prot. N. 168/12/L (England and Wales); Congregation for Divine Worship and the Discipline of the Sacraments, decree, 22 June 2012, Prot. N. 169/12/L (United States); Congregation for Divine Worship and the Discipline of the Sacraments, decree, 22 June 2012, Prot. N. 357/12/L (Australia). The Order of Solemnisation of Holy Matrimony: Congregation for Divine Worship and the Discipline of the Sacraments, decree, 22 June 2012, Prot. N. 359/12/L (England and Wales); Congregation for Divine Worship and the Discipline of the Sacraments, decree, 22 June 2012, Prot. N. 360/12/L (United States); Congregation for Divine Worship and the Discipline of the Sacraments, decree, 22 June 2012, Prot. N. 357/12/L (Australia). The Order of Mass: Congregation for Divine Worship and the Discipline of the Sacraments, decree, 7 May 2013, Prot. N. 274/13/L (United States); Congregation for Divine Worship and the Discipline of the Sacraments, decree, 7 May 2013, Prot. N. 275/13/L (England and Wales); Congregation for Divine Worship and the Discipline of the Sacraments, decree, 7 May 2013, Prot. N. 276/13/L (Australia). The Order of Holy Baptism: Congregation for Divine Worship and the Discipline of the Sacraments, decree, 12 December 2013, Prot. N. 785/13/L (United States); Congregation for Divine Worship and the Discipline of the Sacraments, decree, 12 December 2013, Prot. N. 786/13/L (England and Wales); Congregation for Divine Worship and the Discipline of the Sacraments, decree, 12 December 2013, Prot. N. 787/13/L (Australia). Divine Worship: The Missal: Congregation for Divine Worship and the Discipline of the Sacraments, decree, 27 May 2015, Prot. N. 160/15.

[16] Liturgical Calendar: Congregation for Divine Worship and the Discipline of the Sacraments, decree, 15 February 2012, Prot. N. 76/12/L (England and Wales); Congregation for Divine Worship and the Discipline of the Sacraments, decree, 15 February 2012, Prot. N. 75/12/L (United States); Congregation for Divine Worship and the Discipline of the Sacraments, decree, 30 April 2013, Prot. N. 280/13/L (Australia). Lectionary: Congregation for Divine Worship and the Discipline of the Sacraments, decree, 15 February 2012, Prot. N. 77/12/L (United States); Congregation for Divine Worship and the Discipline of the Sacraments, decree, 15 February 2012, Prot. N. 78/12/L (England and Wales); Congregation for Divine Worship and the Discipline of the Sacraments, decree, 14 February 2013, Prot. N. 280/13/L (Australia).

[17] Congregation for the Doctrine of the Faith, *Statutes of the Interdicasterial Working Group* Anglicanæ Traditiones, 3 October 2011, Prot. N. 536/2012.

The group was co-chaired by Archbishop Augustine Di Noia OP, then an official of the Congregation for Divine Worship, and Monsignor Andrew Burnham, a former Anglican bishop now serving as a priest of the Personal Ordinariate of Our Lady of Walsingham, who served on the Liturgical Commission of the Church of England.[18] The working group itself compiled a *Ratio*—an informal set of working principles—in order to "orient the work and give more specific direction for the selection among the Anglican sources."[19] This *Ratio* provides an important insight into the mind of the group, and its intentions toward what would become the liturgical books of *Divine Worship*. The *Ratio* itself remains unpublished, being an internal document of the working group, but its principles and objectives were enumerated in an article by Monsignor Steven Lopes, an official of the Congregation for the Doctrine of the Faith who served as one of the two coordinating secretaries to the group. These principles are presented here:

1. to preserve for Catholic worship the worthy Anglican liturgical patrimony, understood as that which has nourished the Catholic faith throughout the history of the Anglican tradition and prompted aspirations towards ecclesial unity;
2. to preserve such features and elements as are representative of the historic Anglican Books of Common Prayer (in the first place) and the Anglican Missals (in the second place), in conformity with Catholic doctrinal and liturgical norms;
3. to propose an Order of Mass at once distinctively and traditionally Anglican in character, content, and structure, while also being clearly and recognizably an expression of the Roman Rite, in both its ordinary and extraordinary forms;
4. to identify the patrimony from "the liturgical books proper to the Anglican tradition" (*Anglicanorum Cœtibus* III), rather than composing new liturgical texts or devising new liturgical forms;

[18] In addition to the co-chairmen, the original members of the Interdicasterial Working Group comprised: the Reverend Uwe Michael Lang CO (Coordinating Secretary of the Congregation for Divine Worship and the Discipline of the Sacraments), Monsignor Steven Lopes (Coordinating Secretary of the Congregation for the Doctrine of the Faith), the Most Reverend Peter Elliott (Auxiliary Bishop of Melbourne), the Most Reverend Salvatore Cordileone (Bishop of Oakland, California), Professor Hans-Jürgen Feulner (University of Vienna), and Professor Clinton Brand (University of Saint Thomas, Houston). In addition the Reverend Aidan Nichols OP and the Reverend Jeremy Driscoll OSB were named as Consultors.

[19] Steven Lopes, "A Missal for the Ordinariates," 119. On 24 November 2015 Monsignor Steven Lopes was appointed as bishop-ordinary of the Personal Ordinariate of the Chair of Saint Peter. I am grateful to the aforementioned Dr Brand for the clarification that the *Ratio* was not conceived as a static document but "a set of operational rules of thumb that emerged rather organically."

5. to combine, consolidate, and harmonize wherever possible the diversity of Anglican liturgical usage for the sake of assuring the continuity, integrity, and pastoral utility of the liturgical provision;
6. to minimize the number of options, except where clearly justified by the need for pastoral flexibility in respecting the various constituencies coming together in Catholic unity;
7. to respect received texts in their integrity in as far as possible;
8. to offer an instrument for the sanctification of the faithful who come to the Catholic Church from the Anglican tradition while promoting their unity with one another, with their fellow Catholics in the wider Church, and with the See of Peter.[20]

It is through the lens of these principles, then, that we are bound to read and consider the texts of *Divine Worship* in light of the idea which this paper lays before us: *Divine Worship* as an example of liturgical text preservation.[21] First, a comment on the format of the *Ratio* principles themselves. In a number of cases these principles provide both an objective and subjective element. That is to say there is an element which may be commonly perceived, and an element that retains a subjective judgement to the members of the *Anglicanæ traditiones* working group; a judgement which would ultimately be accepted or rejected by the legislator. Let us take the first paragraph as an example:

> to preserve for Catholic worship the worthy Anglican liturgical patrimony, understood as that which has nourished the Catholic faith throughout the history of the Anglican tradition and prompted aspirations towards ecclesial unity;

The first part of this paragraph indicates that the intention is "to preserve for Catholic worship the worthy Anglican liturgical patrimony." Here the term "worthy" might at first be understood not as subjective, but laudatory; echoing the words of Pope Paul VI. And it is true that the preservation of certain texts and translations of the Anglican liturgical heritage, present in *Divine Worship*, will undoubtedly cause the worshipper to perceive a particular Anglican character, perhaps due to familiarity with the text or translation. The *Collect for Purity*, for instance, is a familiar translation of a prayer drawn from the *Book of Common Prayer*, of a text found in the wider Latin liturgical tradition.[22] Its use in *Divine Worship* is an unimpeachable preservation in Catholic worship

[20] Lopes, "A Missal for the Ordinariates," 120.

[21] This study will be limited to *Divine Worship: The Missal*. Furthermore, we will focus on the texts of the *Ordo Missæ*, and avoid consideration of the *Rubrical Directory*, pertinent liturgical law, or other ceremonial directives.

[22] Here is the text of the *Collect for Purity*, taken from *Divine Worship: The Missal*: "Almighty God, unto whom all hearts be open, all desires known, and from whom no secrets are hid: cleanse the thoughts of our hearts by the inspiration of thy Holy Spirit, that we may perfectly love thee, and worthily magnify thy holy Name; through Christ our Lord. Amen."

of a well-loved element of the Anglican liturgical patrimony. Yet the second part of the paragraph adds a further layer to this consideration. This indicates that the preservation of such texts is indicative that they have "nourished the Catholic faith throughout the history of the Anglican tradition and prompted aspirations towards ecclesial unity." The inclusion of this clause means the term "worthy" is in fact subjective, and so not a direct reference to Paul VI's phrase. To what degree a particular oration or text might be said to have achieved the lofty goal enunciated by the statement at the start of the principle, is clearly a subjective consideration. Taking again the text of the *Collect for Purity*, for instance, let us briefly ask if this can be said to have explicitly or even implicitly been a vehicle for this desire for unity? In a sense we can say yes; the text is preserved in the Anglican liturgical tradition from the Sarum Missal, and it also appears in the *Missale Romanum*. Certainly, then, as a text with origins in Catholic worship its preservation in Anglican worship is an explicit preservation of Catholic forms, which can easily be understood to have provided Anglicans with an implicit prompting toward reunion with the See of Peter, to say nothing of its invocation of the Holy Spirit. In another sense, however, we must say no; this text was intentionally removed from its original Catholic source, translated into the vernacular, and then included in liturgical books that of their very nature are at odds with the liturgical and doctrinal positions of Catholic Church. Thus, any decision about which of these possible outcomes triumphs over the other either requires extensive and precise evidence-based research, or a subjective consensus brought about by the deliberations of a necessarily limited group of people. My observation is manifestly not intended to criticise the decision—indeed it is perhaps impossible to judge whether the final call is right or wrong. Instead, as we consider *Divine Worship* as an example of liturgical text preservation, it is precisely this sort of understanding of the complexities of the work that brings about a high degree of sympathy toward the final text.

In speaking of examples of textual preservation in the liturgical books of *Divine Worship*, three principal categories can easily be identified: texts of original composition, of translation, or centonization, from Anglican sources; texts from Anglican sources which have been altered for *Divine Worship*; texts of new composition or translation not included in Anglican sources.

First, then, those texts which are removed in their integrity from Anglican sources, such as the historic prayer books or the Anglican missals.[23] These may

[23] Lopes notes the following regarding the selection of sources for Anglican liturgical texts considered for inclusion in *Divine Worship* by the working group: "Given its use as an approved Catholic liturgical text for the parishes of the Pastoral Provision in the United States, the *Book of Divine Worship* has been accorded primacy of place in the selection of texts. In the second place, the classic Prayer Book heritage (represented by England 1549, 1662, and 1928,

be texts composed by the framers of the Anglican liturgical books, texts translated from other sources for inclusion in official or unofficial Anglican liturgical books, or texts that have undergone a process of alteration or centonization, either translated or originally in English, for inclusion in Anglican liturgical books. The common factor in this category, though, is that the text in question appears in an Anglican source, be it an edition of the *Book of Common Prayer*, an Anglican missal, or even the *Book of Divine Worship*.[24] Texts in this first category undoubtedly "preserve for Catholic worship the worthy Anglican liturgical patrimony"; they maintain for Catholic worship distinctive elements of the Anglican tradition; they lend a "distinctively and traditionally" Anglican character and content to the *Order of Mass*; their use indicates either a common textual heritage across the Anglican liturgical books, or a choice that gives preference to one version of the text over others; they clearly, as part of the Order of Mass, "offer an instrument for the sanctification of the faithful" who have become members of the personal ordinariates. Subjectively speaking, however, we are bound to ask what scrutiny has been applied to these texts to ensure that they are "in conformity with Catholic doctrinal and liturgical norms"? Given the various competing interpretations given by Anglicans to standard texts (the so-called "historic formularies"), is it possible or even desirable, let alone reasonable, to accept one interpretation over another? Does the process of analysing and conforming these texts to "Catholic doctrinal and liturgical norms" require the removal of all ambiguity regarding a particular point, and (given the breadth of Anglican churchmanship and theological interpretations) from every perspective? And does the alteration of the text itself, even for these best of intentions, bring into question the authenticity of the final text as a true vehicle and means for the preservation of the Anglican patrimony in the Catholic Church? Still more, is the scrutiny applied to the texts in question applied to them in their original context and place, that is within the various Anglican liturgical rites, or is the text considered apart from this? What are the benefits and limitations of such a process? In respect of the third principle of the *Ratio*, for instance, is it primarily the intention of *Divine Worship* to preserve "an Order of Mass at once distinctively and traditionally Anglican in

USA 1928, Scotland 1929, South Africa 1954, and Canada 1962) has been taken into account. In the third place, consideration was given to *The English Missal* (1958) and *The Anglican Missal* (1961). If a consultation of the above sources did not provide the necessary material for a particular liturgical celebration, then *Common Worship* (2000) or the *Roman Missal* were consulted." Lopes, "A Missal for the Ordinariates," 121.

[24] *The Book of Divine Worship* is the liturgical book produced for the use of communities erected under the provisions of the 1980 Statute, the so-called Pastoral Provision, in the United States. See Lopes, "A Missal for the Ordinariates," 121. See Congregation for Divine Worship, decree, 13 February 1987, Prot. N. 1038/83, in *Bishops' Committee on the Liturgy Newsletter* 23 (March 1987).

character, content, and structure," or to ensure that it is "clearly and recognizably an expression of the Roman Rite"?

A brief example of a text from this category illustrates something of the conundrum that the working group faced in its work. Here is the Collect for the Second Sunday before Lent (Sexagesima) as it appears in *Divine Worship: The Missal*, alongside the Latin text as found in both the Sarum Missal and the pre-conciliar *Missale Romanum*:[25]

Sarum Missal & Missale Romanum	Divine Worship
Deus, qui conspicis, quia ex nulla nostra actione confidimus: concede propitius; ut, contra adversa omnia, Doctoris gentium protectione muniamur. Per Dominum.	O Lord God, who seest that we put not our trust in any thing that we do: mercifully grant that by thy power, we may be defended against all adversity; through Jesus Christ.

From the time of Pope Saint Gregory the Great (d. 604) the Roman stational church for this Sunday was the basilica of Saint Paul outside the Walls. The epistle on that day, taken from the Second Letter to the Corinthians and appointed in the Sarum Missal, the pre-conciliar *Missale Romanum*, and the classical editions of the *Book of Common Prayer*, reflects this by recalling the trials undertaken by Saint Paul for the propagation of the faith. The Collect, too, identical in both the Sarum Missal and the *Missale Romanum*, refers to Saint Paul as *Doctoris gentium*. Yet despite the inclusion of this ancient Collect in the 1549 *Book of Common Prayer*, the reference to Saint Paul is removed. This remains the case in subsequent revisions of the Prayer Book. The Collect devoid of the reference to Saint Paul is inoffensive; it certainly cannot be said to contradict Catholic theological principles or norms. Yet at the same time, if the reason for the removal of this reference is because of a rejection of the cult of the saints, then from a Catholic perspective one might reasonably ask: as the text is re-appropriated for Catholic worship in *Divine Worship*, should the text be preserved in its integrity as found in the *Book of Common Prayer*, or restored to the ancient form of the Collect found in Catholic liturgical books?[26]

[25] F. H. Dickinson, *Missale ad usum insignis et præclaræ ecclesiæ Sarum* (Burntisland: J. Parker & Co., 1861-83), 114; *Missale Romanum ex decreto SS. Concilii Tridentini restitutum Summorum Pontificum cura recognitum*. Editio typica 1962, edizione anastatica (Vatican City: Libreria Editrice Vaticana, 2007), 135.

[26] It is of note that the Prayer Book version (i.e., minus the reference to Saint Paul) also appears in the 1961 Anglican Missal and editions of the English Missal, where are often characterised as highly "Romanizing," that is heeding too much attention to Catholic sources, rather than Anglican.

Secondly, *Divine Worship* contains texts taken from Anglican sources which have been altered for inclusion in *Divine Worship.* The *Ratio* gives various reasons for such a change. It may be to bring about conformity with Catholic doctrinal and liturgical norms, to make the liturgical rite more clearly an expression of the Roman Rite, or to harmonize a text found in a range of versions in different Anglican liturgical books for inclusion in the single source of *Divine Worship.* In this the *Ratio* also underscores this principle as part of its work: "to respect received texts in their integrity in as far as possible." Steven Lopes comments that this relates to certain features of Prayer Book worship, namely the *Decalogue*, the *Collect for Purity*, the *Comfortable Words*, and the *Prayer of Humble Access.*[27] However, once more a high degree of subjectivity exists. We are not dealing here with the selection of a single version of an Anglican liturgical text from a particular Anglican source. Instead this scenario sees the adaptation of an existing text—a received part of the Anglican liturgical patrimony—specifically for inclusion in *Divine Worship.* Whatever the reason for this, a similarly persistent question remains: to what extent can even a subtle alteration represent continuity or preservation of a liturgical text-based culture?

Finally, there are texts in *Divine Worship* which are of new composition or translation, and are not included in Anglican sources. Chief amongst these are the orations for saints canonised in the Catholic Church and not provided for in Anglican sources. The addition of such texts has obvious merit and pastoral worth, but there are still interesting questions raised. First, what is the source for the base texts? Were these orations included in *Divine Worship* translated from the Latin originals, or "translated" into hieratic so-called "Prayer Book English" from translations already provided in the English edition of the 2002 *Missale Romanum*? Were, and if so to what extent, the provisions of *Liturgiam authenticam* taken into consideration in this process?[28]

---

[27] Lopes, "A Missal for the Ordinariates," 124. Lopes refers to "elements found in the 1549 [*Book of Common Prayer*] which still have wide currency in the Anglican tradition, such as the preparatory prayers of the priest, the Last Gospel, and a special form of the *Agnus Dei* for funeral Masses." However, these are not found in the *Book of Common Prayer* from 1549 onwards. Certain elements are restored in later editions of the Prayer Book, most notably the proposed *Book of Common Prayer* in England (1928) and the Canadian edition of the *Book of Common Prayer* (1962).

[28] *Liturgiam authenticam* is the fifth instruction issued by the Congregation for Divine Worship and the Discipline of the Sacraments for the implementation of the constitution on the sacred liturgy of the Second Vatican Council. The instruction concerns the use of vernacular languages in the publication of the book of the Roman liturgy. *See* Congregation for Divine Worship and the Discipline of the Sacraments, instruction *Liturgiam authenticam*, 28 March 2001: *AAS* 93 (2001): 685–726. A further question might be whether the mandatory inclusion of all of the saints of the General Roman Calendar in the particular calendar of each ordinariate is necessary, especially given the wealth of saints in the pre-Reformation English, Welsh, and

It is perhaps harder at first to see texts in this third category as examples of textual preservation. They are insertions into an existing liturgical patrimony. Yet in a sense it is in this seemingly incongruous situation that we perhaps understand more clearly the underlying concept of the entire *Divine Worship* project. Particularly in the case of the Eucharistic liturgy, the wholesale approval of a liturgical rite which exists in multiple forms, and which from its origins is in distinction to Catholic liturgical and doctrinal norms, is not the object. Instead it is to make provisions for a liturgical life for the communities of the personal ordinariates, and to maintain their liturgical, spiritual and pastoral traditions in order to offer "a precious gift nourishing the faith of the members of the ordinariate and as a treasure to be shared" (*AC* III). This is ultimately a new context for new communities, albeit formed from a series of broadly similar Anglican ecclesial cultures. That *Divine Worship* is not the result of a "drag and drop" or "copy and paste" process of liturgical text preservation, avoids something as arbitrary and potentially damaging as its opposite: the invention of something from naught. Given the circumstances, and the immediate and particular pastoral need presented by *Anglicanorum cœtibus*, *Divine Worship* instead seeks to provide an intelligent approach to a specific situation. I believe that it is broadly successful in achieving this. That not everyone will agree with every conclusion reached, or with every choice codified within is perhaps less a sign of failure, and more that *Divine Worship* has achieved what, as we have seen, is an almost impossible task.

None of this is to say that there is no need to revisit these principles and texts in the future. Indeed, the very fact that the communities of the personal ordinariates are so new, and the need for this liturgical provision so immediate, will undoubtedly require a developing understanding of what is appropriate, of what "works," and of what is needed in the pastoral care of the faithful concerned. Legitimate questions of distinctiveness from and conformity with other Catholic communities and liturgical rites abound, and the needs of ordinariate faithful in North America and Australia and Britain, to say nothing of Japan and the Melanesian islands, will undoubtedly bring other issues to the fore. As these communities and parishes grow into their new ecclesial reality, however, the form of worship and the link between the identity of the community and the texts with which they pray will only become more important. And in this respect, we can conclude with these words of Augustine Di Noia, one of the co-chairmen of the *Anglicanæ traditiones* working group:

> With the inclusion of such a liturgical provision in *Anglicanorum Cœtibus*, the Holy See acknowledges the legitimate patrimony of ecclesial communities coming into full communion. An essential part of that patrimony must be

Scottish liturgical traditions, which are now rarely given any liturgical commemoration or mention.

liturgical since worship expresses in a most tangible way not only the ethos of a community, but also the faith that prompted it to seek full communion in the first place. Just as it would be unthinkable to describe the Catholic Church without reference to its liturgical and sacramental life, so it would in some sense be for every ecclesial body. The manner in which an ecclesial community worships uniquely expresses its inner life.[29]

[29] Augustine Di Noia, "*Divine Worship* and the Liturgical Vitality of the Church," *Antiphon* 19, no. 2 (2015): 110.

LITURGICAL TEXT AS MANDORLA: WINDOWS FROM THE EVERYDAY TO THE SACRED, FROM THE SACRED TO THE EVERYDAY*

Stephen Morgan
(University of Saint Joseph, Macau)

ABSTRACT

In the iconographic tradition of the Christian East, it is the convention that icons featuring representations of the person of Christ show him placed in front of a gold ovaloid disc. This disc—called a 'mandorla' after the disc's almond-like shape—is understood to represent the uncreated light of heaven bursting through a breach, a tear in the veil between Heaven and Earth, between the sacred and the everyday: the former illuminating and sanctifying the latter, the latter drawn inexorably to the former. The figure of Christ—the God-Man—is depicted as the personal embodiment of this dynamic: he is the man whose death effects the breach in the veil and the God who shines forth through it.

By considering images of glory in a sample of euchological texts from several ancient Christian rites, this paper will seek to establish that these texts function as windows from the everyday to the sacred, from sacred to the everyday in a manner analogous to that represented visually in the iconographic tradition. By considering the semantic fields of the terms in the source languages that are rendered into English as "glory" (and its cognates), it will be argued that the texts themselves should be understood as seeking to evoke and achieve exactly the same Christ-dependent dynamic and, it is proposed, these expressions of divine glory in liturgical texts serve precisely as textual mandorlas.

**

During the T'ang Dynasty (618–907CE), Chinese influence on Japanese Culture was perhaps at its zenith. Religious images of the Buddha present in T'ang Chinese silks were replicated in three-dimensional form in significant Buddhist shrines across Japan. The most significant and longest surviving such image dates to the early eighth century of the Common Era at the Nigatsu-dō, in Tōdai-ji, nt far from Osaka. This image, carved between 729 and 748,[1]

* Acronyms: CCSL = *Corpus Christianorum Series Latina*; PG = *Patrologia Graeca*; PL = *Patrologia Latina*; SC = *Sources Chrétiennes*; ST = *Summa Theologiæ*

[1] The present image was recarved after a fire destroyed the original in 1667. See Angela Falco Howard, *The Imagery of the Cosmological Buddha, Studies in South Asian Culture*, vol. 13 (Leiden: E.J. Brill, 1986), 65.

shows the Eleven Headed Buddha in front of and surrounded by an almond-shaped disc, representing an incision in the śākyamuni, the three worlds of existence, the three spheres of desire, form and formlessness. The three worlds refer to the following destinations for karmic rebirth: *Kāmaloka* is the world of desire, of humans, animals, ghosts etc.; *Rūpaloka* is the world of form, predominately free of baser desires, populated by dhyāna-dwelling gods, a possible rebirth destination for those well practiced in dhyāna. *Arūpaloka* is the world of formlessness, a noncorporeal realm populated with four heavens, possible rebirth destination for practitioners of the four formlessness stages.[2] The incision reveals each world to the other and becomes, thereby, an image of transcendence and the transfiguration of the Buddha associated with his enlightenment or awakening.[3] The disk, originally circular—hence the Sanskrit name *mandala*: literally "circle"—had been a staple of Buddhist iconography for at least 1800 years by the time that the Kannon at Tōdai-ji was made and the Hindu *yantra*, from which it may be derived, dates back further still, where it functions "as [a] revelatory [symbol] of cosmic truths and as instructional charts of the spiritual aspect of human experience."[4]

Whether there is any lineal connection between these Asian iconographies and the term *mandala*, on the one hand, and the use of the *mandorlas* to depict the apotheosis of a dead person in Roman pagan late antiquity and subsequently in Christianity, on the other, has not, as far as I have been able to establish, been demonstrated. Indeed, *mandorla*, the Italian word for the nut known in English, derives directly from the Greek *amygdalos*, for the name of the tree from which it came. Yet, given the generally-accepted linguistic hypothesis of proto-indo-european dependency of origin of most modern European languages, it seems likely that the Sanskrit *mandala* and modern *mandorla* words are related, if only distantly. Although, since the use of *mandorla* to describe the almond-shaped discs in Christian iconography dates only to the middle of the nineteenth century, the specific religious overtones of the Sanskrit term cannot be reliably said to form any part of the semantic influences on the use of the Italian word, which seems to be merely figurative and descriptive.

Icons bearing an almond-shaped (or occasionally round or even irregular) disc behind significant figures, first appear in Christian art in the fifth century. In the Basilica of St Mary Major, Rome, there is an icon of the appearance of the three angel figures to the Patriarch Abraham at the Oak of Mamre (Gen.18:1–8). This icon has been reliably dated to the building of the church

[2] *The Shambhala Dictionary of Buddhism and Zen* (Boston; New York: Shambhala, 1991), 230.

[3] Howard, *The Imagery of the Cosmological Buddha*, 65–68.

[4] Madhu Khanna, *Yantra, the Tantric Symbol of Cosmic Unity* (Rochester, VT: Inner Traditions, 2003), 12.

by Pope Sixtus III in the mid-430s, and in it the central Angelic figure is surrounded by an oval disk of light. By the sixth century, the use of these discs was restricted to figures identifiably of Christ, usually at the Transfiguration and later of the Resurrection, although given the patristic view that the Oak of Mamre account was a Trinitarian theophany, this convention may well have been honoured in icon in the Esquiline Basilica. Later still, these *mandorlas* came to be used in icons of Christ in Majesty and even in those of his Mother at her Assumption. In other words, they become used to signify moments in the Christian account of salvation that reveal the transcendent action of God in the world. Like the images in Japan, they represent an incision in the screen between the Sacred and the everyday, but here, given a specifically Christian context. The incision is understood to represent the uncreated light of heaven bursting through a breach, a tear in the veil between Heaven and Earth, between the sacred and the everyday: the former illuminating and sanctifying the latter, the latter drawn inexorably to the former. The figure of Christ—the God-Man—is depicted as the personal embodiment of this dynamic: he is the man whose death effects the breach in the veil and the God who shines forth through it. In these icons the *mandorlas* function in such a way that it is the God-man, Jesus Christ, who occupies the space between the brightness, which becomes eventually the apophatic darkness of Heavenly glory, and the events illuminated by it.[5]

This hesychast tradition of negation, of apophasis—so strong in the Greek Christian East—derives in part from the work of the late fifth and early sixth century CE neo-platonist philosopher known to us as Dionysius the Areopagite, or more reliably, given the uncertainty concerning the identity of the authorship of the works traditionally ascribed to him,[6] as Pseudo-Dionysius, and particularly in his *On the Divine Names*. Here the author writes that, although seemingly oxymoronic, we can say that the Divine Light is in fact dark: "... because it so exceeds the visible light."[7] Whilst the positive theology of Latin Christianity in the High-Middle Ages and beyond has often been accused of lacking this apophatic sense and eschewing even the apparently contradictory

---

[5] Vladimir Lossky, *The Mystical Theology of the Eastern Church* (Crestwood, NY: St. Vladimir's Seminary Press, 1976), ch.2, "The Divine Darkness."

[6] For a one modern treatment of the identity of the author, see Kevin Corrigan and L. Michael Harrington, "Pseudo-Dionysius the Areopagite," in *The Stanford Encyclopedia of Philosophy*, ed. Edward N. Zalta (Metaphysics Research Lab, Stanford University, 2019), last modified April 30, 2019, accessed July 20, 2019, https://plato.stanford.edu/archives/sum2019/entries/pseudo-dionysius-areopagite/.

[7] "Intangible and Invisible Darkness we attribute to that Light which is Unapproachable because it so exceeds the visible light." *Pseudo-Dionysius, Dionysius the Areopagite On the Divine Names; and, the Mystical Theology*, ed. W. J. Sparrow-Simpson, trans. by C.E. Rolt (Kila, MT: Kessinger Pub. Co., 1992), 150.

in favour of making ever greater distinctions, it should be noted that the use of the analogy of being (*analogia entis*) by the Scholastics and their descendants was predicated precisely on an apophatic foundation. The Fourth Lateran Council's second canon, *On the Error of Abbot Joachim* (of Fiore), encapsulates the principle in stating that "for between creator and creature there can be noted no similarity so great that a greater dissimilarity cannot be seen between them."[8] In this case, that which we call bright of the Divine is more unlike natural brightness than like it. In any event, the fact that the *mandorla* is often extremely bright on its outer edge and seemingly darkens behind the figure of Christ is an expression of this mystical reality of the nature of the Uncreated when seen by the created. This visual property of *mandorlas* in much Christian iconography betokens a truth that will not be unimportant to keep in mind as I come to consider the often cataphatically and rationally unsatisfying account of the mechanism, the causality of liturgical *theosis*. If we must attempt an account in terms of positive theology, then we may have to take refuge in the Aristotelian category of final causality, of *telos*, and accept that this works by attraction rather than agency. I think it more helpful, however—at least on this occasion—to side with an apophatic acknowledgement of the limits of analogy when speaking of something ultimately beyond our comprehension, otherwise we may find ourselves forced into the silence Wittgenstein envisaged when he wrote, "Whereof one cannot speak, thereof one must be silent."[9]

I want to turn now to the thesis of my paper, for which this account of visual iconography provides a necessary point of departure. I want to suggest to you, that the textual images evoking Divine glory in Christian liturgical texts, at least those texts of the traditional Eucharistic rites of Western and Eastern Christianity, function as *mandorlas*: as points at which the veil between the Sacred and the everyday is torn apart, in order to mediate the one to the other; to illuminate the everyday with the eternal light of Heaven: to bring into the view of the Sacred, the joys and travails of the everyday. To do that comprehensively would require a lengthy monograph and so, given the constraints of this paper, I will have to content you with some indications derived from a very limited number of texts. I will confine myself largely to looking here at one example taken from the texts associated with the central act of Christian ritual worship: the Eucharist, together with a few allusions to some other liturgical texts.

---

[8] "... quia inter creatorem et creaturam non potest similitudonotari, quin inter eos maior sit dissimilitudo notanda," Concilium Lateranense IV, 1215, in *Decrees of the Ecumenical Councils*, ed. Norman P. Tanner, vol. 1 (London: Sheed & Ward; Washington, DC: Georgetown University Press, 1990), 232. See also ST Ia, 13, 3 ad 2.

[9] Ludwig Wittgenstein and Bertrand Russel, *Tractatus Logico-Philosophicus*, trans. C. K. Ogden (London: Kegan Paul, Trench, Trubner & Co, 1922), 90.

St Thomas Aquinas helpfully reminds us of Aristotle's dictum that "words are signs of thoughts and thoughts are likenesses of things."[10] The Philosopher, as Thomas calls Aristotle (here and almost everywhere else), gives a lengthier treatment of the same subject in *De Anima*, "To the thinking soul images serve as if they were the contents of perception.... That is why the soul never thinks without and image."[11] Aristotle is, though, anxious to recognize the limits of this account and to draw the distinction between concepts and images, asserting that they are not identical, "though they necessarily involve them."[12] Assuming for our present purposes that this idea that words are supposed to suggest images to the mind is correct, then I want to argue that the use in the liturgy of the Christian churches of terms which evoke what we might best translate into English as "glory," is intended, when predicated of the Divine, to suggest to the mind the image of that breach in the veil between the created order and the uncreated. In other words: "glory words" are textual *mandorlas*.

Liturgy is both word and actions, *gestis verbisque*— the reference here is to the Constitution on Divine Revelation of the Second Vatican Council *Dei Verbum*, which locates Divine Revelation not only in the words of Christ but in His actions too.[13] Since Catholic Christianity has long recognized the Liturgy as both a vehicle for the custodianship and transmission of Divine Revelation and as a *locus theologicus*, indeed as the first place in which theology is done (*theologia prima*), I would want to argue that the gestures and actions of the Liturgy that evoke Divine Glory also function as *mandorlas*. Nevertheless, for the present purposes—and given that here we are concerned with Comparative Literature not ritual studies—I will confine the remainder of my remarks, as far as possible, to the words and not the actions of the Liturgy.[14]

Both the Latin Thomas Aquinas (1225–1274) and his Greek near contemporary Gregory of Palamas (1296–1359) understand the process of divinisation, of theosis, deification, of becoming like unto God, as one whereby the human soul is transformed by the encounter with God, specifically the

[10] ST Ia, 13, 1, Resp, quoting Aristotle, *De Interpretatione*, ch.1, 16a3, see Aristotle, *The Basic Works of Aristotle*, ed. Richard McKeon (New York: Random House, 1941), 40.

[11] *De Anima*, III, Ch.7, 431a, 14–17, in Aristotle, 592.

[12] *De Anima*, III, Ch.8, 432a, 14f, in Aristotle, 596.

[13] "*Haec revelationis oeconomia fit gestis verbisque intrinsece inter se connexis*." "Dei Verbum," §. 2, accessed July 19, 2019, http://www.vatican.va/archive/hist_councils/ii_vatican_council/documents/vat-ii_const_19651118_dei-verbum_lt.html.

[14] For a detailed consideration of the relationship between ritual solemnity and the inspiration of devotion in the liturgy, see Sr. Thomas Augustine Becker, "The Role of Solemnitas in the Liturgy according to Saint Thomas Aquinas," in *Rediscovering Aquinas and the Sacraments: Studies in Sacramental Theology*, ed. Matthew Levering and Michael Dauphinais, Hillenbrand Books Collections Series (Chicago: Hillenbrand Books, 2009), 114–35.

encounter with Divine Glory or Divine Light. They are both faithful to the patristic consensus that this can take place only by way of "perceptible images"[15] in the ascending and uplifting "gaze upon the divinizing splendor of God"[16] or, as the twentieth century French Dominican theologian Marie-Dominique Chenu, put it "not-God's journey towards and in union with God, of the created's participation in the Uncreated."[17] Before looking at the small selection of texts that the constraints of this paper permit, we need to consider—as broadly representative of the Western and Eastern, the Latin and Greek liturgical traditions—the theological synthesis offered by Aquinas and Palamas.

In considering this movement towards union or into union with God, together with the Divine medium or cause of that journey, Gregory of Palamas confines himself to the use of the word *light*, whereas, at least in this regard, Thomas Aquinas uses *gloria* and *claritas* almost interchangeably, which is of particular interest given that claritas is also understood by him as *beauty*, one of the transcendentals predicated of God. Gregory is here very heavily reliant on Maximus the Confessor (c.580-662) whom he quotes as saying, "Deification is an enhypostatic and direct illumination ... [in which mortals] observing the light of the hidden and more-than-ineffable glory become able to receive the blessed purity in company with the celestial powers."[18] This is enhypostaic in the sense that the union with God being accomplished is such that the human is entirely dependent upon and subsistent to the Divine. Gregory goes further and locates the primary place of that direct illumination not in some purely rational process of intellectual speculation but in the contemplative activity of the Divine Liturgy. Here he draws on a rich patristic heritage (dating back as far as Origen, at least)[19] that sees the encounter with Christ, at least for those who come after His Ascension, as mediated by, as taking place in a privileged and unique manner in the Sacramental economy of the Liturgy: "What was

[15] Pseudo-Dionysius, *Pseudo-Dionysius: The Complete Works*, ed. Paul Rorem, trans. Colm Luibhéid, The Classics of Western Spirituality (New York: Paulist Press, 1987), 197.

[16] Daria E. Spezzano, *The Glory of God's Grace: Deification According to St. Thomas Aquinas*, Faith and Reason: Studies in Catholic Theology and Philosophy (Ave Maria, FL: Sapientia Press of Ave Maria University, 2015), 352.

[17] See A. N. Williams, *The Ground of Union: Deification in Aquinas and Palamas* (New York: Oxford University Press, 1999), 158.

[18] Ibid., 105n6. Here Williams is quoting Gregory Palamas, *The Triads*, ed. John Meyendorff and trans. Nicholas Gendle, 2 vols., Classics of Western Spirituality (New York: Paulist Press, 1983), 610, III.1.28. Gendle locates the quotation from Maximus—which Meyendorff was unable to do, in Maximus the Confessor, *Ad Thalas*, 61, in J.-P. Migne, ed., PG 90, 636C and Scholia, 6, ibid., 644C.

[19] Origen and Rowan A. Greer, *Origen*, Classics of Western Spirituality (New York: Paulist Press, 1979), 25.

visible in Christ has passed over into the Church in her mysteries," as Pope St Leo the Great observed.[20] Thomas Aquinas, finds himself in the same territory, albeit by a different route (which need not concern us today). Wanting to maintain that "Nature is not done away, but perfected, by glory,"[21] in the *Tertia Pars* of his *Summa Theologiæ*, he claims this to be not only an encounter with but a sacramental and hence liturgical or ritual participation in Christ's glory understood as his human self-offering. He writes:

> The whole rite of the Christian religion is derived from Christ's priesthood. Consequently, it is clear that the sacramental character is especially the character of Christ, to Whose character the faithful are made like unto Him by reason of the sacramental characters, which are nothing less than certain participations in Christ's priesthood, flowing from Christ Himself.[22]

Glory in Judaeo-Christian thought has long been understood as the particular property of God.[23] We have already seen how Thomas Aquinas understands it as *claritas*, how Gregory of Palamas identifies it with light and how they both stand in the patristic tradition of interpreting it as operating as a cause of theosis/deification through the liturgy. However, the term "glory" has a much longer theological history and wider semantic field than explored in this paper thus far and we needs must consider some of that now.

Faced with the sight of observant Jews dancing before the Western Wall of the former-temple complex in Jerusalem after the siren sounds for beginning of *Shabbat* שַׁבָּת, one might reasonably ask what the celebration was all about. Imprecatory prayers sung mournfully or uttered close to the wall, or slipped into gaps in the masonry itself can easily be understood in simple human terms of longing by Jews for the restoration of God's presence on Mount Zion, true pole of all the earth, as the Psalmist has it (Ps.47(48): 3). The exuberant dancing at dusk on a Friday evening must surely betoken something else and indeed it does. The presence of God in the Holy of Holies in the Temple goes by the Hebrew term שכינה, *Shekinah*, a word whose etymology gives the term the literal sense of "the settling" or "the resting." What rested in the Temple was the

---

[20] Leo the Great, *Sermo* LXXIV, II.

[21] "est quia natura non tollitur per gloriam, sed perficitur," ST, IIa IIae, 26, 13 sed contra. Here he repeats the claim in ST Ia, 1, 8 ad 2, that "gratia non tollit naturam sed perficit eam" but now "gratia" has become "gloria."

[22] "Totus autem ritus Christianae religionis derivatur a sacerdotio Christi. Et ideo manifestum est quod character sacramentalis specialiter est character Christi, cuius sacerdotio configurantur fideles secundum sacramentales characteres, qui nihil aliud sunt quam quaedam participationes sacerdotii Christi, ab ipso Christo derivatae," ST, IIIa, 63, 3 resp.

[23] Arthur Michael Ramsey, *The Glory of God and the Transfiguration of Christ* (London: Longmans, Green and Co, 1949), 10.

glory of God, the glory that had accompanied the People of Israel in that Exodus from Egypt, the historicity of which is disputed, but which becomes the foundational myth of the entire Jewish nation. When Titus destroyed the Second Temple in 70CE and carried away many of the ritual artefacts used in the Temple cult, this was widely understood by Jews as marking God's departure from his Sanctuary. Since the nineteenth century emergence of Zionism, however, other theologies have emerged. Asked recently for an explanation of these eve of *Shabbat* revels, Rabbi David Mitchell explained that the term for glory in Hebrew was כָּבוֹד *kabod* and it was this that rested on Zion. It is a term that originally meant simply heavy or weighty or even valuable but, when applied to God, it acquired the sense of Divine majesty or glory.[24] The Rabbi explained that modern Jews typically understand the glory of God that rested on the temple as having such weight that the destruction of Titus could not dislodge it from the very stones of the Temple. Margaret Barker, in her seminal "Temple Themes in Christian Worship" notes that this notion of the abiding Divine presence was a constant feature of the Jewish liturgical horizon against which the Christian cult emerged.[25]

When confronted with the two hundred occurrences of the word כָּבוֹד *kabod* in the Hebrew text, the translators of the Septuagint chose cognates of the Greek word δοξα on all except one occasion and that in Is.5:13—where the rendering πληθος, honourable, retains the sense in the Greek of "weighty."[26] *Doxa* has an extraordinarily wide semantic field in Greek literature. Its meanings range from "a notion, true or false" and "an expectation" in the Homeric literature, through "an opinion" or "conjecture" in Aeschylus, to "good repute" in Thucydides, Solon and Democrates.[27] Clearly this later, developed meaning influenced the Septuagint translators and by the time of the writing of the New Testament, *doxa* had come to be understood within the nascent Christian communities—at least as far as can be established by its use in their scriptures, as having the sense of the Latin *gloria*: glory, fame, renown, praise, honour, whilst not losing its associations with God's presence.[28] This is how St Paul

[24] Walther Eichrodt, *Theology of the Old Testament*, The Old Testament Library (Philadelphia: Westminster Press, 1967), 29–35.

[25] Margaret Barker, *Temple Themes in Christian Worship* (London; New York: T & T Clark, 2007).

[26] Henry George Liddell and Robert Scott, *A Greek-English Lexicon*, s.v. Πλῆθος, accessed July 19, 2019, http://www.perseus.tufts.edu/hopper/text?doc=Perseus:text:1999.04.0057:entry=plh=qos.

[27] Henry George Liddell and Robert Scott, *An Intermediate Greek-English Lexicon*, s.v. Δόξα, accessed July 19, 2019, http://www.perseus.tufts.edu/hopper/text?doc=Perseus%3Atext%3A1999.04.0058%3Aentry%3Ddo%2Fca.

[28] Charlton T. Lewis and Charles Short, *A Latin Dictionary*, s.v. Glōrĭa, accessed July 19, 2019, http://www.perseus.tufts.edu/hopper/text?doc=Perseus%3Atext%3A1999.04.0059%3Aentry%3Dgloria.

uses the term repeatedly—sixty six times in the *Corpus Paulinum* (arguments about pseudepigraphy aside) and in the Fourth Gospel and the Book of the Apocalypse the word is used in this sense thirty two times. As the Christian cult developed and its texts came to be fixed, the repeated use of "glory words" clearly came to convey a sense that was well understood by the nascent Church and with associations that placed those words and the images they evoked firmly in the sense of something associated with the presence of the Divine.

The interdependence of the Eucharistic and other liturgical texts of the various rites (understood as specific rituals) in each of the broad families of Christian Rites (understood as local expressions of that cultus) is readily demonstrable and the idea of "glory" disclosing the presence of God in them is virtually ubiquitous. Those who created the various liturgical traditions across the Christian world of late-antiquity appear to have striven to use the same texts in several ritual settings, in order to create a common thought-world or imaginative-world that, nevertheless, related to and reflected the many differing local or temporal circumstances. There is an abundance of texts that could be considered here: from the various *psalmi idiotici* or private hymns, such as the *Phos Hilarion*, the *Te Deum* and the eponymous *Gloria in Excelsis Deo*, the texts of which were, it seems, more or less settled by the middle of the fourth century; through the collections of *preces* and orations which formed the variable parts of the Christian liturgies; and the litanies and antiphons which accompany the various entrances and processions that mark the ancient Rites.

The first-mentioned of these texts, the *Phos Hilarion*, will have to stand duty for these various texts. It is a hymn for the Great Entrance at the Solemn Evening Office of Vespers in the Liturgy of Byzantium and, as a result of the historical influence of that City, now of the wider Orthodox world. Not well-known in the Latin west, it had no settled part in the Roman Rite until a bowdlerized translation was added to the Liturgy of the Hours following the liturgical reforms of the late-twentieth century. Nevertheless, its powerful imagery had attracted the religious imagination and translation genius of the nineteenth century Anglican divine, John Keble, who fashioned the hymn "Hail gladdening light" from its ancient origins. The *Phos Hilarion* appears first in the fourth century *Apostolic Constitutions*, and expresses a deifying dynamic of the encounter with the glorious light of the Divine presence in Jesus Christ. Its imagery is such that it bears quoting in full, such is its correspondence to my contention that these images of glory serve as textual *mandorlas*:

> O Gentle Light of the holy glory of the immortal, heavenly, holy, blessed Father, O Jesus Christ: Having come to the setting of the sun, having beheld the evening light, we praise the Father, the Son, and the Holy Spirit: God. Meet it is for Thee at

all times to be hymned with reverent voices, O Son of God, Giver of life. Wherefore, the world doth glorify Thee.[29]

Other practices developed alongside the doctrinal controversies of the fourth and fifth centuries that both served to underline what became, after the first councils at Nicaea, Constantinople, the Trinitarian orthodoxy of the majority of Christian churches, and also repeatedly to assert the motif of "glory" in the liturgical texts used throughout the liturgy. Prominent amongst these is the use of the minor-doxology "Glory be to the Father and to the Son and to the Holy Spirit" to begin liturgical services, to mark the entrance into the Divine action of the liturgy, and to complete the psalms and responsories. There are minor local textual variants: notable amongst these is the use both amongst the East Syrians and—at the very other end of the Christian world of the time—the Mozarabic Christians of a version that reads "Glory and honour to the Father and to the Son and to the Holy Spirit," which, given the semantic field of the word *doxa* that we encountered earlier, may, in an original and now lost Greek form, have served as a superlative formed by the common practice of doubling—familiar, at least, to those of you who speak Semitic or Sino-Tibetan languages.

The practice of using the minor doxology in these liturgical locations had become near universal by the time of the Council of Constantinople in 381AD and its frequent use may have served to provide for that Council evidence of the faith of the Church in the divinity of the Holy Spirit, alongside the Trinitarian baptismal formula, against the claims of the so-called *pneumatomachians*, those who "fought the Spirit." Whatever else this minor doxology did, it repeated brought the Christian worshipper face-to-face, so to speak, with the image of Divine glory as the daily round of the liturgy progressed.

At the heart of the Christian *cultus* is the Eucharistic liturgy: the ritual enactment, in the form of a sacrificial meal, and representation, *anamnesis*—a remembering-that-makes-present—of the Paschal Mystery by which, Christians believe, Jesus Christ effected their redemption and the possibility of their union with God, from whom the sin of their first parents had separated them. It is, above all things (and in a way that transcends inter-Confessional disagreements about its modalities) a ritual of the celebration of the presence of the Divine. We should not be in the least surprised that ideas derived from the vocabulary of glory should predominate—both in terms of the use of that vocabulary and in the use of terms, texts and rhetorical devices (to say nothing here of the ritual acts, decoration and artifacts) designed to evoke glory. Common to all these various Rites, as local expressions of the Christian *cultus*, however, is the adoption at the centre of the Eucharistic liturgy of a textual (and ritual) format that appears designed to draw the individual worshipper

[29] *The Unabbreviated Horologion* (Jordanville, NY: Holy Trinity Monastery, 1997), 192f.

from the everyday into close contact with the Sacred, with כָּבוֹד *kabod*, δοξα, gloria, "glory." This format occurs in the three-fold textual structure of Preface-Sanctus-Canon that is common to the main families of ancient Christian Rites and it is a series of prayers that use a vocabulary rich in images of glory, in terms closely related to or associated with the word and clearly designed to "conjure up" imagery of the celestial.

The preface, αντηαναφορα or *praefatio*, is the first limb of this *prex triplex*—which in some Rites has hundreds of variants, in others is fixed to a single or relatively small selection of texts.[30] It begins with a dialogue, which, minor variations in vocabulary aside, has the same shape and serves the same purpose in all the major ancient liturgies. It proceeds by way of a three-part verse and response:

V. The Lord be with you;

R. And with your Spirit;

V. Lift up your hearts;

R. We lift them up to the Lord;

V. Let us give thanks to the Lord our God;

R. It is right and just.

Elements of this introductory dialogue can be reliably traced back to the third century[31] but has little to offer of interest to our current enquiry, save and except to say that it has its remote origins in both Temple worship and in the public rituals of late-Roman paganism. It's ritual purpose is to serve as a unifying or gathering exchange between the priest (although in some places some

[30] Alan Griffiths, *We Give You Thanks and Praise: The Eucharistic Prefaces of the Ambrosian Missal* (Norwich: Canterbury Press, 2000), xv.

[31] Cyprian of Carthage refers to the priest's exhortation "*Sursum corda*" and the people's response "*Habemus ad Dominum*" in his Cyprian of Carthage, *De dominica oratione*, 31: CSEL 3,289. *The Traditio Apostolica* has the entire Roman introductory dialogue, except for the addition "*Deo nostro*" to the celebrant's last exhortation: see *Traditio apostolica* 4,3: P.F. Bradshaw, M.E. Johnson, L.E. Philips, ed., *The Apostolic Tradition: A Commentary*, Hermeneia (Minneapolis, MN: Fortress Press, 2002), 38. The people's final response "*Dignum est iustum*" belongs to the kind of acclamations that were a common feature of popular assemblies in the ancient world. Such acclamations confirmed an important decision or election, including that of a Roman Emperor: "*Aequm est, iustum est*"; cf. the references in Eizenhöfer, Canon Missae romanae, 25. Later they were also used to approve the election of a bishop. See J.A. Jungmann, *The Mass of the Roman Rite: its origins and development*, trans. Francis Brunner, vol. 2 (Christian Classics: Notre Dame IN, 2012), 111–2, who also points to a similar response in Jewish morning prayer.

parts of it included interpolations by the deacon serving the Liturgy) and people that establishes their common purpose.

The final response of this dialogue "*Dignum et iustum est* .../ It is right and just ..." is then taken up and echoed by the celebrant in the first part of the preface-proper (also known by its technical term the "protocol"), with the first of a series of ascending and intensifying phrases, clearly designed to heighten the sense of anticipation: "It is truly right and just, our duty and our salvation, always and everywhere to give You thanks" and then, in a memorable rhetorical crescendo, in which the shorter invocation precedes the longer: "Lord, holy Father, almighty and eternal God."[32] In English this ascent is one of one, four and eight syllables, in the Latin of one, four and nine: the rhetorical effect is, however, the same. In the Greek liturgy of Byzantium a different technique is used to effect the same sense of ascent. Here an gradually intensifying list of verbs is used, "to hymn you, to bless you, to praise you, to give you thanks, to worship you in every place of your dominion." These crescendos are similar to that in the *Gloria in Excelsis Deo*: a hymn of such complexity and richness in its images of glory that I have deliberately shied away from a detailed consideration of it in this paper. In the *Gloria*, God is first acclaimed and then acknowledged and worshipped in a four-fold ascending Latin trope—laudamus te, benedicimus te, adoramus te, glorificamus te—of four, six, five and six syllables, a form similar to that in the Greek original—where the ascent is of four, five, five and six syllables.

The central part (or "embolism") of the Preface provides the motive why the Church renders praise and thanks to God and provides yet further rhetorical focus on the mystery of salvation. It may be brief or extended but the Roman Rite and other Western variants (such as the Ambrosian and the Mozarabic) differ from the practice in the East, at Alexandria or Antioch, for example, where the Preface remains the same at all times. In the Roman Rite it changes, the variants serving to identify the reason for thanksgiving particular to the day concerned. A particularly beautiful example is the ancient preface for Christmas:[33] it is a sublime expression of the human birth of the Son of God and is used on one of the most solemn days of the liturgical year. It retains the spare, even terse form of Roman public speech that is a characteristic of the Roman Rite. It reads:

---

32 In the *Missale Romanum* of 1570 and its subsequent editions, this was printed as "Domine sancte, Pater omnipotens, aeterne Deus." However, it has been shown conclusively that this punctuation is not correct, and so this has been changed in the editio typica of 1962; see Christine Morhmann, "Problèmes de Ponctuation Dans Le Préface," in *L'ordinaire de La Messe*, ed. Bernard Botte and Christine Morhmann, vol. 2, Études Liturgiques (Louvain: Du Cerf, 1953), 105.

33 Prefaces of the Nativity I in *Missale Romanum* 1970/2008 and Preface of the Nativity in *Missale Romanum* 1570/1962.

For in the mystery of the Word made flesh
a new light of your glory has shone upon the eyes of our mind,
so that, as we recognise in him God made visible,
we may be caught up through him in love of things invisible.

The text clearly draws on the Gospel of John, especially on its prologue (Jn.1:1–14) and more generally on the Johannine theology that presents Christ as the light of the world. There is also a detectible echo of the apparition to the shepherds of the Heavenly Host announcing the birth of the Saviour. The themes of this preface resonate particularly in the writings of Gregory the Great, whose influence on the Roman Rite, though difficult to pin down precisely, is uncontroversially held to have been definitive.[34]

The concluding part (or "eschatocol") invokes the continuous praise rendered by the angels and saints to God in heaven and invites the earthly community to join in it, thus providing the transition to the *Sanctus*. A characteristic feature of many prefaces is the reference to the choirs of angels, which developed from the Church Fathers' exegesis of Holy Scripture (e.g. Genesis 3:24, Ezekiel 28:14–16, Isaiah 6:2–3, Ephesians 1:21 and Colossians 1:16). Thus, a fittingly solemn prelude to the great acclamation of the thrice-holy God is provided. It is here that the language is deliberately structured to evoke images of encounter with Divine Glory.

To take but two examples, that used in the Common Preface of the traditional Roman Missal and that used in the Antiochene form of the Byzantine Liturgy of St John Chrysostom, we read—and thus hear—first in Rome:

> Through whom the Angels praise Your majesty, the Dominions adore You, the Powers tremble: the Heavens and the Hosts of Heaven, and the blessed Seraphim together celebrate in exultation, with whom, we pray You, command that our voices also be admitted in confessing You, saying....

and, in the characteristically prolix form of Constantinople:

> For You are praised by the angels, archangels, thrones, dominions, principalities, authorities, powers, and the many eyed Cherubim. Round about You stand the Seraphim, one

[34] See, for example, Gregory the Great, In *Ezech.* II, I, 15: SC 360, 80; *Moralia in Iob*, XVIII, li, 83: CCSL 143, 946, and also Fulgentius of Ruspe, *Ad Trasimundum*, 2, 6: PL 65, 252B. For a full list of these biblical and patristic references, see Anthony Ward and Cuthbert Johnson, *The Prefaces of the Roman Missal: A Source Compendium with Concordance and Indices* (Rome: Cong. for Divine Worship, 1989), 72–74.

with six wings and the other with six wings; with two they cover their faces; with two they cover their feet; with two they fly, crying out to one another with unceasing voices and ever resounding praises: singing the victory hymn, proclaiming, crying out, and saying....

In response to this peroration, the action of the liturgical prayer immediately moves on to a hymned response by the entire body worshippers in the *Sanctus*, the *Trisagion*, where the allusion is directly to the image of the worship of the glory of God in the Heavenly Temple,[35] taking up the words of the angels in the book of the Prophet Isaiah:

> Holy, holy, holy is the Lord God of Hosts.
>
> Heaven and earth are full of your glory
>
> Hosannah in the Highest. (Isaiah 6:3)

The theological vision textually and ritually expressed in the *Sanctus* marks a dynamic moment in the liturgy: the heavenly Church's presence is invoked, in all its Divine illuminated, deified glory and the earthly assembly is united with it as together they sing an identical hymn of praise. Here again we can detect a ritual practice carried over from the Jewish Temple cult into Christian worship, in which the earthly, the everyday, is united with the Sacred, the Heavenly, gathered, as in the Temple on Mount Zion, either side of the veil between the world and the Holy of Holies.[36] Furthermore, these words, common both to the celestial and the mundane, to the already-sacred, deified Church in Heaven and the becoming-sacred, being-deified Church on earth, enables the latter to join the former in "stand[ing] before the divine majesty ... in his glory and [with] the right to stand in his court."[37]

The final part of this Eucharistic *prex triplex*, is the Canon, the Eucharistic prayer, the Anaphora, in which, by means of the words of consecration the Church in its priest brings about the sacramental presence of Christ, crucified, risen and glorified, under the appearance of bread and wine—everyday gifts given Sacred reality. Although often seen as the sublimely and supremely theologically significant component of the Eucharistic ritual, for our present textual considerations this is, perhaps, the least interesting part of the Liturgy—although it is ritually of unsurpassable significance and provides visual

---

[35] Barker, *Temple Themes in Christian Worship*, 222.

[36] Ibid., 222.

[37] *A Commentary on the Order of Mass of the Roman Missal: A New English Translation Developed under the Auspices of the Catholic Academy of Liturgy*; General Editor, Edward Foley; Associate Editors, John F. Baldovin, Mary Collins, Joanne M. Pierce; Foreword by Roger Mahony, ed. Edward Foley et al. (Collegeville, MN: Liturgical Press, 2011), 265.

mandorlas aplenty: at least when celebrated in the eastward orientation common to the traditional practice of the ancient rites. Suffice it to say that this is the ritual moment when the veil between the Sacred and the everyday—a veil which has become ever thinner in the imaginative conception of the gathered worshippers by use of the images of Divine Glory in the preceding prayers—when that veil is torn by the Eucharistic Mystery of Christ. In the terms of my thesis in this paper, this is the moment when the *mandorla* between the Sacred and the everyday opens, when the veil between the realities is ripped open: the uncreated light of the former now illuminates the latter, the latter made eternally present and acceptable to the former, in the person of the God-man of the acceptable sacrifice. This whole ritual act is one couched in the language of "glory" and which functions precisely as the medium for the rupture in the veil between the sacred and the everyday, an incision in the worlds of existence revealing each to the other in an image of transcendence and transfiguration.

My thoughts on this subject are, I have to admit, still somewhat conjectural. Much more work needs to be undertaken, many more texts and sources of those texts need to considered if I am to establish whether the thesis is sustainable in the terms of a study in comparative literature. When considered alongside the ritual practices surrounding these texts—perhaps I should say, once again, given the subject matter, the words and actions—I am sure, even if only in the illative sense, that the thesis does hold water as a piece of liturgical theology. You will, I suppose, have to take that assertion on trust. I hope, though, that I have made a sufficient case for the contention, in terms of literary analysis, that textual images of glory in the Christian liturgy function as *mandorlas*, as incisions in the fabric of mystical reality between the sacred and the everyday in the context of that act central to Christian worship.

Sacred Time—Sacred Text: The Sanctification of Time as Evidenced in the Liturgical Texts of the Roman Rite

Monsignor Andrew R. Wadsworth
(International Commission on English in the Liturgy, Washington DC)

Time is something we live with; it is inseparable from our human experience. Time so envelops our existence from birth to death that we are often unaware of it and scarcely able to examine it. St. Augustine of Hippo [d.430] tells us that time itself is a creature of God when he writes: "You have made all times, and you are before all times, and not at any time was there no time."[1]

It is evident that God has enfolded all of His material creation in time, from the brilliant stars that endure for billions of years to the flower "that blossoms in the morning and withers in the evening."[2] All material creation comes to be and passes away, including we humans, whose "span is 70 years or 80 for those who are strong."[3] Our lifespan is bound by time, and yet it seems that God "has put the timeless into our hearts."[4]

In his Confessions (Book XI), Augustine ponders the mysterious nature of time. He seeks to explain the passage of time: "If we conceive of some point of time which cannot be divided into even the minutest parts of moments, that is the only point that can be called the present; and that point flees at such lightning speed from being future to being past, that it has no extent of duration at all."[5]

Augustine frames the essential question for us when he asks, "where does time come from, and by what way does it pass, and where does it go to while we are measuring it?" Where is it from? Obviously time comes from the future. "But by what means does it come to us? It comes by means of the present.

[1] James J. O'Donnell, *Augustine: Confessions* (Oxford: Oxford University Press, 1992) in *The Confessions of Augustine: An Electronic Edition*, ed. James J. O'Donnell, Stoa Consortium, November 24, 1999, accessed 20 July, 2019, http://www.stoa.org/hippo, Bk XI, Ch. 13. My own English translation for this paper.

[2] Ps. 90:6.

[3] Ps. 90:10.

[4] Eccl. 3:11.

[5] *Confessions*, XI, 15.

Where does it go? It goes into the past. In other words, it passes from that which does not yet exist, by way of that which lacks extension, into that which is no longer."[6] Time is certainly elusive. We are also reminded here of the Pre-Socratic philosopher Heraclitus (c.500 BCE), who said, "You cannot step twice into the same rivers; for fresh waters are flowing in upon you."[7] At this point, we can certainly sympathize with Augustine when he says, "what then is time? If no one asks me I know; if I want to explain it to a questioner, I do not know."[8] Yes, we can agree with Augustine, for while we recognize time's passage, we are hard pressed to say what it is.

That time exists somehow through memory we also learn from Augustine. After showing that the only time that has any real existence is the present moment, he offers yet another way of explaining time. "It might be appropriately said that there are three 'times': a present of things past, a present of things present, and a present of things future."[9] This Christian understanding of time is itself inherited from Judaism and takes us back to the first verses of the Book of Genesis, where God's creative activity is divided into as yet undefined sequences of time which are called days:

> וַֽיְהִי־עֶ֥רֶב וַֽיְהִי־בֹ֖קֶר י֥וֹם אֶחָֽד׃
>
> And there was evening and there was morning, one day.
>
> Gen. 1:5b.

It seems slightly counter-intuitive to the modern mind, but it would not be so to the ancients, that this primordial day begins with evening and follows through to the morning, and so throughout the day until the next evening. This pattern continues throughout five indeterminate "days" of the material creation, up to, and including the creation of animals.[10] Then, the sixth day sees the creation of human beings, and with the advent of human life, time itself seems to enter a new moment, linked, as it were, to human life. This is, in every sense, the culmination of the creation account and brings forth an expression of God's satisfaction in his completed work:

---

6 Ibid., XI, 21.

7 "ποταμοῖσι τοῖσιν αὐτοῖσιν ἐμβαίνουσιν ἕτερα καὶ ἕτερα ὕδατα ἐπιρρεῖ· καὶ ψυχαὶ δὲ ἀπὸ τῶν ὑγρῶν ἀναθυμιῶνται" H. Diels, *Herakleitos von Ephesus*, 2nd ed. (Berlin: Weidmann, 1909); *The Fragments of the Work of Heraclitus of Ephesus on Nature*, trans. with introduction by G. T. W. Patrick (Baltimore: N. Murray, 1889); *Fragment 12: Arius Didyne dans Eustèbe, Préparation évangélique*, XV, 20, 2, as cited at http://philoctetes. free.fr/heraclitus.htm [last updated September 25, 2006, accessed 20 July, 2019].]

8 *Confessions*, XI, 14.

9 Ibid., XI, 20.

10 The Hebrew text here uses the indefinite article: one day, a second day, a third day etc. up until the creation of the human beings on the sixth day which takes the definite article.

וַיַּרְא אֱלֹהִים אֶת־כָּל־אֲשֶׁר עָשָׂה וְהִנֵּה־טוֹב מְאֹד
וַֽיְהִי־עֶרֶב וַֽיְהִי־בֹקֶר יוֹם הַשִּׁשִּׁי׃

And God saw every thing that He had made, and, behold, it was very good. And there was evening and there was morning, the sixth day.

Gen. 1:31.

The Genesis creation account gives us the shape of a week that culminates in the שַׁבָּת (sabbath), the seventh day, upon which God rested after the work of creation and which became a perpetual ordinance, as a day differentiated from the rest and characterized by worship and rest. As God reveals himself progressively to the nation which becomes the holy people of Israel, there is established a pattern of worship which depends largely on the consecration of time. Observances such as the sabbath[11] (marking the passing of one week and the beginning of another), the new moon[12] (similarly the ending of one month and the beginning of another), the seasons, the notions of (the sabbati [13]שמיטה cal year) and (the jubilee year), evening, morning, and afternoon that [14]יובל bring with them the daily call to prayer, all of Judaism's first rituals are rooted in the marking of times and days. While the festivals celebrate events that happened in time, the date of the month assigned for each festival in the calendar is determined by life in nature.סֻכּוֹת[16] the (Passover) and [15]פֶּסַח (the Feast of Tabernacles), for example, coincide with the full moon, and the date of all festivals is a day in the month, and the month is a reflection of what is happening continually in the realm of nature, since the new month begins with the new moon, with the reappearance of the lunar crescent in the evening sky. In contrast, the sabbath is entirely independent of the month and unrelated to the moon. Its date is not determined by any event in nature, such as the new moon, but rather by the act of creation. Thus, the essence of the sabbath is completely detached from the world of space. The meaning of the sabbath is to celebrate time rather than space. It is a day on which we are called upon to share in what is eternal in time, to turn from the results of creation to the mystery of creation, from the world of creation to the creation of the world.

One of the most significant words in Scripture is the word קֹדֶשׁ, holy; a word which more than any other is representative of the mystery and majesty of the divine. It is significant when we consider the first holy object in the history of

[11] Ex. 20:8–11.
[12] Ps. 81:3.
[13] Ex. 23:10–11.
[14] Lev. 25:8–13.
[15] Lev. 23:5–8.
[16] Cf. Neh. 8:13–18; Zech. 14:16–19; Lev. 23:34–44.

the world. Was it a mountain? Was it an altar? At the end of the creation account in Genesis, we are told that the adjective "holy" is first applied to time:

> וַיְבָרֶךְ אֱלֹהִים אֶת־יוֹם הַשְּׁבִיעִי וַיְקַדֵּשׁ אֹתוֹ כִּי בוֹ שָׁבַת מִכָּל־מְלַאכְתּוֹ אֲשֶׁר־
> בָּרָא אֱלֹהִים לַעֲשׂוֹת׃
>
> And God blessed the seventh day and made it holy, for it was the day when he rested from all his work of creation.
>
> Gen. 2:3

There is no reference, in the Scriptural record of creation, to any object in space that would be endowed with this quality of holiness. We might expect that, after heaven and earth have been established, God would create a holy place, a holy mountain, whereupon a sanctuary is to be established. Yet it seems that in the Bible it is holiness in time, the sabbath, which comes first. This is the primordial holiness, for when the world was created, there was only one holiness, holiness in time. When, at Sinai, the word of God was about to be proclaimed, it was as a call for holiness in human beings that it was proclaimed:

> וְאַתֶּם תִּהְיוּ־לִי מַמְלֶכֶת כֹּהֲנִים וְגוֹי קָדוֹשׁ
>
> And you shall be to me a kingdom of priests and a holy nation.
>
> Exod. 19:6a

It was only after the people had succumbed to the temptation of worshipping an idol, the golden calf, that the erection of a tabernacle, a place of holiness in space, was commanded. Sanctity of time came first, sanctity of people came next, and the sanctity of space came last. Time was hallowed by God; space, in the form of the tabernacle, was consecrated by Moses.

These notions of the primacy of the sanctification of time are immediately brought by the first Christians, the vast majority of whom are Jewish, to the worship of the Church as it emerges as a separate community from those who worshipped in the Temple and the synagogues. The liturgical day, beginning with evening seems to have been the earliest pattern of Christian worship[17] and the establishment of celebrations which have as their focus the sanctification of days and seasons are in direct continuity with the experience of Judaism. The evening, morning and afternoon times for daily prayer informed the development, over time, of a pattern of prayer which became the *Liturgia Horarum*,[18] the Liturgy of the Hours, which marked the hours of the day, linking

---

[17] Cf. Paul F. Bradshaw, *The Search for the Origins of Christian Worship: Sources and Methods for the Study of Early Liturgy*, 2nd ed. (New York: Oxford University Press, 2002).

[18] *Liturgia Horarum*, editio typica altera (Vatican City: Libreria Editrice Vaticana, 1985 & 2000) with draft English translations, copyright International Commission on English in the Liturgy, Washington D.C., 2019.

them with various moments of salvation history, beginning with the creation account of Genesis. The Latin hymns attributed to St Gregory the Great [d.604] for Evening Prayer (Vespers) of each day present the finest examples of this genre. These hymns follow a simple four strophe pattern in which the first two strophes draw strongly on the Scriptural narrative for each day of creation, while strophes three and four offer a short παραίνεσις (exhortation) in terms of how this account might be applied to our lives. The hymn for Sunday Vespers is based on Genesis 1:1–5:

Lucis creátor óptime, lucem diérum próferens, primórdiis lucis novæ mundi parans oríginem;	Sublime Creator of the light, in bringing forth the light of day, you form the fabric of the world from fountains of your pristine light.
Qui mane iunctum vésperi diem vocári prǽcipis: tætrum chaos illábitur; audi preces cum flétibus.	The morning joined to evening hour is named the day at your command: as formless dark steals over us, in mercy heed our prayers and tears.
Ne mens graváta crimine vitæ sit exsul múnere, dum nil perénne cógitat seséque culpis ílligat.	Let not our soul, weighed down by faults, be exiled from the gift of life and, heedless of eternal good, ensnare itself in bonds of guilt.
Cælórum pulset íntimum, vitále tollat prǽmium; vitémus omne nóxium, purgémus omne péssimum.	But let it knock at heaven's gate to gain the prize of lasting life; let us avoid all harm from sin and purge away all base desire.

Wednesday's Vesper hymn, based on Genesis 1:14–19, evokes the placing of the sun and moon and so the marking of days and months:

Cæli Deus sanctíssime, qui lúcidum centrum poli candóre pingis ígneo augens decóri lúmina,	Most holy God in heaven above, who paints the sky with gleaming ray, the glowing dome of heaven's vault, adorning with resplendent lights
Quarto die qui flámmeam solis rotam constítuens, lunæ minístras órdini vagos recúrsus síderum,	On this fourth day you set in place the flaming circle of the sun and made the wandering paths of stars to serve the orbit of the moon,
Ut nóctibus vel lúmini diremptiónis términum, primórdiis et ménsium signum dares notíssimum:	That you might set for night and day a boundary keeping them apart and mark with clear, unfailing sign each new beginning of the month.
Illúmina cor hóminum, abstérge sordes méntium, resólve culpæ vínculum, evérte moles críminum.	Enlighten every heart and mind and wipe away all shameful thoughts; deliver us from bonds of guilt and ease the burden of our sin.

An anonymous hymn of the 6th or 7th century, intended for singing at the night office or at dawn, offers a similar reading of the creation story:

Primo diérum ómnium, quo mundus exstat cónditus vel quo resúrgens cónditor nos, morte victa, líberat,	On this the first of all the days, when God began to make the world, the day our Maker conquered death and rose again to set us free,
Pulsis procul torpóribus, surgámus omnes ócius, et nocte quærámus pium, sicut Prophétam nóvimus,	Now let us banish drowsy sloth and rise from sleep without delay to seek by night the loving God, as we have learned from David's psalm,
Nostras preces ut áudiat suámque dextram pórrigat, et hic piátos sórdibus reddat polórum sédibus,	That Christ may hear our humble prayers, and stretching forth his strong right hand, restore to their celestial home those cleansed from evil here below.
Ut, quique sacratíssimo huius diéi témpore horis quiétis psállimus, donis beátis múneret.	So may he grant his gracious gifts to us who rise when all is still, to sing him psalms and hymns of praise at this most sacred time of day.

The same principle is at work within the course of each day, assigning to the specific hours of Terce (midmorning prayer), Sext (midday prayer) and None (midafternoon prayer) the commemoration of events that are believed to have happened at that time. This hymn, written before the 6th century, is assigned to Terce and commemorates the descent of the Holy Spirit at Pentecost:

Certum tenéntes órdinem, pio poscámus péctore hora diéi tertia trinæ virtutis glóriam,	We keep the order of the day with loving heart and earnest prayer; at this third hour we humbly beg the glory of your threefold power,
Ut simus habitáculum illi Sancto Spirítui, qui quondam in apóstolis hac hora distribútus est.	That we may be a dwelling place where God the Holy Spirit dwells, who at this hour, in parted tongues, on each Apostle came to rest.
Hoc gradiénte órdine ornávit cuncta spléndide regni cæléstis cónditor ad nostra ætérna prǽmia.	Throughout the course of daily hours the Author of the heavenly realm with splendor has adorned all things to be our everlasting crown.

If we go even further back, we come to the hymns originally assigned to these hours, hymns traditionally attributed to St Ambrose of Milan (d. 397). These three hymns, later assigned respectively to Terce, Sext and None, may well have originally been a single text. They register three moods of the ordinary working day, assumed, for the purposes of argument, to be a fine day, as it is experienced in a Mediterranean clime (St Ambrose knew his audience). There is the freshness of morning, there is the glaring heat of midday, there is the languid cool of early evening. And behind these three distinct moments of the day, and making use of the imagery of those moments, they register three moods of an entire human life: the ardour of youth, the concentrated effort of middle life, and the slackening and recreation which comes in later life. It is a commonplace to use the idea of a day representing an entire life-time—we get up in the morning (birth); the activity of the day gets under way (adolescence); we reach the height of our natural powers (early adult life); as we consolidate our experience we start to feel an intimation of decline (middle age); as we get older there comes a mellowness of maturity (old age); finally we decline and become dependent upon others (extreme old age and death). Perhaps in the hymn at Terce the point is made less clear; that is because, as already stated, the Church can never forget that Pentecost happened about nine o'clock in the morning, and so at that hour, every day, she must invoke the Holy Spirit.

Aemiliana Löhr OSB (d.1972), in her commentary on the hymns of the Monastic Breviary, says of the hour of Terce:

> It was with prayer that the Church received the new-born day from the womb of the night; prayer has accompanied the day in its steady growth; and now that the day has attained to its fullness, it is ready to receive its solemn consecration.[19]

By the ancient Roman reckoning, the third hour (9am) was the time of the morning sacrifice in the temple and therefore, the high point of the morning. Christian tradition holds that it was the hour at which the disciples of Jesus went up to the temple to pray, the hour at which Christ was condemned by Pilate and ascended the Cross, and the hour at which the Holy Spirit descended at Pentecost, all these commemorations add further resonances to this "consecration." This introduces to us, in the unfolding pattern of each day, the notion that the sanctification of time as evidenced in the *Liturgia Horarum* is intrinsically linked to a conscious *imitatio Christi*, and in particular, in its commemoration of the various moments of the story of salvation in the different hours of the Church's prayer:

Nunc, Sancte, nobis, Spíritus, unum Patri cum Fílio, dignáre promptus íngeri nostro refúsus péctori.	Now, Holy Spirit, come, descend, one with the Father and the Son; come swiftly in and fill our hearts with your full flood of holiness.
Os, lingua, mens, sensus, vigor confessiónem pérsonent, flamméscat igne cáritas, accéndat ardor próximos.	In mind and mouth, with heart and tongue, with strength and sense, may praise resound. May charity with ardor blaze and kindle others with its flame.

[19] Aemiliana Löhr OSB, trans. by Chrysogonus Waddell OSCO, "The Holy Sacrifice. Terce and Hymn of Terce," *Liturgy* 15, no. 3 (October 1981): 5.

In the second strophe, we reach the substance of the prayer: "Flammescat igne caritas, Accendat ardor proximos"; "May charity with ardor blaze, and kindle others with its flame." The ardour of youth; its eagerness to found and start new projects, its enthusiasm in trying to get other people involved; its impatience to make everybody see the world with its own eyes. That is the mid-morning of life, and it is something of that the Church asks to recapture when this hymn is prayed at Terce.

By the time we get to Sext (midday), we have to learn to make allowances. Most of us are so accustomed to living in a reasonably temperate climate, that we forget the conditions under which the Scriptures were written, and, for the matter of that, the conditions under which these early hymns were written. In Mediterranean countries, at any rate during the summer months, the midday sun is something of an enemy; you ask to be delivered from "the pestilence that stalks at noon,"[20] and you expect a special bonus if you have borne the burden and heat of the day. That is why Christ says his heavenly Father "makes his sun rise on the evil and equally on the good, his rain fall on the just and equally on the unjust."[21] Most people miss the order of the words here; the point is that God makes his uncomfortable hot sun rise on those who are evil, but equally also on those who are good; he lets the nice cool rain fall on the just, but equally on the unjust. At Sext, then, we pray to the God who controls all these changes of temperature, who lights up the morning with brightness, and the noon with burning flames, and our prayer is "Aufer calorem noxium," "all harmful passion take away."

Rector potens, verax Deus, qui témperas rerum vices, splendóre mane ínstruis et ígnibus merídiem,	O mighty Ruler, God of truth, for days and seasons setting bounds, you clothe with splendor morning light and midday skies with brilliant heat.
Exstíngue flammas lítium, aufer calórem nóxium, confer salútem córporum verámque pacem córdium.	Extinguish flames of bitter strife, all harmful passion take away, grant health unto our mortal frame, and on our hearts bestow true peace.

This hymn takes the fire of the noonday sun and compares it to that fiery time in our own life, that moment when we realize that we have got to grow up, and see things as they are, and make allowances for other people's points of view; the time in which we must settle down both mentally and emotionally. Otherwise, we will be a perpetual focus of strain and conflict; that is why we pray "Extingue flammas litium," "extinguish flames of bitter strife"; we have got to learn to fit in with other people, particularly if they do not see things from our point of view. "Confer salutem corporum," "grant health unto our mortal

[20] Ps. 91:6.
[21] Mt. 5:45.

frame," here, no doubt, the hymn is thinking of the hot noon and all its literal dangers. But when it goes on to mention "Veramque pacem cordium," "and on our hearts bestow true peace," it is thinking of our life, and the more temperate judgments which ought to come with middle age. Not readiness to compromise just in order to gain peace at any price; it speaks of "true peace," not just any kind of peace.

So far we have seen hymns for Terce and Sext; and now we come to the midafternoon office of None, and the hymn which is arguably the finest of them all. Of the *hora nona,* Aemiliana Löhr OSB writes:

> The oppressive midday heat is no longer with us; we can breathe more freely. The air is growing cool, the shadows are lengthening. The sun has lost its baneful power to burn and sear. Something of the pure clarity of early morning light seems to return; and light recovers its transparency, though this is a transparency different from that of morning—the more mature, ripe clarity of eventide. Created realities are retiring once more into their domain of mystery, but for a moment they are clothed in a clear light that has about it almost nothing of the earth. This time of day is decked out with waning beauty; but this is a decline which is not experienced as decline. This is no smile before a final separation, but the mature plenitude of a life which has no fear of death itself.

There is one unique death which has hallowed this hour, and it is as though this hour has received from that death that brightness of life which will remain with it for all time.[22]

Rerum, Deus, tenax vigor, immótus in te pérmanens, lucis diúrnæ témpora succéssibus detérminans,	O God, our firm and steadfast strength, remaining in yourself unmoved, you rule the span of daily light and guide the course of all the hours.
Largíre clarum véspere, quo vita numquam décidat, sed prǽmium mortis sacræ perénnis instet glória.	Bestow at eventide a light by which our life may never fail; may endless glory be the crown that follows on a holy death.

"Rerum Deus tenax vigor" is a very difficult line to translate. In the new ICEL translation of the hymns of the Liturgy of the Hours, we settled on "O God, our firm and steadfast strength." The literal meaning of the Latin is probably is something like: "O God, the persistent sap of things," which starts to sound

[22] Aemiliana Löhr OSB, "Light at Eventide," trans. by Chrysogonus Waddell, *Liturgy* 15, no. 3 (October 1981): 53–54.

rather pantheistic. The idea would seem to be that as sap lends life to the tree, so God lends all things their existence. He is what gives reality its realness; if he did not exist, things just would not be there. If God ceased to exist, creation would not fade out slowly, it would just no longer be there.

"Immotus in te permanens," "remaining in yourself unmoved"—God, unlike us, is unchanging and while God is everything to his creation, his creation is, strictly speaking, nothing to him. He has a life of his own, altogether outside time, into which no echo of our earthly jarring can intrude. "Lucis diurnae tempora Successibus determinans"; "you rule the span of daily light and guide the course of all the hours"; God, the timeless one, the unchangeable one, maps out our existence, by the unfolding of time which is the measure of change. And each day is a working model, as it were, of that mysterious truth. The sun marks out the hours for us, casts the shadow that creeps over the dial, yet (as we know) the sun is not really moving; it is, as far as is possible for a created and material thing, "immotus in se permanens." No wonder, then, that as we see the sun verging towards the western horizon, we should be reminded of our own mortality; the thought of God's eternity casts over our brief lives the shadow of impermanence. At None, we must be thinking of how our time must come to an end and eventually we all pass on, and God remains.

Our prayer at this stage is "Largire lumen vespere," "Bestow at eventide a light" and it is all about a summer evening. The sun has lost its strength, it has become something to be contemplated, rather than an influence to be felt; a chill has crept into the air; the light is fading, and before long it will be impossible to read. And yet, as we know, the dying sun has reserved some of his greatest splendours for the last moments of a glorious sunset. Hopefully, there is a calm about us too when we reach this time of day, a coolness, a sense of completion, which evaded us earlier in the day. Numerous poets and painters have immortalized the picture, but even so, a sunset is a new revelation every time. Will not old age, we ask, offer us compensations of the same kind? Inevitably a person's powers decline with time; and we find that there tends to be less enterprise about our decisions as we get older, less originality in our thought, there is certainly less of an opportunity for making new friendships, and so on. But surely there is also a kind of mellow radiance about old age which can compensate us, if only in part, for those things which we had and which we have lost. Our passions will have cooled, the demands we make upon life will tend to be fewer, and we shall have gathered wisdom with the years; the experience of living may be less rich in some ways, but there will be a peace of mind, a calmness of view, which will help to compensate for all that. The sunshine of our days will have gained in splendour what it has lost in intensity.

We seem to live two lives simultaneously; and one of them, the natural life, is of its nature destined to decline. The machinery of our bodies, like all machinery, eventually wears out, and that has its effect even on the mind; our memories become weaker, our attention is less capable of sustained effort, and so on. But Christians believe that the supernatural life which grace implants in us is not subject to these physical laws, and that all that is spiritual in us will survive the decline of our natural powers. We might even suppose that it will shine out more clearly than ever in old age. As the shell of the natural wears thin, all the more visibly will the light of the supernatural shine out in us. Most of us have met people in whom something of that kind seems to have taken place; in them old age seems to have eaten away their natural personalities, leaving nothing but grace. "Largire lumen vespere, Bestow at eventide a light"; how attractive a thing, when you see it, is that evening splendour "Quo vita numquam decidat"; "by which our life may never fail," so the hymn goes on to pray, and we can understand what it means. Symptoms of decline there must be in the physical order; hair and teeth and eyesight don't seem to be built for eternity. But in the spiritual order, the life of any person should lead up to something of a crescendo, so that its last years will be its crowning years, which then find us ripe for heaven.

And so, as the day draws to a close, and with night in view, the Church has traditionally thought of that suspension of time which sleep is, that state which in its suppression of consciousness has always be seen as prefiguring death. And yet, the interval is still to be used wisely and in this ancient hymn for Compline, we ask to dream of God during the hours of night, until light returns and the activity of the day is resumed. This hymn was born of a time when the night was long and dark, unaided by artificial light. Often considered a time that can induce fear, night is full of snares and potential dangers, and it brings to completion the idea of each day being in itself a lifetime, all of whose moments can be sanctified as they pass.

Te lucis ante términum, rerum creátor, póscimus, ut sólita cleméntia sis præsul ad custódiam.	To you before the close of light, Creator of all things, we pray: Be our protector, keep us safe in your unfailing clemency.
Te corda nostra sómnient, te per sopórem séntiant, tuámque semper glóriam vicína luce cóncinant.	Incline our hearts to dream of you, to sense your presence as we sleep; as light returns, so let us sing your praise and glory evermore.
Vitam salúbrem tríbue, nostrum calórem réfice, tætram noctis calíginem tua collústret cláritas.	Grant us the grace of health and strength, renew our warmth and joy of life; and let your radiant light dispel the dreaded darkness of the night.

With this hymn, our brief consideration of sanctification of time as evidenced in the hymns of the Liturgy of the Hours, commonly experienced in the course of an ordinary day, draws to a close. There is much more to be said and much evidence to be considered, particularly from the hymns that mark the seasons of the Church's Year. In closing, I would like to leave the final word to Aemiliana Löhr OSB, whose detailed study of some of the hymns we have considered here unlocks many of their secrets and helps us to grasp rather more fully the manner in which these sacred texts express notions of sacred time:

For us, time courses on in the literal sense of the word: the time which we experience and live through—the hour, the day, the year—escapes us. Where does it go? We do not know. We only see it progressing in a straight line and going on and on before us without coming to an end. There is no hope of ever seeing again any particular point of time. The hour, the day which meant so much to us, has passed without any possible hope of being seen again. This is why we cling so to the present moment, why we strive to grasp it and bring it to a halt, why we are worried about the time we have lost. The ancients had other ideas. They spoke of the cycle of time; and they saw it under the image of the serpent biting its own tail. The day flows back on itself; the year returns periodically. During the night the sun is plunged into the chill waters of the sea; but in the morning it comes forth with new life from its nocturnal bath. Each day, Helios began his course again, and with it began again the cycle of time. It ran, not in a straight line, but in a circle; and this is why that which had been could return. There was a certain "perennity", or better, an eternal presence of things and events. Upon its cyclic return, the day brought with itself the event which had marked it as noteworthy, the deed which had rendered it memorable. This endued life in the temporal order with something of the repose of the eternal.

It was on this conception of time that worship in the ancient times was based, as well as the worship of the Church. When in the course of the cycle of the year the day returns on which, in times past, the Redeemer's saving act took place, that divine act returned with the day, and salvation was renewed ...

In this mystical "today" of the Church the ancient conception of time receives its Christian fulfillment: the cycle of the terrestrial year filled and crowned with the manifestation of salvation as day succeeds to day.[23]

[23] Ibid., 41–43.

Part III
The Sacred and the Everyday in Literature

THE SACRED AND ITS CONNECTION TO HUMAN LIFE IN FRANÇOIS CHENG'S WORK

Lucie Bernier
(Independent Scholar)

Notre vraie vie, c'est l'itinéraire de notre âme[1]
François Cheng, *La République des livres*. March 14, 2017.

In France since 1948, François Cheng (Cheng, Chi-hsien, Cheng, Bàoyī for his writings in Chinese) the first Franco-Chinese member of l'Académie Française (2002), is a writer, poet, essayist, painter, calligrapher, translator and philosopher who chose French to express himself.

Born in 1929 in Shandong (Confucius' native province) into a family of literate and university scholars which was forced to flee to Sichuan because of the Sino-Japanese war (1937–1945), François Cheng did his high school studies in Chongqing (Sichuan) and then, at the Nanjing University.

Cheng has, like other families of the time, a Confucianist foundation if not education.[2] A traditional Confucianist cultural education meant to master three skills: painting, poetry, and calligraphy and sometimes music.

... la calligraphie est une pratique artistique. Un art du trait fondé sur l'idée du souffle—qui est à la base de la pensée chinoise.[3]

True to his early education, François Cheng will nurture those three skills while developing his thought toward Taoism and, ultimately Catholicism (voie christique).

Aged 19, having obtained a UNESCO grant, he arrives in France with his family. Unable to return to China because of political turmoil, François Cheng stays in Paris to pursue his studies while his family moves to the USA. He then begins his life as an exiled in what will be "une longue expérience de néantisation terrible" (*Le Dialogue*).

[1] "Interview with François Cheng," La République des livres de Pierre Assouline, March 14, 2017, accessed June 25, 2019, http://larepubliquedeslivres.com/notre-vraie-vie-cest-litineraire-de-notre-ame/.

[2] Madeleine Bertaud, "François Cheng, Du Tao à la 'voie christique,'" *Transversalités* 124, no. 4 (2012): 131.

[3] François Cheng, *Le Dialogue* (Paris: Desclée de Brouwer; [Shanghai]: Presses littéraires et artistiques de Shanghai, 2002), 95. Thereafter *Dialogue*.

… l'exilé éprouve la douleur de tous ceux qui sont privés de langage, et se rend compte combien le langage confère « la légitimité d'être »[4]

Still, he becomes one of the most successful francophone writers and imposes himself has a prolific and versatile author. His love for another country and its language seen through poetry makes him the winner of several prizes, among others in 1998, the Femina literary Prize for his first novel, *Le Dit de Tianyi* while his book on the landscape painter Shitao won him the André Malraux Prize (1998). In 2001, one year before becoming a member of the l'Académie Française, Cheng won the Grand Prix de la Francophonie de l'Académie Française. Since then, he published more than fifteen books (poetry, monographs, novels).

At the crossroads between Chinese and French cultures, as Daoist and Christian, François Cheng mediated through universal themes such as love, separation, beauty and death, meditating on the sacred and its relationship to everyday life.

In this paper, we shall examine how this connection is developed through what he called the ternary composition of our Being, that is, body, soul and spirit. The focus of this study shall be on his work in general, the aim being not to summarise any of his books—one has to read them—not to analyse but to give a mere glimpse on the philosophical aspect of François Cheng's work, and to demonstrate the originality of his thought.

"Un homme de dialogue"[5]

In the first pages of his *Dialogue*,[6] François Cheng explains how he became a *porteur* (carrier) and *passeur* (ferryman in Taoist terms) of two so utterly different languages and their cultures, their literary and humanist ideals. In trying to link two different linguistic and cultural worlds—his mother language whispering and nourishing him unconsciously while his love for an adopted language brings him to a *dialogue*, an intercultural "Way," the thematic of his lifelong *cheminement* (journey)—Cheng learns to "apprendre à désapprendre" and ultimately to reach a cultural and philosophical symbiosis:[7]

> Nommer chaque chose à part
> est le commencement de tout
> Mais dire ce qui surgit d'entre elles
> toujours neuf

[4] Ibid., 29.

[5] François Cheng, "Discours prononcé le 16 octobre 2007 lors de la cérémonie de remise des insignes de Docteur Honoris Causa de l'Institut Catholique de Paris," *Transversalités* 105, no. 1 (2008): 167. Thereafter, *Discours*.

[6] *Dialogue*, 7–8.

[7] Ibid., 14.

et imprévu
C'est
chaque fois
re-commencer le monde
Entre arbre et nuage
Que passe oiseau blessé ou vent ravi
Que l'éclat furtif s'inscrive
entre les yeux
entre les lèvres
À la vraie vie
indéfiniment
nous re-naissons[8]

This dialogue between two cultures to a symbiosis of the three schools of thought, that is, Confucianism, Taoism and Christianity and their three respective components can be explained through Cheng's life experience. The dialogue will be conducted at the intellectual level between Europe (West/Occident) and China and as lived by someone whose consciousness has been formed by the Chinese thought. According to Cheng, a literate can be a Confucian in his community and privately a Taoist. Family life lies on Confucian ethics while Taoism brings a cosmological notion that is, the *qi* problematic in *Yin* and *Yang* which allow man to live in nature and cosmos.[9] This is how the literary and poetics work Cheng creates is this Tao "vide suprême" generating a "vide médian," the space in between, between the here and there, beyond cultures.[10] For several reasons, François Cheng dissociates himself from Confucianism but shows that, like Taoism and Catholicism, it has a tertiary component that will be displayed throughout his work. While not ignored, Buddhism plays a complementary role.

FRANÇOIS CHENG'S TERTIARY COMPONENT IN BUDDHISM, CONFUCIANISM, TAOISM, AND CHRISTIANISM.

François Cheng establishes a connexion between what he calls the ultimate phase of his intellectual development and his designation of "le Trois"—the Three[11]—, based on Taoism and Confucianism and his coming to a third level

[8] François Cheng, *Le livre du vide médian* (Paris: Albin Michel, [2004] 2009), 37.

[9] "Culture chinoise et christianisme. Interview de François Cheng, de l'Académie Française," May 6, 2005, accessed June 25, 2019, http://culturainformations.over-blog.fr/article-culture-chinoise-et-christianisme-interview-de-fran-ois-cheng- de-l-academie-fran-aise-54687934.html. No page numbering. Thereafter, *Cultura Vox*.

[10] François Cheng, *Vide et plein* (Paris : Editions du Seuil, 1991), 59. Thereafter *Vide*.

[11] *Dialogue*, 85–87.

of his spirituality, that is, an intimate relationship with Christianism, *le fait christique* —as he calls it.[12]

While the roots of Confucianism and Taoism go back to the 5th and the 4th century BC respectively, Buddhism or Chan is introduced into China between the 3rd and 4th century A.D. and was in many ways compatible with Taoism. "Dans ma création, le Chan et le Tao ne font qu'un."[13] From the 7th century on, the three schools of thought are officially recognised and coexist thus, showing that China is flexible and tolerant toward different philosophies. The heart of this Chinese cosmology is the basis of a cohabitation enabling each philosophical stream to reinforce a ternary component:

Buddhism brings to China awakenings, compassion and soul redemption. Compassion was until that moment almost unknown in China and might have helped Cheng to hear the Christian message. Compassion appears in two of his novels, *Le dit de Tianyi*[14] and *L'éternité n'est pas de trop.*[15] In both novels, the spouse, the lover or the mother are compassionated and comforting.[16]

Confucianism has *Heaven-Earth-Man.* Taoism has *Yin-Yang-Vide médian* (the emptiness in between). Both triads are corresponding: Heaven is Yang, Earth is Yin and Man thanks to his spirit can be regulated by the space in between:

> De fait, il y a correspondance, terme à terme, entre les deux triades, étant donné que le Ciel relève du principe Yang, la Terre du principe Yin, et que l'Homme, par son esprit, est capable de la régulation par le Vide-Médian.[17]

In his book *Vide et plein,*[18] Cheng explains at length Taoism and its three components:

> … un système binaire qui serait ternaire; un système ternaire unitaire (TAO) : 2=3, 3=1. Tel est le ressort apparemment paradoxal mais constant de la pensée chinoise.[19]

---

[12] *Discours*, 167.

[13] François Cheng, *Chu Ta 1626–1705, le génie du trait* (Paris: Phébus, [1986] 1999), 13.

[14] François Cheng, *Le dit de Tianyi* (Paris: Albin Michel, 1998).

[15] François Cheng, *L'éternité n'est pas de trop* (Paris: Albin Michel, 2002).

[16] Bertaud, "François Cheng," 138–9.

[17] *Dialogue*, 16

[18] *Vide*.

[19] Ibid., 60.

According to Cheng, Christianism is the most demanding religion.[20] It came to China at a bad time and was synonymous with China's decline through colonisation. One has to go back more than four centuries ago to see a fruitful exchange between China and Christianism through the Jesuit Matteo Ricci (1552–1610). While in Beijing, Ricci discussed with all the great scholars of the time. In the *Analects*, Confucius states that one has to be ready to die for the virtue of humanity. Ricci died in a Confucian way, out of exhaustion having met scholars from morning to evening to share ideas.

Contrary to the three other philosophies, a dialog between Chinese culture and Christianism was impossible but is nowadays necessary then China knows how to interchange and its spirit is flexible. This is how Buddhism was assimilated.

Many Chinese who convert to Christianity accept Trinity and the Holy Spirit. Triad and "qi" belong to Chinese culture as much as tai-chi and qi gong. According to Cheng, perfection, that is harmony, action and elevation, is in the Three.[21]

In 1969, two years before receiving French citizenship, Cheng was baptised and became François, like Francis of Assisi (François d'Assise)[22] and being French (François in old French). Cheng doesn't like much to speak about himself but regarding his conversion, he will states that he doesn't think much in terms of belief but of **adhesion** that is, a complete bond to Christ with whom he sees a true friendship. "Ce n'est pas une croyance mais l'adhésion à la personne du Christ, une amitié complète.":[23]

> À un moment donné, j'ai compris qu'au sein de l'humanité, il a fallu que Quelqu'un vînt pour dévisager le mal absolu et envisager le bien absolu. Non seulement dévisager l'un et envisager l'autre, mais réellement les prendre en charge, cela au prix de sa vie, offerte comme un don total, afin de démontrer que le bien absolu est possible, que l'absurdité et le désespoir ne sont pas sans issue. C'est ce que l'on appelle une vérité incarnée; c'est ce qu'a accompli le Christ en qui le bien absolu s'est manifesté comme amour absolu. Ce qu'il a accompli est proprement surhumain ... Que cet accomplissement fût porté par le divin, qu'il révèle par là la part divine de la destinée humaine, c'est là une vision que j'accepte aussi. C'est dire que

[20] *Cultura Vox.*

[21] Ibid.

[22] See, François Cheng, *Assise: une rencontre inattendue* (Paris: Albin Michel, 2014).

[23] *Cultura Vox*, 3.

> j'épouse volontiers et sans réserve la voie christique. Mon engagement relève, non de ce que l'on appelle la « croyance », mais bien d'une adhesion.[24]

It is not contradictory for Cheng to be a Taoist and a Christian. With its qi/spirit concept, Taoism offers a unitary and organic conception of the universe where everything is related and held together in a vast life network (Tao/way). The Tao is in a continuous process of transformation. Cheng feels closely related to the Tao and will never leave it, doesn't have to as it allows him to live "la voie christique" fully. Since the Chinese thought, as mentioned above, is ternary, it was natural for Cheng to have an intimate relationship with the Christian idea of Trinity—human—divine.

NOTRE VRAIE VIE, C'EST L'ITINÉRAIRE DE NOTRE ÂME.[25]

In his book entitled *De l'âme*,[26] François Cheng writes about the soul as being beauty and goodness or kindness. It is a superior order, dominating body and spirit and is the mystery that defines and survives us when body decays and spirit is deficient:[27]

> Comment, en effet, pourrait-on parler de l'âme sans parler de l'esprit ? Comment ne pas affirmer … le principe justement incarné par la triade corps-âme-esprit ?[28]

And it is exactly this triad—body—soul—spirit that, according to Cheng, provides us richness and openness because the soul can take in charge body and spirit. The soul is irreducible and indivisible and shows the unicity of our being permanently. The soul allows to show one's value no matter his/her origin. Soul beauty goes beyond physical beauty. Soul beauty shows limitless generosity and compassion, it opens the way to charity and the sacred, provides nature and world consciousness.[29] This is a teaching Way in Taoist terms which allows to see everyone's life as an adventure, as an exchange between spirit and from soul to soul. The soul is Chinese because it is related to the Tao and its qi which is life in itself, translated the sacred in our daily life through the up and downs of human's life.

---

[24] *Discours*, 168.

[25] "Interview with François Cheng."

[26] François Cheng, *De l'âme* (Paris: Albin Michel, 2016).

[27] Ibid., 149.

[28] Ibid., 39.

[29] Ibid., 75, 88–90.

Cordelia's Love and Sustainability of Familial and Social Elderly Care in China: A Religious and Ethical Interpretation

Shi Xiaoli

Abstract

The paper is a case study of philia love from the biblical perspective. The discussion on philia love is on the rise due to family disputes over supporting aged or disabled parents or grandparents in an aging society which has developed on the basis of one-child family in the last several decades. By doing a biblical study of Cordelia's love for her father, King Lear, the paper aims to explores the role that equality plays in ensuring the work of philia love against discrimination against the old when age has stripped parents or grandparents of their health and social influence.

Lord, make a channel of Thy peace
that, where there is hatred, I may bring love;
that where there is wrong, I may bring the spirit of forgiveness;
that, where there is discord, I may bring harmony;
that, where there is error, I may bring truth;
that, where there is doubt, I may bring faith;
that, where there is despair, I may bring hope;
that, where there are shadows, I may bring light;
that, where there is sadness, I may bring joy.
Lord, grant that I may seek rather to comfort than to be comforted,
to understand than to be understood;
to love than to be loved;
for it is by forgetting self that one finds;
it is forgiving that one is forgiven;
it is by dying that one awakens to eternal life.
St. Francis of Assis

I

The prayer of St. Francis of Assis was quoted by Mother Teresa in her Nobel Peace Prize acceptance speech. It was cited to confirm her statement that helping the poor and miserable is helping oneself to grow spiritually mature. What needs to be stressed here is the last part of the prayer, which talks about the reward of loving the poor and miserable. That reward of love, in Mother Teressa's words, shows in the form of many beautiful things poor people taught her. For that reason, she called poor people "great!" Obviously, the love for the poor and miserable, as described in St. Francis's prayer and testified by

Mother Teressa, is reciprocal in nature. It is showcased by Cordelia's love for King Lear. As much has been discussed about King Lear's salvation through Cordelia's filial love while little on Cordelia's salvation through it, this paper focuses on the much less talked, aiming to highlight the biblical view that "It is more blessed to give than to receive" (*NIV* Acts. 20.35). Hence the question the paper tries to answer is: In what way Cordelia is blessed when she reaches out to her father who is deprived of sound judgement and health, power, glory and wealth due to old age? I hope the discussion on the reciprocal nature of love might shed ethical light on supporting parents of old age and social senior care, which have become social issues with the aging of China's population.

To answer the question about the reward Cordelia gets from her filial love, first, an analysis of the nature of her love is to be made in accordance with St. Francis's prayer. That is to say, the analysis will make her reward show itself.

Her filial love is of self-denial nature if it is put under a comparative study with her sisters'. For she brings truth where they tell lies at the expense of her own immense interests. Cordelia claims in King Lear's court that she is a maid "so young, my Lord, and true" (Lr. 1.1.105). The truth she points out to her king father contains two points. First, her sisters' promise of total devotion to him is a lie that sounds much like idolatry. Cordelia tells her father plainly that their promise is impossible to keep due to the fact that they have made their commitment to their husbands: "Why have my sisters husbands, if they say / They love you all?" (1.1.99–100); "Sure I shall never marry like my sisters, / To love my father all" (1.1.102–03). Second, she explains to him the nature of filial love by defining it in plain language: "You have begot me, bred me, lov'd me; I / Return those duties as are right fit" (1.1.96–7). In other words, filial love is in essence duties that should be repaid to parents whether children like or not; it involves "respect" required or "obligatory tasks, conduct, service, or functions that arise from one's position (as in life or in a group)"("Duty," def.1; 2a). Hence, it is self-denying in nature to her. What is more, Cordelia puts filial love in relation to other kinship. She tells Lear that her love for her future husband is as equally important as her love for him: "That lord whose hand must take my plight shall carry / Half my love with him, half my care and duty" (1.1.101–02). Her speech on even distribution of her love for her father and husband reveals her view of filial love as being impartial and non-discriminative, free from personal preference. And that further stresses self-denying nature of filial love. In this sense, Cordelia's understanding of filial love echoes the biblical definition of love: "it does not boast . . . it is not self-seeking" (1 Cor. 13.4–5).

The self-denying nature of filial love is highlighted against the context in which Cordelia makes the above statement: she makes it in response to Lear's aggressive demand of her love vow in exchange for power and wealth and to rebuke her sisters' exuberant expression of idolatry of Lear. Materially, the truth of filial love costs Cordelia inheritance of the central part of the kingdom.

But she seems not care at all, which can be inferred from her straight refusal to be Duchess of Burgundy: "Since that respect and fortunes are his love, I shall not be his wife" (1.1.249). That underlines her belief in filial love as self-denying in essence.

Behind Cordelia's courage to deny herself for holding up the truth might lie her strong faith in better reward brought by real filial love than material gains. As she admits upon her departure from Lear, "That hath depriv'd me of your grace and favor, / But even for want of that for which I am richer" (1.1.229–30). Her acknowledgment of richer reward awaiting her is confirmed by Prince of France: "Fairest Cordelia, that art most rich, being poor; / Most choice, forsaken; and most loved, despised!" (1.1.250–51). He calls her "unpriz'd precious maid," who "losest here, a better where to find" (1.1.259–61). His words may be seen as an echo of St. Francis prayer that "it is in forgetting self that one finds."

Then what does she find? Or what is the reward of her sacrifice? Wisdom. To be more specific, possession of truth of filial love. In Lear's words, "Thy truth then be thy dower," and "Let pride, which she calls plainness, marry her" (1.1.108;129). Her marriage to truth, as Kent sees it, means "The Gods to their dear shelter take thee, maid, / That justly think'st and has most rightly said!" That is to say, the reward of self-denial is spiritual holiness; her loss of her father's favor for the sake of truth puts her on the way of sanctification.

As an old Buddhist saying goes: wisdom goes in parallel with good deeds to make a man holy.

Cordelia's sanctification is completed by her turning her understanding of filial love into self-denying deeds, which, in St. Francis's words, means bringing forgiveness, faith, hope, light, joy, comfort, understanding to where there is wrong, doubt, despair, shadow, sadness, discomfort, and misunderstanding. Kent's prediction that she would be taken into holy shelter is fulfilled in the gentleman's description of her eyes as heavenly and her tears as holy water and of her compassionate reaction upon hearing her father's misery. As the gentleman says, her "clamor" and "grief," together with a flood of tears prove that she keeps no record of terrible wrongs her father has done to her, including "unkindness / That stripp'd her from his benediction, turn'd her / To foreign casualties, gave her dear rights / To his dog-hearted [sisters]" (4.3.43–46). Her sympathetic understanding of Lear's misery is better illustrated by her candid imagination of what Lear has gone through after being abandoned by her sisters: "Was this a face / To be oppos'd against the warring winds? / To stand against the deep dread-bolted thunder? / In the most terrible and nimble stroke / Of quick, cross lightning?"; "And wast thou fain, poor father, / To hovel thee with swine and rogues forlorn, / In short and musty straw?" (4.7.31–35; 38–40). To put it in St. Francis words: she seeks rather to comfort than to be comforted, to understand than to be understood; to love than to be loved.

Apart from standing in Lear's shoes feeling his misery, she devotes herself to the work of rescuing him from the wilderness and curing him of his madness. She engages her men in the rescue work of Lear: "A century sent forth; / Search every acre in the high-grown field, /And bring him to our eye"(4.4.6–8). She reaches out to her father not to mock him and take pleasure in his "burning shame" (4.3.47) but to pay evil with all kindness she could think of. She is willing to pay "all my outward worth" to anyone who is capable of "restoring his bereaved sense"(4.4.9). She tries every possible means to save him from misery, praying that "All bless'd secrets, / All you unpublish'd virtues of the earth, Spring with my tears! be aidant and remediate / In the good man's distress!" (4.4.15–18). That is to say, metaphorically speaking, she is in possession of a filial love that has life-sustaining power like the earth does. That also explains why she believes her kiss has the healing power that "Repair those violent harms that my two sisters / Have in thy reverence made" (4.7.26–29). The possession of healing power may be seen as another reward she gets from her self-denying love for her father. The kindness overwhelms evil in that it heals pain and suffering the latter causes no matter how terrible they can be.

One more thing that deserves the reader's attention is her determination to wage a war against her sisters' ruled England in the name of her father. She explains her motive to go to war this way: "O dear father!/ It is thy business that I go about; / Therefore great France / My mourning and importun'd tears hath pitied./ No blown ambition does our arms incite, / But love, dear love, and our ag'd father's right"(4.5.23–28). Obviously, in her filial devotion, there is no sign of any grudge she bears against her father, nothing at all self-seeking. Her love for her father is not untainted by any wrongs or harm incurred on her by him. In that sense, her love is the love advocated in the Bible, a love that "does not delight in evil," but overwhelms whatever evil or sinful that stands in the way (1 Cor. 13. 6).

With the strength to overcome evil and sinful temptations, Cordelia can treat her father exactly as he asks her to in their reunion: "You must bear with me. / Pray you now, forget and forgive" (4.7. 83–84). As for the reward brought by such forgiving love, it may be summed up in St. Francis's words: "it is forgiving that one is forgiven." With her sins purged, she is holy, which is testified by Lear: "Upon such sacrifices, my Cordelia, The Gods themselves throw incense" (5.3.20–21). What better reward can anyone get than that in this world?

What comes with being holy is eternal life, which is implied in Lear's description of her death: "Thou'lt come no more, / Never, never, never, never, never!" (5.3.308). Here, one "no more" and five "never'[s]" are used to make an emphatic declaration about her departure from this world for good. What follows is a verse containing five verbs that refers to the same action, the action of looking at Cordelia: "... Do you see this? Look on her, look, her lips, / Look there, look there!" (5.3.310). The action of looking is also highlighted by the syntactic form of the verse, which is a combination of a rhetorical question and a command. Thus, Lear announces to the whole world the good news of Cordelia's resurrection to eternal life upon her death and her ascendance into heaven. Hence, the quoted verses can be seen as a dramatic repetition of St. Francis words that "it is by dying that one awakens to eternal life." To put it another way, eternity is the ultimate reward Cordelia gets from her living up to the truth of filial love through self-denial.

It may be such spiritual sanctification Mother Teresa went through in helping the poor and miserable that makes her appreciate the greatness of the underprivileged. Their misery gives saints like Mother Teresa, St. Francis their chances to become saints. No misery, no saints. That may also be seen as a personal significance of Cordelia's unfailing filial love.

II

What is the familial and social significance of the discussion of Cordelia's filial love to parent supporting and social senior care in an aging society like China? That is the question to be answered in this part of the paper.

First, it might be helpful to tackle domestic dispute or fight in connection with parent supporting.

The cause of such domestic dispute and abuse is vividly depicted in the scenes in which King Lear and his daughters have a bitter argument over the number of knights he should keep. In those scenes, "old " and "foolish" are the two words repeatedly used by the daughters to describe Lear. To Goneril, his foolishness is shown in his refusal to hand over his authorities: "Idle old man, That still would manage those authorities / That he hath given away!" (1.3.17–19). Similarly, Fool uses the word "fool" to comment on Lear's ignorance of his loss of his royal privileges that go with his kingship: "thou hadst little wit in thy bald crown when thou gav'st thy golden one away" (1.4.169–71). Hence it is inevitable that his authoritative presence in court angers his daughters. For instance, Goneril complains much about his overstepping of his bounds: "By day and night, he wrongs me; every hour / He flashes into one gross crime or other, / That sets us all at odds." "His knights grow riotous, and himself upbraids us /On every trifle" (1.3.4–8). No doubt, the way Lear behaves in court is that of a king; he "overrules" Goneril who is in possession of kingship (1.3.15–21). That is why Goneril uses the word "abused" to describe his behavior (1.3.21). And she attributes it to foolishness associated with old age. In a word, Lear is an old fool in that he still acts the way a king does after his abdication?

Goneril's view of her father is confirmed by Regan's. She puts it this way: "O, Sir! you are old; / Nature in you stands on the very verge of her confine: you should be rul'd and led / By some discretion that discerns your state / Better than you yourself" (1.4.148–50). She thinks he should succumb to Goneril's rein because his old age has deprived him of sound judgement. The tone here indicates criticism of his holding firm on power or authority in an old age, which, as they see, has made Lear an old fool.

Behind Lear's lust for power is the fact that he is a "wilful m[a]n" (2.4.304). That means, in the light of St. Francis's prayer, he is being self-centered. His inability to forget self is best exemplified in his wrath over Cordelia over her refusal to flatter or idolize him the way her sisters do. His self-possessiveness has gone to such a degree that Kent calls him a "mad" man, who "bows" to "flattery" and "falls to folly" (1.1.146, 147, 149). In a word, self-love has made Lear a fool. Kent even condemns his treatment of Cordelia as "evil" (1.1.166). And Lear seems to endorse Kent's comment by calling himself "Dragon," which is "a symbol of savage ferocity" according to Kenneth Muir's notes on *King Lear* (Shakespeare 11). Seen in this light, his relentless vanity or ferocious self-love will inevitably lead him into fight with his two elder daughters when they stop flattering him and bring to his face the truth about his position in court. Therefore, it can be said that Lear lives in contrary to St. Francis's prayer that a person should forget himself; he is too self-centered to seek not to be comforted but to comfort, not to be understood but to understand. Consequently, he brings discord where there should be harmony, which is evidenced by his refusal to make comprise with his daughter by reducing his train by half or more although their request sounds reasonable: "Hear me, my Lord, / What need you five-and twenty, ten, or five,/ To follow in a house where twice so many/ Have a command to tend you?" (2.4.263–64).

His self-centeredness is further shown in his being over-reacting to their request against his will. He curses Goneril for cutting his train to half vehemently: "All the stor'd vengeances of Heaven fall / On her ingrateful top!"; "You nimble lightnings, dart your blinding flames / Into her scornful eyes! Infect her beauty, / You fen-suck'd fogs, drawn by the pow'rful sun, / To fall and blister her!" (2.4.162; 166–69). And Regan's response to his bad curse on Goneril points out his self-willed nature: "O the blest Gods! So will you wish on me, When the rash mood is on" (2.4.170–71). As Regan predicts, Lear does curse her later in spite of his promise to her that "thou shalt never have my curse" (2.4.172). When he finds Regan standing on Goneril side trying to persuade him to give up his knights, he put curse on her too. In a word, Lear, being self-willed in nature, is partly to blame for family dispute with his two daughters and his subsequent self-exile in the wildness.

Of course, as Lear's daughters, Goneril and Regan should be accounted for much of the blame for the family dispute and Lear's misery. The reason? Ethically, they should take good care of their aged father. In Cordelia's words, that is the commitment they have made, duties they must fulfill. Second, all the power and wealth they are in possession with was handed over to them by their father, let alone their lives. Therefore, they have every reason to be obedient to and respectful of him. Yes, they were full of gratitude upon receiving kingship from Lear, which can be inferred form the conversation between Lear and his knight. The knight reported to Lear that "to my judgement, your Highness is not entertain'd with that ceremonious affection as you were wont; there's a great abatement of kindness appears as well in the general dependants as in the Duke himself and your daughter" (1.4. 61–63). His report agrees with Lear's observation: "I have perceived a most faint neglect of late" (1.5.71). But, on the other hand, the point the conversation tries to make is one key to the development of the plot: the daughters have got slack in filial service!

Behind their slack treatment of Lear lies their ferocious self-seeking intention. Goneril justifies her filial negligence this way: "... my sister, whose mind and mine, I know, in that are one, / Not to be over-rul'd ... Now, by my life, Old fools are babes again, and must be us'd / With checks as flatteries, when they are seen abus'd" (1.3.15–21). Obviously, they take the presence of Lear and his knights in court as a challenge to their rein. To check his authority or power, they demand Lear first to cut down on the number of his train, then to dissolve it, for which Regan argues: "fifty followers / Is it not well? What should you need of more? / Yea, or so many, sith that both charge and danger / Speak 'gainst so great a number? How, in one house, / Should many people, under two commands, / Hold amity?" (2.4.239–44). In a word, Lear and his men have posed an aggressive threat to their maintenance of their royal households. To put it another way, their lust for power trumps their respect for their father, motivating them to take measures to curb his power and authority in court.

So, it can be said that behind their negligence of filial duty is their attempt to establish their maternal authority by usurping the fraternal one represented by Lear. As Fool has expected, the reverse of family roles is inevitable once Lear gives up his kingship: "e'er since thou mad'st thy daughters thy mothers; for when thou gav'st them the rod and putt'st down thine own breeches" (1.4.179–81). Hence, the family dispute in Lear's case can be described as a fight over household authority. In this sense, *King Lear* is a game of family authority.

Similar games of authority are on in many Chinese families, although not in such a dramatically tragic scale as it is in Lear's. A typical illustration is a metropolitan household whose master has his retired parents or parent-in-laws move in to support them or to help him tend his children. The game of authority is unlikely to avoid in such a household for the following reasons. First, the older generation, or the aged parents or parent-in-laws, having been in guardianship of the younger ones for at least twenty-years, have difficulty in fitting into the household where the younger generation are in charge. In other words, they have grown into their authoritative family roles to be at beck and call of the younger generation. Second, the younger generation, in their attempt to manage life the way they think is good for all in the household, have to make decisions which the older generation might find disagreeable or even offensive.

In many cases, a fight for authority is carried on between the younger and older generation without their being aware of it until key issues like how to raise the third generation come into play.

Now the paper goes back to the question put forward at the beginning of this section: in what way Cordelia's filial love may shed light on dealing with family fight over authority, which is unavoidable when more than two generations living under one roof? Cordelia's filial love, being self-denying in nature, is the solution to the family authority problem. Without it, family strife is inevitable. As the above analysis of Lear's family crisis shows, self is the main culprit of family dispute over authority; the attempt to deny pure self-seeking motives, especially in the part of the younger generation, will cease much of the family fight, bringing peace home. Aged parents might also be recommended to deny self so that compromise can be made when a dispute arises. This way, peace is likely to be maintained in a household with more than two generations living together.

And peace at home, by ancient Chinese wisdom, is the foundation to peace in a society and state, for which Lear's family offers a typical negative example. His family strife over authority leads to the death of the whole family, genetically speaking, consequently the ruin of the kingdom. That shows how catastrophic self-possession can be and how significant self-denial in Cordelia's style is to the maintenance of peace in a household, society and state. Maybe that is why self-edification, which involves much of self-denying work, is put as the premise for good management of a household, a society and a state in the Confucius culture.

The social impact of Cordelia's filial love may be great in an aging society like China where family fight over authority appears to have gone rampant due to the fall of its filial tradition underpinning the family care of aged parents, a Confucius tradition that advocates absolute submissiveness to parental authority in family life. Reports on family abusive cases of the old caused by such fight are common on media, so common that only extreme cases can drive a surge of search interest on the internet. Also, dramatic presentation of such family fight in the form of soap opera are broadcast on as many as half of the TV channels available in prime time almost five days a week. What is more, scenes of such fight make up for more than fifty percent of the gossip or complaint among married women as my experience told me. Hence, it can be said without exaggeration that family discord caused by the authority issue has become a social ill that needs to be addressed now. A proof is the going viral on the internet recently of the defense argument for the first criminal trial of Zhao Koukou, who committed a serial murder to revenge on his mother's death. What attracted the public attention, as I perceive, is the emotional plea by the defense lawyer who described Zhang's filiality as the motivation of his killing of three; to justify his plea, the lawyer even resorted to an ancient historical case of a criminal who was pleaded not guilty due to his crime being of filial revenge type. Obviously, behind the public appeal to the defense argument lies their grave concern for the decline of traditional filial tradition in the process of China's modernization. That also explains why varied promotion programs of filial tradition has been pushed forward actively by national and local authorities countrywide. A case in point is the legislation of mandatory regular visit of one's aged parents, a move taken by the national authority in its effort to revive filial family tradition. Seen in this light, discussion on Cordelia's love might be of some help.

More than that, study on Cordelia's self-denying love might also be inspiring to social care of the older people in China, a rising social service whose development both local and national authorities are engaged in now. The reason? Self-seeking motivation has gravely undercut the public faith on social senior care, which is evidenced by frequent official sanction and media exposure of shocking Ponzi schemes associated with senior care programs and products. To show the role that Cordelia's love could play in ensuring the development of senior social care on the right track, the care work of old patients I witnessed in a hospital in a metropolitan city may serve as an illustration. But before further exposition on the topic, the senior care service in that hospital is briefed as follows.

The senior care service in that hospital is not conducted by its professional nurses but by the staff of a private enterprise in connection with it. Most of the staff, poorly educated and middle aged, having been lowly paid migrant blue-collar workers or farmers before, turned to the service purely for its much higher pay, about RMB250/day, with the intention to earn quick money to pay off the heavy debt incurred on them by the great expenditure on their children's marriage and housing. That means they engaged in the service totally out of pressing economic concerns, which means their top agenda was to keep the job by satisfying those who were in charge of them. As their daily performance was checked by their company's supervisors, who could discharge them from their work if a complaint from a nurse or doctor or patients' family reached them, they had to try hard to keep their job by doing it the way doctors, nurses and patients' families are satisfied with. As for the patients? Most of them were bed ridden, too sick to think and talk clearly or even move their bodies in bed, let alone put an eye on their work. Hence, the carers arranged their work schedule in accordance with that of the doctors and nurses. That might explain why time for bathing or body cleaning is set not at night, but early in the morning right before the daily check of the doctors and nurses. For the same reason, breakfast and medicine were often seen shoveled down the throats of old patients so that enough time is saved for cleaning away and tiding up. In a word, they tended the patients so that they are physically presentable when the doctors, nurses, and families were around.

This complete money-oriented work ethic, naturally, led to their indifference to or negligence of patients' needs when nurses, doctors and families were not around, which occurred often at night. The following scenes I witnessed personally within my month stay there may serve as proof: a care taker slept soundly without stirring while his patient kept shouting and moaning in pain almost the whole night; another one watched soap operas on the mobile phone attentively totally ignoring his patient who was battering the bed rail noisily for straight two hours almost without stop; another carer was out till late midnight leaving the patient who was in deep coma unattended for at least six hours; another one talked to me about his co-worker in an envious tone saying that she had made a big fortune by tending her patient for seven years and he did that right after that patient died and was moved out of the ward to the mortuary. These scenes show what is missing in the social senior care service: work ethic; that is where Cordelia's love comes into play. Without it, negligence of duty among care takers is unavoidable. Without it, old people who need social care are nothing but money-producing machines to their care takers. That may be the reason why many old people who originally planned for social senior care have settled with family care after their short stay in senior care centers.

Then how to make Cordelia's love the work ethic of senior care service? It takes personal, familial, social and national efforts to work together to make it happen. And it is a time-consuming undertaking which involves the patient work of cultural education and moral edification of the whole society before sufficient qualified staff becomes a possibility. In terms of personal and familial efforts in social senior care, children should set an example for care takers by trying to tend old parents as much and as considerate as possible. Filial love children showed to their parents on their sick or dying beds, as I observed in the above-mentioned hospital, was what impressed the care takers and moved them to serve the patients more tenderly and considerately. For instance, the caretaker I hired told me about how he was moved by a son's love for his dying father and by a doctor's devotion to his gravely ill former boss. And he is not an exception. As love can only be won by love, which is what money cannot buy, the compassion needed in the work ethic of senior social care can only be obtained through Cordelia' filial love. Without filial love from children first, how can compassion be expected from money-oriented care takers? No way! Just as *King Lear* presents, Lear would not be given a slack treatment by the court dependents if his daughter Goneril paid him due respect out of filiality. In this sense, Cordelia's filial love is key to building up the work ethic among care takers in the short run. As a nurse told me, with the joint work of filiality and compassionate service from care takers, the old patients, troubled by mental hallucination or the Alzheimer's disease, may stand a better chance of recovery. In a word, Cordelia's love might work magic in the recovery of old patients the way it does in the cure of Lear's madness.

In conclusion, Cordelia's love has its significance in personal edification, maintenance of familial peace, and assurance of better social senior care, especially in an aging society. Without filiality, a man ceases to be a man, a home, no longer a home, a society, no longer a society. Only in Cordelia's type of love, a man may find eternity, a home, peace, a society, harmony, as love overwhelms all hardship and difficulty and heals all pain and suffering.

Finally, the paper ends with St. Paul's words on love to highlight once again the importance of Cordelia's love to one's personal, familial and social life as well as to remind the readers of St. Francis prayer:

> If I speak in the tongues of men and of angels, but have not love, I am only a resounding gong or a clanging cymbal. If I have the gift of prophecy and can fathom all mysteries and all knowledge, and if I have a faith that can move mountains, but have not love, I am nothing. If I give all I possess to the poor and surrender my body to the flames, but have not love, I gain nothing.
>
> Love is patient, love is kind. It does not envy, it does not boast, it is not proud. It is not rude, it is not self-seeking, it is not easily angered, it keeps no record of wrongs. Love does not delight in evil but rejoices with the truth. It always protects, always trusts, always hopes, always perseveres.
>
> Love never fails. (1 Corinthians 13:1–8)

BIBLIOGRAPHY

Brown, Guy Story. *Shakespeare's Philosopher King: Reading The Tragedy of King Lear*. Macon: Mercer UP, 2010.

Chen, Lei. "Regulations Made by Local Authorities in Many Places Against Unfilial Acts," Fazhi Daily. Xinhua Net, July 25, 2019. Accessed July 25, 2019. www.xinhuanet.com/2019-07/25/c_1124795323.htm

Custer, Charles. "The Aging Population in China," ThoughtCo, May 25, 2019. Accessed July 16, 2019. www.thoughtco.com/elderly-in-china-4077065.

Dang, Xiaofei. "Testing the Emerging Senior Care Market," China Today, May 15, 2018. Accessed July 6, 2019. www.chinatoday.com.cn/cteng-lish/2018/sl/201805/t20180515_800129473.html.

Deng Xueping. "Every One Is Unique in the World: First Trial Defense Statement for Zhoukoukou's Case." Jinan Criminal Defense Lawyers Net, January 8, 2019. Accessed July 25, 2019. www.lxlvshi.com/arti-cle/1558.html.

"Duty." Def. 1& 2. Merriam-Webster's Collegiate Dictionary. 11th ed. 2003. Print.

Haines, Bill. "Confucius on the Family as Model," Warp, Weft and Way, June 17, 2016. Accessed July 20, 2019. warpweftandway.com/confucius-family-model/#comments.

Humphries, Richard, et.al. "Social Care for Older People: Home Truths," King's Fund, September 15, 2016. Accessed July 20, 2019. www.kings-fund.org.uk/publications/social-care-older-people.

Liu, Caiyu. "'Hero' Status for Murderer Sparks Online Controversy: Man Allegedly Killed Three Men in Act of Revenge for Mother's Death," Global Times, February 21, 2018. Accessed July 14, 2019. http://www.global-times.cn/content/1089998.shtml.

Mother Teresa. "Nobel Peace Prize Acceptance Speech," December 11, 1979 Oslo, Norway. Address. Catholic Education Resource Center, accessed July 10, 2019, www.catholiceducation.org/en/religion-and-philosophy/social-justice/mother-teresas-nobel-peace-prize-acceptance-speech.html.

Shakespeare, William. *King Lear*. Edited by Kenneth Muir. The Arden Shakespeare. 8th ed. London: Methuen, 1961.

Zondervan NIV Study Bible. Edited by Kenneth Barker. 10th anniversary ed. Grand Rapids, MI: Zondervan, 1995.

PRIDE AND PREJUDICE: JANE AUSTEN AND THE HERMENEUTICS OF 'SCRIPTURAL REASONING'

Christopher D. Hancock
(Oxford House & St. Mary's University, London)

ABSTRACT

The novelist George Eliot is better known than Jane Austen for acute theological insight and informed philosophical opinions. But the ever-engaging Austen was no slouch in her reading and interpreting of the Bible, and took a view on complex theological and moral issues. Indeed, her skillful interweaving of the 'sacred' and the 'everyday' provide timeless wisdom for a world that still struggles to define human roles and values, and an individual's relationship to the great questions about self, life and God. In this paper I engage Austen's character, characters, novels and other writings as resources to refresh the tired science of biblical hermeneutics.

INTRODUCTION

The 1913 edition of the *Life and Letters* of the English novelist Jane Austen (1775–1817) includes the endearing, and for our purposes illuminating, account of a visit her elder brother (and later literary executor), Henry (1771–1850), made to the rather unimpressive, establishment Bishop of Winchester, Brownlow North (1741–1820), for verbal examination prior to his being ordained into the Church of England.[1] "That dignitary," we are told, "after asking him such questions as he thought desirable, put his hand on a book lying near on the table, which happened to be a *Greek Testament*, and said, 'As for *this* book, Mr. Austen, I dare say it is some years since either you or I looked into it.'"[2] It is possible the Bishop's remark reflects his own, or his examinees, ignorance of, or lack of interest in, the Greek text of the New Testament. It may also be, though, the Bishop had in mind Henry's checkered past as the co-editor (with his oldest brother James [1765–1819]) of a short-lived literary

---

[1] Ordination is a major theme in Austen's novel *Mansfield Park*. Edmund Bertram, who seeks ordination, says of this role: "I cannot call the situation nothing, which has the charge of all that is of the first importance to mankind … the guardianship of religion and morals, and consequently of the manners which result from their influence." *The Complete Novels of Jane Austen*, vol. 1 (New York: The Modern Library, 1992), 621.

[2] William Austen-Leigh, *Jane Austen – Her Life and Letters: A Family Record* (London: E.P. Dutton, 1913), 333.

magazine *The Loiterer*, as a dashing young captain in the Oxfordshire militia, and as a recently failed banker. The bank of Austen, Maude and Tilson in Covent Garden, London, which he had founded, went bankrupt in 1816, the year Henry turned to the church for a new career. It may also be the Bishop is revealing his own theological orientation or the religiously low-wattage character of Georgian society at large. However we interpret this exchange, the incident illustrates a world in which the Bible is *not* a central text for daily life: if you like, the 'sacred' text of the Bible does *not* shape the 'secular' reality of the everyday.

The issue for us in this paper is whether that was also true of Henry's better-known sister, Jane, and whether our answer to that question should, or should not, shape the way we read her writings. Put another way, in light of the hermeneutical interests of this roundtable, what kind of world did Austen inhabit? And, did the Bible shape the way she read that world, so that Austen-ian textual hermeneutics are, or should also be, essentially biblical? Given her profile as the creator of a set of global literary classics (now reproduced in popular films and television series), Austen's attitude towards, and use of the Bible directly and indirectly shapes the way millions consciously and unconsciously read their world today and, thence—albeit unwittingly, perhaps—imbibe a 'biblicized' reality. In relation to 'Scriptural Reasoning', that pursues a sympathetic, comparative reading of religious texts, the 'pre-understanding' (or A.N. Whitehead's 'prehension') created by Austen's particular view of the world and the Bible challenge the presumption that religious texts are, or can ever be, read *tabula rasa*; that is, without pride or prejudice. Austen's life and legacy suggest, I would argue, this is rarely, if ever, the case.

To address these complex issues in this short paper, I want to look first at Jane Austen's world (and method of engaging it), then at her religion (and way of expressing it) and, finally, at her hermeneutic method (for its impact on discussion of 'Scriptural Reasoning').

Jane Austen's World—and Her Method of Engaging It

Austen's brief life spans some extraordinary events in the Western world: the American Declaration of Independence of 1786, the incorporation of India to the British Empire in 1783, the start of the French Revolution (1789) and the founding of the first French Republic (1793), Napoleon Buonaparte's overthrow of the French Directory (1799) and the Act of Union in Great Britain (1800), the Battle of Trafalgar (1805), Napoleon's failed invasion of Russia (1812) and the historic Battle of Waterloo (1815). Nearer to home: the anti-Catholic 'Gordon Riots' of 1780, the legal battle in 1781 over the murder of slaves on the trading ship *Zong*, the appointment of the 23-year old William Pitt as Prime Minister in 1783, the campaign against slavery and the slave trade that began formally in 1787 and ended in 1833, the launch of *The Times* newspaper (1788), the 'Regency Crisis' provoked by the madness of King George

III, the founding of radical artisan groups like the 'London Corresponding Society' (1792), and 'Society of United Irishmen' (1798) to fight British rule. And, so we might go on. It was an age of conflict, confusion, change and disorder—but you wouldn't know it from Austen's novels. With a few exceptional allusions, the wider world has little impact on the little world she inhabits and portrays. Even the very public impeachment of a family friend, Warren Hastings (1732–1818), *de facto* first Governor-General of India (1774–1785), did not intrude on Austen's literary labours. Hers is, superficially at least, a world of ordered calm and principled peace. Indeed, to many in our insane, violent, progressive, lax, immoral, disordered societies, Austen is a haven for literary retreat, rational debate and bucolic pleasure. In so far as she illuminates our everyday world, it is because she extruded much of hers to profile with piquant wit what she clearly believed *really* mattered.

Lives of Austen are, like her novels, studies in minutiae. Born on 16 December 1775, she lived and died in Hampshire in the south of England. She was the eighth and youngest child of the poorly paid but well-connected gentry cleric, Rev. George Austen (1731–1805) and his wife Cassandra Leigh (1739–1832). It was while her father was Vicar of Steventon and Deane in Hampshire that Austen began to write seriously. The clerical references in much of Austen's writing reflect an environment she knew well. Her so-called *Juvenilia* of often 'boisterous' and 'anarchic'[3] poems and stories for her family and friends, written between 1787 and 1793, and her first novels, which would later be published as *Sense and Sensibility, Pride and Prejudice* and *Northanger Abbey*, were begun and worked on in the Vicarage at Steventon between 1795 and 1799. Hers was, as Janet Todd has written, "a thickly clerical environment, the very heartland of Anglicanism, where church attendance was central to almost everyone's existence."[4] Though she, and her watercolorist older sister Cassandra (1773–1845), enjoyed brief spells of formal education in Oxford, Southampton and Reading, and were regularly exposed to fine libraries, domestic theatricals and a wide range of cultural media, because of ill-health and domestic finances, after 1786, as her biographer Deidre Le Faye points out, Austen "never again lived anywhere beyond the bounds of her immediate family environment."[5] This was her world; whether it be in Bath (where her father retired from 1800 to 1806), Clifton, Southampton, or from early 1809,

[3] Cf. Richard Jenkyns, *A Fine Brush on Ivory: An Appreciation of Jane Austen* (Oxford: OUP, 2004), 31.

[4] Cf. Janet Todd, "Review: Laura Mooneyham White, *Jane Austen's Anglicanism* [Farnham: Ashgate, 2011]," *Religion & Literature* 44, no. 2 (2012): 233–5 (233).

[5] Deirdre Le Faye, *Jane Austen: A Family Record*, 2nd ed. (Cambridge: CUP, 2004), 52. See also, Deidre Le Faye, *Jane Austen: The World of her Novels* (New York: Harry N. Abrams, 2002).

Chawton, nr. Alton, in Hampshire, in a modest red-brick house gifted to her, and her mother and sister, by her well-off brother Edward (1768–1852). Life in Chawton, as the autobiographical quality of so much of her writing reveals, was determined by finance, physical weakness, family expectations and gentry delights. As her niece Anna observed, it was "a very quiet life, according to our ideas, but they were great readers, and besides the housekeeping our aunts occupied themselves in working with the poor and in teaching some girl or boy to read or write."[6] Though more sophisticated—at times incomplete—works appear after 1794, this was the small, genteel world Austen studied, mocked, re-imagined and portrayed, from as early as 1790, as a self-conscious writer and free social commentator. The extent to which she was deliberately, or angrily, socially 'subversive' is a matter of dispute.[7] From her early teens, Austen was driven by a need to voice her thoughts and, ideally, support her family financially.[8]

If we ask about the world Austen inhabited, it is the world of her novels, of balls and marriage, of dashed hopes and finite joys, of witty banter and ingrained social mores. To Austen, it is also a silly world of excessive sensibility and stifled opinion, of moral ambiguity and stiff relations. She engages that world as a mirror and erstwhile mentor; albeit, when her first novel *Sense and Sensibility* appeared in October 1811, it was published anonymously 'By a Lady', such was her sense of the limitation custom imposed on the art and artifice of frail women. When *Pride and Prejudice* appeared in January 1813, *Mansfield Park* in May 1814 and *Emma* in December 1815, Austen's name and reputation began to spread. But she did not live to see the appearance of *Northanger Abbey* and *Persuasion*, which her brother Henry prepared for the press after her death, or the wider acclaim that accompanied the 1833 edition of her works, or the publication of her nephew's *A Memoir of Jane Austen* in 1869, and the explosion of Austen adulation in the mid- and late-twentieth century; such that Austen's world is now surely part of our world, and her perspective on love, life, women and men, relations and human relationships

[6] Quoted in J. David Grey, A. W. Litz, B. C. Southam & H. A. Bok, *The Jane Austen Companion* (London and New York: Macmillan, 1986), 38.

[7] For an overview of this debate, see Terry Lovell, "Jane Austen and the Gentry: A Study in Literature and Ideology," *The Sociology of Literature*, ed. Diana Laurensen (Keele: Sociological Review Monographs, 1978), 21f.

[8] Cf. Park Honan, *Jane Austen: A Life* (New York: St. Martin's Press, 1987), 93. N.B. also, Austen's comment in a 1 April, 1816, letter to James Stanier Clarke, "I could not sit seriously down to write a serious romance under any other motive than to save my life, and if it were indispensable for me to keep it up and never relax into laughing at myself or at other people, I am sure I should be hung before I had finished the first chapter" (in James Edward Austen-Leigh, *A Memoir of Jane Austen* [London: Richard Bentley & Son, 1871], 117).

embedded in postmodern consciousness.[9] If we ever doubt the power of texts and ideas, Austen disabuses us of such folly. Central to Austen-ian hermeneutics is profound confidence in the power of words.

Austen died of the degenerative 'Graves Disease' in the arms of her sister Cassandra on 18 July 1817. She was buried in Winchester Cathedral four days later. The simple plaque on her tomb makes but passing reference to her greatness and the "extraordinary endowments of her mind." Perhaps Virginia Woolf was right, she is the writer above all others whom it is hardest to catch in the act of greatness.[10] The 'sacred' and the 'secular' find definition and redefinition here.

There are two particular features of Austen's world, and engagement with it, that deserve note: both have attracted considerable scholarly debate, and impact Austen's indirect contribution to discussion of the hermeneutics of 'Scriptural Reasoning'. First, as the Victorianizing, and then the 20th-century romanticizing of Austen reveal, our perception of the world she both inhabited and represented is the object of hermeneutic complexity. That is, as intimated above, not only pride and prejudice, but priorities and projection influence what we see, appreciate, criticize and miss in Austen's writing. The Victorian era, that eschewed what it saw as the vanity and immorality of Georgian society, cauterized Austen's literary impact with its own, dullard, cultural prejudice. Ironically, for much of the later 20th century, Austen was read and received as an enlightened, secular, neo-Victorian romantic. The publication of Marilyn Butler's acute contextual study *Jane Austen and the War of Ideas* (1975) heralded a new era in Austen studies, in which the nature and reality of Georgian society and religiosity become the matrix for informed interpretation. Indeed, as we will see in the next section, it is only in context that we see Austen's remarkable insight and appreciate her place in understanding and discussion of the 'sacred' and 'secular'.

Second, Austen's much-studied literary artistry is a masterclass in the developing genre of the British novel. Here character and caricature are formed and indelibly etched on global, literary consciousness. Jane, Darcy and Mr. Collins in *Pride & Prejudice*, and the eponymous *Emma*, are characters who are rarely forgotten because personally provocative or amusingly recognizable. Here, too, characters develop, but not through self-discovery (as in modern fiction) as much as through 'rational' (to use a preferred Austen-ian term) and

---

[9] On the complexity of 'Austen-ian [literary] exceptionalism' and the 'malleability' of Austen-ian 'reception', see Nicole Peters, "Austen's Malleability: Fans, Adaptations, and Value Production," in "Crossing the Boundaries of Reception," special issue, *Reception: Texts, Readers, Audiences, History* 10, no. 1 (2018): 74–95.

[10] Cf. Virginia Woolf, "Jane Austen at Sixty," *The Nation*, 15 December 1923, 433; reproduced in *Jane Austen: A Collection of Critical Essays*, ed. Ian Watt, Twentieth-century Views series (Englewood Cliffs, NJ: Prentice-Hall, 1963), 15.

'moral' enquiry. Elinor Dashwood in *Sense & Sensibility*, like Fanny Price in *Mansfield Park*, longs for 'the relief of quiet reflection'. The heroine becomes effectively co-reader of the novel and world that she inhabits. We read alongside her as she ponders, comments, learns and listens. Here is Elinor in the process of re-appraising Willoughby:

> [She is] ... resolved not only upon gaining every new light as to his character which her own observation or the intelligence of others could give her, but likewise upon watching his behavior to his sister with such zealous attention, as to ascertain what he was and what he meant.[11]

But—and herein lies part of the winsome power and lasting attractiveness of Austen's figures—though many learn along life's way, they are neither saved from (all) their foibles nor free from the embrace of Austen's confined, and at times confining, secure, little world. Mr. Knightley's enduring love for Emma is ultimately the assurance we have that though her follies persist she will in the end survive.

In the process of defining and refining her characters, Austen made a major contribution to the art of the novel and the science of interpretation. For, as we have seen, solitary thought, inward reflection, 'third person' narrative and the repositioned author as commentator and participant in the drama, create a 3D effect in the text. While the German Liberal Protestant theologian Friedrich Schleiermacher (1768–1834) was shaping the tools of modern hermeneutics in his rich admixture of aesthetics, ethics and philosophy, Austen was paralleling him in English literature. The subjective view is accorded by her with new critical and constructive priority. So, when Mr. Knightley finally proposes to Emma, we read: "While he spoke, Emma's mind was most busy—and yet without losing a word—to catch and comprehend the exact truth of the whole."[12] Such articulate consciousness, for good and ill, staged at times in quiet soliloquies or violent inner explosions (such as Jane's on discovering she has so profoundly mis-read Darcy), is pivotal for Austen's psychology and art. As Fanny says to Henry Crawford in *Mansfield Park*, when he asks for her advice: "We have all a better guide in ourselves, if we would attend to it, than any other person can be."[13] This is the voice of Austen's heroine. It is also her own view of the world and way of engaging it, especially in her later works. Life, however small and inconspicuous, is the raw material to shape identity,

[11] *Sense and Sensibility* (London: Richard Bentley & Son, 1882), 132.

[12] *Emma* (London: Macmillan & Co., 1920), 386.

[13] Cf. Richard Brimley Johnson (ed.), *Jane Austen's Novels* (London: J. M. Dent & Co., 1894), 184.

nurture morality, develop family and, finally, discover eternity.[14] The deep, settled, mature, self-conscious person knows and perpetuates this ideal. The fused horizons of 'secular' and 'sacred' this approach creates is central to Austen's literary greatness and lasting appeal.

JANE AUSTEN'S RELIGION—AND HER WAY(S) OF EXPRESSING IT

We have noted the clerical context of Austen's life and alluded to her attitude toward religion. We return to both now as crucial elements in the character and development of her writing. The extent to which the Church and Christianity impact Austen are much disputed. Here, too, pride and prejudice, secularism and religious enthusiasm, inveigle their way into hermeneutics. As Janet Todd writes in her review of Laura White's *Jane Austen's Anglicanism*, decisions about the traditionalism or progressivism of Austen lie in the commentator as often as the author.[15] To White, Austen's piety is genuine and very different from the willful secularizing of her by many modern critics; and, indeed, from the popularizing of her in films and TV series as a light-weight author, who tells romantic tales of country life. No, here is a sophisticated social commentator, who addresses deep themes with disarming wit *and* decisive rigor. Faith is the fire in her soul: her programme of publication after 1813 intentionally religious. But we should not see religion and comedy as alternatives in Austen; as C. S. Lewis noted,

> [T]he hard core of morality and even of religion seems to me to be just what makes good comedy possible. 'Principles' or 'seriousness' are essential to Jane Austen's art ... Unless there is something about which the author is never ironical, there can be no true irony in the work. 'Total irony'—irony about everything—frustrates itself and becomes insipid.[16]

In other words, the interplay of religious sincerity and secular wit are essential to Austen's art.

[14] Cf. also, the penitent Marianne towards the end of *Sense and Sensibility*: "[My] feelings shall be governed and my temper improved. They shall no longer worry others, nor torture myself. I shall now live solely for my family ... [I]f I do mix in society, it will be only to show that my spirit is humbled, my heart amended, and that I can practice the civilities, the lesser duties of life, with gentleness and forebearance. As for Willoughby, ... [h]is remembrance ... shall be regulated, it shall be checked by religion, by reason, by constant employment." *The Novels of Jane Austen* (Edinburgh: John Grant, 1905), 234.

[15] Cf. Janet Todd, "Review: *Jane Austen's Anglicanism* by Laura Mooneyham White," *Religion & Literature* 44, no. 2 (Summer 2012): 233.

[16] C. S. Lewis, "A Note on Jane Austen," in *Selected Literary Essays by C. S. Lewis*, ed. Walter Hooper (Cambridge: CUP, 1969), 175–86 (185).

A series of BBC broadcasts in 1962 by Angus Wilson, entitled *Evil in the English Novel,* inspired greater attention to the religious element in Austen's life and writing.[17] In time, Michael Giffin's monograph *Jane Austen and Religion: Salvation and Society in Georgian England* (2002) took that discussion in an important new direction.[18] In line with modern hermeneutics, Giffin called for analysis to "place [the] critical focus on the didactic intensions of the author."[19] This is, he says, particularly plausible where the author's reflective voice, heard so often in first- and third-person interventions, is such a feature of Austen's new, evolving, novelistic style. Her authorial intensions are clear, claims Giffin, and clearly inextricable from contemporary Georgian religion in general and from her own moral and spiritual agenda in particular. The price of this, to Giffin, is that her figures are "prototypes" of the supremacy of reason, "vehicles of discursive rhetoric" or "tropes in a discursive rhetoric, rather than literary approximations of 'real' people."[20] Read thus, the paucity of explicit references to faith or religion in Austen are arguably, therefore, less significant than the spirit that drives Austen's work. She is clearly not the secular rationalist or caustic critic some still claim. She is rather more, as her family said (and encouraged her to be), a self-aware Christian soul seeking to use her gifts for the glory of God and well-being of others. As Irene Collins observes, Austen's "characters who experience true happiness are those who think about others."[21] Furthermore, Richard Whately (1787–1863), Archbishop of Dublin, noted in a *Quarterly Review* article of 1821, that to him the power of Austen's religious emphases and moral injunctions lay in their being not "too palpably prominent" and, crucially, shown in life-like characters. As a contemporary, he should know. To him, 'secular' and 'sacred' blend easily here.

To some scholars, the admission of religion into Austen studies compromises their preferred view of her secularity;[22] to others, it kills, or contradicts, textually her spirited wit and scathing socio-personal commentary. To others, following Wilson and Giffin, we cannot grasp Austen's genius or intentions

---

[17] Austen is referred to in Wilson's first talk, cf. *The Listener*, 27 December, 1962. On these talks and religion in Jane Austen, see also Mary Watts, "God and Jane Austen," *New Blackfriars* 53, no. 620 (1972): 15–22.

[18] For a review of Giffin's work, see Franklin E. Liebenow, Jr., *Religion & Literature* 38, no. 2 (Summer, 2006): 121–3.

[19] Cf. Michael Giffin, *Jane Austen and Religion: Salvation and Society* in *Georgian England* (Basingstoke: Palgrave Macmillan, 2002), 4.

[20] Giffin, *Jane Austen and Religion*, 5.

[21] Collins, *Jane Austen and the Clergy*, 50. See also, John Wiltshire, *The Hidden Jane Austen* (Cambridge: CUP, 2014), 79.

[22] For a relatively recent study of Austen against the background of the secular Enlightenment, see Peter Knox-Shaw, *Jane Austen and the Enlightenment* (Cambridge: CUP, 2004).

apart from the religious world she inhabited and Christian faith she owned. Perspective, preference and/or prejudice, will shape the way we read her. We should, perhaps, note in passing too, though, that (*contra* Auerbach) Austen does not intentionally, or nervously address the 'sacred' comedically: the professional, relational and psychological tragicomedies she creates are full of moral and spiritual urgency. Humor helps, more than hinders, her aims.

If Austen's religion remains, for some, hard to evaluate, this is not surprising: her views change. There is throughout her life, as Peter Leithart maintains, "an Anglican reticence about religious affections."[23] She is certainly more 'rational' than some fluffy-headed pietists in her day; as she wrote in 1809 of a novel by the Christian writer and social commentator Hannah More (1745–1833), "I do not like the Evangelicals."[24] But by 1814, her views have, it seems, changed and her attitude to Evangelicals mellowed. She writes to her niece Fanny Knight (1793–1882): "I am by no means convinced that we ought not all to be Evangelicals, & am persuaded that they who are so from reason & feeling, must be happiest & safest."[25] This is important. It reflects Austen's growing respect for Evangelical leadership of the campaign against slavery by her social peers. It also testifies to her new, growing sense that God and the Bible were more vibrant witnesses to truth than the Christian establishment offered. But, if Austen is not, as some have claimed, a secular, progressive, feminist even, voice for the 'Long Enlightenment', that gripped European intelligentsia from ca. 1660 to 1830, how specifically does her faith shape her art? and, in light of our conference theme, what light does this shed on 'sacredness' and 'secularity'?

Scholars who take Austen's religion seriously focus on three specific ways in which her Christian faith manifests itself in the content and methodology of her writing.

First, *God is to her both immanent and omniscient.* He is all-present and all-knowing. As one of three prayers attributed to Austen, from the period after her father's death in 1805, states:

> Give us grace, Almighty Father, so to pray, as to deserve to be heard, to address thee with our hearts, as with our lips. Thou art everywhere present, from thee no secret can be hid. May the

[23] Peter J. Leithart, *Miniatures and Morals: The Christian Novels of Jane Austen* (Moscow, ID: Canon Press, 2004), 31.

[24] Letter to Cassandra, 24 January, 1809, in Deidre Le Faye, *Jane Austen's Letters*, 4th ed. (Oxford: OUP, 2011), 177. On Austen, More and evangelicalism, see also Irene Collins, *Jane Austen and the Clergy* (Hambledon & London Hambeldon Press, 1994), 145–7, 186–8, 216–7.

[25] Letter to Fanny Knight, 18–20 November, 1814, in Le Faye, *Jane Austen's Letters*, 292.

> knowledge of this, teach us to fix our thoughts on thee, with reverence and devotion that we pray not in vain.[26]

Though the verbal style is old Prayer Book Anglicanism, the spirit and tone are anything but the perfunctory religiosity of the Bishop who examined her brother Henry prior to his ordination. A recently discovered note by Austen on the back of one of her brother's sermons confirms this. She writes: "Men may get into the habit of repeating the words of our prayers by rote, perhaps without thoroughly understanding—certainly without thoroughly feeling their full force & meaning."[27] Religious sincerity[28] is of a piece with her quest for balanced self-awareness, and her belief in the liberating power of integrity. God is not alien to authentic human existence: he is foundational for it and integral to it. Austen's oft-noted neo-classical critique of the disruptive impact of romanticism on a person, a community and a nation, is bolstered by a conviction that the re-ordering she seeks is rooted in the structural givenness of an Almighty God and Father. Her God provides the framework and ground of life for individuals, families and societies. This is no new truth to Anglicanism: but it is, for Austen, an old truth in need of recovery. If her novels are, as often argued, 'condition of England' novels, in which life in a domestic, parish and local level are merely microscopic tropes of larger issues, the need for God to be repositioned at the centre of national life is all too clear in Austen's writings. Her growing sympathy for Evangelicals appears to be in part the consequence of their contribution to the transformation of faith and morality. As Austen wrote during the latter stages of the War of 1812:

> If we are ruined, it cannot be helped—but I place my hope of better things on a claim to the protection of heaven, as a religious nation, a nation in spite of much evil improving religion, which I cannot believe the Americans to possess.[29]

Years ahead of Auerbach and Leiris, Austen sees the essential inter-relatedness of the 'sacred' and the 'secular'; as Giffin rightly notes: "While Austen is often thought of as a secular author, state and church were still an organic unity to the Georgians, so it is not possible to separate her literary

[26] On this prayer, see William Austen-Leigh and R. A. Austen-Leigh, *Jane Austen: Her Life and Letters* (London: E. P. Dutton, 1914), 274 n. 57. Cf. also, Margaret Dodds and Douglas Murray, eds., *Jane Austen: Catharine and Other Writings* (Oxford: OUP, 1993), 283–4.

[27] Bruce Stovel, "'A Nation Improving in Religion': Jane Austen's prayers and the place in her life and art," *Persuasions* 16 (1994): 193.

[28] NB. Prayer is, according to Stuart Tave, often termed 'serious reflection' in the Austen corpus.

[29] Letter to Martha Lloyd, 2 September, 1814, in Le Faye, *Jane Austen's Letters*, 285.

commentaries into distinct secular and religious spheres."[30] Absolutely. Even the omniscience of Austen's third-person voice is a reflection of knowledge that transcends time.[31] Hence Giffin concludes: "In Austen's world, religious issues are indivisible from secular issues; and religious observance still has a public importance and is not a matter of private observance or psychological journey as it is now considered to be."[32]

Secondly, scholars recognize *a redemptive strain* in Austen. Not only does the prayer quoted above refer to Christ's saving work ("Hear us Almighty God, for his sake who has redeemed us"), as the hope for the world in the face of human sin, failure, doubt and 'evil', but her novels more generally address, as Giffin notes, the 'economy of salvation' (Gk. *oikonomia*) as it is played out in the daily life of men and women in church and state, estate and parish, family and marriage. Though Austen follows British social philosopher John Locke (1632–1704) in accrediting human reason and will in moral choice, and in secularizing 'salvation' as the redemptive power of a good marriage, a vibrant friendship or a fruitful harvest of crops and goods, she still sees truth, thought and action ultimately referable to the righteousness of God and redemption of Christ. In this we see again a natural inter-play of the 'sacred' and the 'secular': poor judgment like Emma's has higher consequences, pure perception and perfected love, like that of Elizabeth and Darcy, acts to rebuild their life and the lives around them. As in classical Christology there is a teleological dimension to Austen's account of the redemption individuals or situations attain. Her novels are future-oriented towards personal maturity in greater understanding of self and the world. *And*, she is willing to leave a story-line open-ended and unresolved if, or when, the journey towards a better future can be shown to have begun. Emma will repeat her mistakes, yes, but the process of improvement has begun. For all his faults, Mr. Knightley's concern for Emma's father and Miss Bates are the mark and proof, to Austen, of his Christian character.[33] Taste or breeding may nurture Anglican religious reserve, moral probity and integrity do not: they anticipate heaven's rewards. As the final paragraph of the prayer we have cited concludes:

> Above all other blessings, Oh! God, for ourselves, and our fellow-creatures, we implore thee to quicken a sense of thy mercy in the redemption of the world, of the value of that holy

[30] Michael Giffin, "Jane Austen and Religion: Salvation and Society in Georgian England," *Persuasions On-line* 23, no. 1 (Winter 2002): 1–4 (2).

[31] On Austen's 'omniscient voice', see Alison Searle, "The Moral Imagination: Biblical Imperatives, Narrative and Hermeneutics in *Pride & Prejudice*," *Renascence* 59, no. 1 (Fall 2006): 17–32 (esp. 17–19).

[32] Giffin, "Jane Austen and Religion," 4.

[33] Cf. Collins, *Jane Austen and the Clergy*, 194.

religion in which we have been brought up, that we may not, by our own neglect, throw away the salvation thou has given us, nor be Christians only in name.

In other words, a believer's life on earth is to be conformed to the ideals and hope of heaven.[34] Or, as Alistair MacIntyre argues in his influential monograph *After Virtue* (1981), Austen "sees the telos [end] of human life implicit in its everyday form."[35] 'Sacred' and 'secular' coinhere.

Lastly, following on from this, *religion inspires the moral impulse evident in Austen's writings*. Hers is, as Searle records, a 'moral imagination'. Evaluating the marriage of the wayward Lydia and deceitful Wickham in *Pride and Prejudice*, Austen reflects through Elizabeth: "How little of permanent happiness could belong to a couple who were only brought together because their passions were stronger than their virtue, [she] could easily conjecture." However, as Searle also argues, the moral 'sense' or 'philosophy' that drives Austen's work is implicit in the imaginative forms she adopts. Or, as Martha Nussbaum puts it: "Life is never simply *presented* by a text: it is always *represented as* something."[36] In other words, Austen's narrative fiction is intentional *and* moral. There is no separation of form and content. Her fictional world is throughout *significant*. To Jesse Wolfe, studying the use of third-person omniscient narration and reflection in Austen's novels, there occurs in her texts a blurring of objective morality and individual subjectivity, that creates a 'supple' kind of moralizing.[37] She writes: "The suppleness grows from an honest and thoroughgoing exploration of human psychology." And, thus, "Ambivalence, partial knowledge, confused sexual longing, egocentrism" are integrated unselfconsciously into discussion of the moral quotient of a person or situation.[38] But, the "psychological awakenings, or conversions"[39] in Austen's narratives are not necessarily religious: they are, *contra* Searle and other scholars who admit religion in Austen-ian exegesis, "thoroughly mundane."[40] That is, Christian in moral form, maybe, but non-metaphysical in their basic ontology.

---

[34] On the teleological orientation of Austen's writing, see Searle, "The Moral Imagination," 19f.

[35] Alistair MacIntyre, *After Virtue: A Study in Moral Theory* (Notre Dame, IN: University of Notre Dame Press, 1981), 226.

[36] Cf. Martha Nussbaum, *Love's Knowledge: Essays on Philosophy and Literature* (Oxford and New York: OUP, 1990), 5.

[37] Jesse Wolfe, "Jane Austen and the Sin of Pride," *Renascence* 51, no. 2 (1999), 111–31 (130).

[38] Ibid., 111.

[39] Ibid., 113.

[40] Ibid.

With re-accreditation of Austen's Christian faith, the framework and religious valency of her character studies and narrative line have become more obvious. Hence, Searle and Michael Edwards connect the ideal marriage of Lizzie and Darcy in *Pride and Prejudice* to God's design for life in Genesis 2 and St. Paul's vision of the church as bride in Ephesians 5. As Edwards says, "the marriage of the lovers, which is the success of the comedy, looks towards the supreme success ... in so far as that too is a marriage, both spiritual and eternal."[41] Hence, purity and faithfulness in marriage anticipate their heavenly forms. Here, too, classical Christian dogma affords the moral setting and point of lasting reference for Austen's narratives. Apart from this 'sacred' matrix 'secular' realities become shapeless entities. As a consequence, the slippery Wickham and Elizabeth's father Mr. Bennett are both overtly and covertly censured for their want of spirituality and morality as much as of personality and integrity. Their life on earth is not an anticipation of heaven, it is an evocation of the dreaded deception and indecision of hell.

Jane Austen's Hermeneutics—and Their Relevance to 'Scriptural Reasoning'

Hermeneutics has been a sub-text throughout this paper. What Dennis Davis defines as "the study of understanding, especially through the interpretation of actions or texts,"[42] has, as we have seen directly and indirectly already, a particular place in critical study of Jane Austen. For, in general, as Klaus Bruhn Jensen has written, "any understanding requires a pre-understanding—a 'prejudice' [ed. pre-judgment] in the neutral sense."[43] As noted above, the reader brings to Austen assumptions about the Georgian world she inhabited as much as the reality, or folly, of her view of love and learning and the Christian faith. Indeed, I would argue, the dynamics of the 'hermeneutical circle' apply in a particular way, and to a unique degree, when we read Austen. If it is true, as Jensen argues, that "throughout the activity of reading, people perform minimal or sub-interpretations," which realign their frame of reference for the novel and themselves, and create a "dialogue" with the text and "with other minds, past as well as present,"[44] this is surely true in the reading and 'reception history' of Austen. If not pride, then 'prejudice' has shaped (for good and ill) how she has been viewed as a woman, a character, a believer and a novelist. She is herself a cautionary tale against naively assuming we read texts *tabula rasa*. No, we enter a complex, evolving nexus of interpretations and re-

[41] Michael Edwards, *Towards a Christian Poetics* (London: Macmillan, 1984), 47.

[42] Quoted in S. J. Baran and D. K. Davis, *Mass communication theory: foundations, ferment and future*, 6th ed. (Boston, MA: Wadsworth, 2011), 13.

[43] K. B. Jensen, ed., *A handbook of media and communication research: qualitative and quantitative methodologies* (Abingdon: Routledge, 2013), 22.

[44] Ibid.

interpretations when we read, and allow a text to reframe understanding. This is, perhaps, particularly true of religious texts, and something 'Scriptural Reasoning' risks downplaying when it seems to assume comparative reading is straightforward or agenda-less. Texts and readers are neither 1-dimensional nor static: they have a past, present and future relation to themselves and the texts they read. Austen is an early exemplar of awareness of the dynamic power of texts and textual prejudice.

Austen's writing invites us to take this discussion forward in two specific directions, and with this I end. First, as James Wood maintains in an article in the *New Spectator* in August 1998, Austen is instrumental in what Wood terms 'the birth of inwardness'. That is, as we have seen, she presents her characters not as static 'human beings' but as dynamic 'human becomings' in process of change and decay, and of joyful, or painful, self-discovery. The reader is drawn into the narrative to reflect calmly and intentionally on this process and, at the end, to evaluate it. Here is Elinor in *Sense and Sensibility* as a paradigm of this 'quiet reflection' at work. When she reappraises Willoughby, she is, as we saw before,

> resolved not only upon gaining every new light as to his character which her own observation or the intelligence of others could give her, but likewise upon watching his behavior to her sister with such zealous attention, as to ascertain what he was and what he meant....[45]

Austen's fluid use of different modes of reflective discourse—from first-person soliloquy to third person narration and scraps of dialogue—enables a remarkable development in literary form and in characterization. Unlike Flaubert's taut, controlled interiorization of personality, Austen's style creates a fragmented, urgent, in many ways more plausible, account of the way we behave, change and develop as people. Of course, twentieth-century authors have taken inwardness to new depths, but Austen is at the headwaters of a process of reading and writing that affects us all. She rightly complexifies character and interpretation. As a consequence, the implied 'givenness' of religious people and texts in 'Scriptural Reasoning' is now problematized.

Second, according to Wood, "Austen's heroines do not discover ... what is best in themselves: they discover what is best for themselves and for others."[46] And, in light of this, he maintains: "Austen's work is not therapeutic but

[45] *Sense and Sensibility* (London: Cassell, 1908), 130.

[46] J. Wood, *The Broken Estate: Essays on Literature and Belief* (New York: Picador, 1999), 34.

hermeneutic."[47] If you like, it creates the conditionalities for characters and readers to become more self-aware and, particularly, self-aware *for the sake of others*. So, we share Emma's painful journey of flawed perception and frustration when she cannot read Jane Fairfax: "so cold, so cautious!"[48] she calls her. And complains, "There was no getting at her real opinion. Wrapt up in a cloak of politeness, she seemed… suspiciously reserved."[49] To Austen, open-mindedness is an essential hermeneutic principle. Poor Emma lacked this quality. Likewise, to Austen, readiness to admit error was a *sine qua non*. Hence, Elizabeth's heart-felt cry when she realizes she has mis-read Darcy:

> How despicably have I acted! ... I, who have prided myself on my discernment! I, who have valued myself on my abilities, who have often disdained the generous candour of my sister, and gratified my vanity, in useless or blameable distrust.—How humiliating, is this discovery! —Yet, how just a humiliation!—Had I been in love, I could not have been more wretchedly blind. But vanity, not love, has been my folly.—Till this moment, I never knew myself.[50]

There is a religious, as much as a moral, thrust to Austen's psychological hermeneutics. The on-going quest for new self-awareness is not (or is not to be) selfish: it is (and must be) primarily altruistic. We fulfil the command to love better when we understand self and another better. Likewise, the journey to greater understanding passes through the valley of humiliation and despair. Self-sacrifice and penitence, that Austen's faith honored, are pivotal principles of her hermeneutics in life and literature. She makes a case for all Christian reading of scriptural texts to be rooted not in the confidence of rational comparison, but in the humility of godly listening to God, self and others. If Austen would teach us anything, it is that we know ourselves and another better not in light of social interaction, but in the quiet of private, penitential reflection. In this true wisdom, love and 'rational' religion in daily life are found and kept.

Conclusion

As argued at the start, Austen's life, writing, faith, and sophisticated hermeneutic methodology, have had a lasting global impact. More have been shaped by her thought than are aware of it. She changed the nature of texts and repositioned readers and writers in relation to them. She recrafts a literary 'character' and exposes them to the crosswinds of inner turmoil and outer expectation. She uses her art to advance causes and voice complaints. Hers is,

[47] Ibid.

[48] *Emma* (Edinburgh: John Grant, 1905), 240.

[49] Ibid.

[50] *Pride and Prejudice* (London: T. Egerton, 1813), 165.

perhaps above all, a biblical world, in which biblical truth is articulated with depth, subtlety and integrity. We read the Bible, and every other religious text, differently because of her. She is there before we open a page. She challenges us to ask what other filters inform our judgment as we read texts comparatively and engage in 'Scriptural Reasoning' together.

Ritual and the Sacred in Peter Shaffer's Theatre

Jenny Oliveros Lao Phillips
(University of Saint Joseph, Macau)

Introduction

As one of the most successful playwrights in the British theatre, Peter Shaffer's plays have been analysed from different perspectives. Most of the studies focused on the grand theatricality and dramatic language;[1] the exploration of identity and alienation;[2] and the theme of ritual, worship and the divinity.[3] These themes are closely related to classic Greek theatre. Especially in his 'ritualistic plays' which all include elements central to Greek Tragedies: the use of masks,[4] the concepts of justice, revenge and violence, as well as the sacrificial victim.[5] Therefore, I argue that Peter Shaffer is one of the few playwrights who have successfully brought the sacred and ritualistic significance of Greek Tragedy back to the modern stage. In fifth century B.C. Athens, drama was not merely for entertainment, but "a religious and civic duty" for citizens to participate,[6] rooted from the worship of the wine god Dionysus. This paper explores how Shaffer makes use of ritualistic elements from Greek theatre, and step by step, from *The Royal Hunt of the Sun* (1964), *Equus* (1973), and *The Gift of the Gorgon* (1992) turns his theatre into a religious ritual. Shaffer claimed that he has "never actually been able to buy anything of official

---

1 M. Hinden, "Trying to Like Shaffer," *Comparative Drama* 19, no. 1 (1985): 14–29; M. MacMurraugh-Kavanagh, Peter Shaffer: *Theatre and Drama* (London: MacMillan Press Ltd., 1998).

2 T. Akstens, "Redression as a Structural Imperative in Shaffer's Equus," *Journal of Dramatic Theory and Criticism* 6, no. 2 (Spring 1992): 89–98; MacMurraugh-Kavanagh, Peter Shaffer; M. Torkamani, H. Kohzade and F. Azizmohammadi, "Traces of Self-alienation and Identity Crisis in Peter Shaffer's The Gift of the Gorgon," *Anthropologist* 17, no. 2 (2014): 639–46.

3 J. R. Stacy, "The Sun and the Horse: Peter Shaffer's search for worship," *Educational Theatre Journal* 28, no. 3 (1976): 325–37; M. Hinden, "When Playwrights Talk To God: Peter Shaffer and the Legacy of O'Neill," *Comparative Drama* 16, no. 1 (1982): 49–63; G. A. Plunka, *Peter Shaffer: Roles, Rites, and Rituals in the Theater* (London; Toronto: Associated University Presses, 1988); L. Mustazza, "A Jealous God: Ritual and judgment in Shaffer's Equus," *Papers on Language & Literature* 28, no. 2 (1992): 174–84.

4 J. Lennard and M. Lackhurst, M. *The Drama Handbook: A guide to reading plays* (Oxford: Oxford University Press, 2002).

5 R. Girard, *Violence and the Sacred*, trans. Patrick Gregory (London & New York: Continuum, 2005).

6 Lennard and Lackhurst, *The Drama Handbook*, 57.

religion [but] to [him] a life without a sense of the divine is perfectly meaningless."[7] Through theatre, he attempts to revive in his audience the need to search for the divine, because to him, theatre is "the only religion that can never die."[8]

The Ritual Begins

The Royal Hunt of the Sun, first produced in 1964, has been seen to be about honor, comradeship, a historical recollection of the clash of divergent cultures, or organized versus primitive religion, however, its central theme is actually about the need for worship.[9] As Shaffer's first ritualistic play, *The Royal Hunt* was an experiment in the creation of what the playwright believes theatre ought to be. With the Inca priests wearing masks at all times signifying their lives as a form of ritual to their king and god, a contrast is created with the Spanish priests and soldiers, who, on some level, all wear invisible masks to hide their true intention for gold and conquer rather than for bringing salvation to the primitives. These masks serve as part of the ritual which ultimately leads Commander Francisco Pizarro, whose initial search was for glory and immortality, to understand the dichotomy between the real and pretense, and is finally illuminated of life through his meeting with the Inca sovereign, and sun-god, Atahuallpa.

The use of masks does not only contribute to the spectacle of the play, but enhances the sacredness that is central to Greek Theatre. The masked Inca priests indicate true faith and obedience to their god, having no personal ambition, living their lives as a ritual to worship their god in communion. The Catholic priest, Valverde, on the other hand, uses salvation as his mask to hide his violence and wild ambition to conquer. His true face is revealed when he commands the killing of the unarmed pagans, instead of offering them salvation as he claimed.

Although Pizarro has been fighting and conquering land for his country, he does not feel part of the country or the Church. His sole existence has been to fight for his own glory. Pizarro thinks that "Army Tradition [is] nothing but years of Us against Them. Christ-men against Pagan-men. Men against men."[10] He recognizes the pretence of his country and religion, the masks worn by his people, and yet, he is part of them. But from his first encounter with Atahuallpa, Pizarro finds a mission to meet this god, shown through their first but separate converse:

---

[7] Hinden, "When Playwrights Talk To God," 51.

[8] Peter Shaffer, *The Gift of the Gorgon* (London: Samuel French, 1993), 22.

[9] Stacy, "The Sun and the Horse."

[10] Peter Shaffer, *The Royal Hunt of the Sun* (New York: Ballantine Books, 1966), 31.

Atahuallpa He surely is a god. He teaches my people to praise him.

Pizarro He's god all right. They're scared to hell of him. And a bastard too. That's civil war—bastards against bastards!

Atahuallpa I will see him. Let no one harm these men.

Pizarro Let's see you, then. What's it look like to be the Son of the Sun?[11]

This longing to meet the sun-god changes the purpose of Pizarro's hunt, it is no longer an expedition, but a pilgrimage to encounter a god who offers protection on his journey ordering his Incas to not harm the Spanish.

For the Commander's young page Martin, Pizarro is his god, and chivalry his ambition, he worships Pizarro whom he believes to be a man fighting for his country. Unlike Pizarro, Martin fights for what he believes in, he fights for his god, Pizarro, and this gives meaning to his expedition to Peru, for him, it is also a pilgrimage journeying side by side with his idol. Pizarro, however, does not know what he is fighting for, and in his young page he notices what he is missing, the passion to live for something and to die for something. All Pizarro seeks then was eternal glory, to find an antidote to time, and when he learns about Atahuallpa, he sees possibility:

> He has some meaning for me, this Man-God. An immortal man in whom all his people live completely. He has an answer for time.[12]

But instead of finding an antidote to time, as Pizarro's relationship with Atahuallpa evolves, he finds the significance of life, to have something or someone to believe in. When the play ends with Atahuallpa's death, Pizarro's emptiness is healed, a final enlightenment and liberation of his life long struggle. Pizarro cries for the first time in his life, feeling his loss but also a sense of community, shown in his use of the inclusive word 'we' in his final monologue: "It's over lad, I'm coming after you. There's nothing but peace to come. We'll be put into the same earth, father and son in our own land."[13]

Like the bull in the Dionysian Spring ritual which is sacrificed at the end of the ritual every April,[14] the death of Atahuallpa is not an end, he has to die in order to be one with Pizarro, and this communion sanctifies the old man.

[11] Ibid., 14.

[12] Ibid., 44.

[13] Ibid., 79.

[14] J. Harrison, *Ancient Art and Ritual* (Oxford: Oxford University Press, 1948).

Together they rise again like the new bull selected for the next year; they are resurrected every time the drama is staged, reflecting the original Greek theatre, the ritual of the resurrection of Dionysus who ascended to heaven, and sits at the right hand of Zeus.[15] Just as the Christian believe of the resurrection of Jesus Christ who is "ascended into heaven, and is seated at the right hand of God Almighty" (The Creed).

However, the play is not about religion, but ritual and worship. In contrasting the Catholic ritual at the beginning of the play, a ceremony sending off soldiers to war in the name of God, with each of the characters having their own agenda; and the sacred ritual of the masked Incas, chanting as one, in hope for the resurrection of Atahuallpa, Shaffer enlightens his audience of what ritual has become—meaningless. As Harrison stated "when the emotion dies down and is forgotten, (ritual and art then) become an end in itself, a mere mimicry."[16] The concept of a religious communal experience central to Greek tragedy that ends in a relief of feelings, catharsis,[17] was successfully achieved in Shaffer's first ritualistic play through the primitive ritual at the end. Shaffer recalled the success of this scene:

> I'll never forget the first time they arrived in the theatre, and a couple of the lads who were playing Inca priest put [the masks] on, and the transformation that happened on stage. When there were 16 of them at the end, when they were all assembled round the stage, the temperature in the house rose enormously. And later, when the audience came out of the theatre, they said—how did one get the masks to reflect joy, hope, gloom, and change expression? And what, of course, was happening was not that the masks changed in any way—what was happening was that the changes in the communal imagination and emotion of the audience were being invested in those masks.[18]

The Worship of Life

Shaffer's experiment of masks and worship is further explored in *Equus*, first produced in 1973. His second ritualistic drama is about a 17-year-old boy, Alan Strang, who blinded six horses. Under the psychiatric care of Martin Dysart, Alan slowly reveals his religious obsession with horses which he worships in an attempt to placate his own confused feelings in religion and worship.

[15] R. Graves, *The Greek Myths*, vol. 1 (London: Penguin Books, 1960).

[16] Harrison, *Ancient Art and Ritual*.

[17] T. J. Scheff, *Catharsis in Healing, Ritual, and Drama* (Berkeley, CA: University of California Press, 1979).

[18] Plunka, *Peter Shaffer*, 477.

Alan's sexual encounter with his girlfriend in the stable leads to his attack on the horses, blinding them as he believes they condemn him for his sexual activity, as do the God of organized religion. During his treatment of Alan, Dysart is forced to compare the tedium of his professional and private life with the boy, who represents a force of passion and creativity. Dysart knows that to cure Alan of his equine worship is to reduce the boy to the same meaningless life as his own.

In this play, unlike the use of masks in *The Royal Hunt*, which are part of a primitive ritual, the masks of the horses use in *Equus* transforms the play itself into a ritual similar to the ancient Greek's, which masks were frequently used to represent the presence of the gods. During the formal part of the early Spring Ritual, the annually selected archon basileous (city official in charge of religious activities) would impersonate the god Dionysus "wearing a large mask and lavish robes."[19] After putting on the mask, though the archon was still himself, to the participants of the ceremony he was the god Dionysus. This transformation between ontological categories is significant in *Equus*. With the use of the horse-masks, actors become not just horses, but gods. Thus, the play becomes not merely a play, but a religious ritual which the audience are participants.

Shaffer states in the stage directions that "the masks [of the horses] are put on before the audience with very precise timing—the actors watching each other, so that the masking has an exact and ceremonial effect."[20] Even with their human faces still visible, the audience then see them as horses, not as humans. This transformation occurs only when rapport has been established between actors and audience. It is after Dysart revealed Alan's story that the audience shift into the ritualistic atmosphere of the theatre, and thus, this scene, which in other cases might seem comical, now enters the realm of the sacred. As in ancient Greek drama, the mask "allow the actor to merge or to lose himself in alternative identities ... literally 'standing outside' oneself." When the masks are being worn, actors are not themselves anymore, they are beyond themselves, like the horses in Equus, the masks "empower the wearer by sympathetic magic and symbolic incarnation, overriding divisions of gender (man/woman), species (human/animal), and ontological category (mortal/god)."[21] And in *Equus* the masks have been put to full use to cross such divisions.

Moreover, the ritualistic element in the play is further strengthened by the humming of the chorus that goes hand in hand with every entrance of the

---

[19] R. Rehm, *Greek Tragic Theatre*, ed. John Russell Brown (London; New York: Routledge, 1992), 14.

[20] Peter Shaffer, *Equus* (Harmondsworth: Penguin Books Ltd, 1977), 15.

[21] Rehm, *Greek Tragic Theatre*, 39.

masked horses. The humming is first heard when Alan recollects his initial encounter with a horse at the beach when he was six years old. This humming (representing the hooves and splashing of the horse) serves as the opening of his story, and the beginning of his journey of worship. Like most religious ritual that begins with a song sung by a choir, this humming serves as an entrance song to Alan's ritual, which invites the audience into communion.

Artaud states in his essay *Theatre and Cruelty* that drama with plots dealing with money troubles, social climbing, the pangs of love unspoilt by altruism which appeal primarily to our understanding instead of our senses, "has rendered us unaccustomed to the direct, violent action theatre must have. [Therefore] if theatre wants to find itself needed once more, it must present everything in love, crime, war and madness."[22] In some ways, *Equus* can be seen as a play about theatre itself, a resonance of Artaud's theory of what theatre should be. The experience of catharsis from a play enables the audience to release their emotions and at the same time to realise the value of their existence and their passion for life. Therefore, it is something sacred, it is the awakening of what is inside each individual, it "arouses deep echoes within us ... upsets all our preconceptions, inspiring us with fiery, magnetic imagery and finally reacting on us after the manner of unforgettable soul therapy."[23] In this sense the role of Dysart is more than a character in the play; he represents 'theatre' itself. Theatre which is deprived of its real meaning as a result of the bourgeois plays about everyday life. At the same time Equus symbolises the ritualistic element, the sacredness in ancient theatre. This conflict is expressed in Dysart's opening monologue:

> Is it possible, at certain moments we cannot imagine, a horse can add its sufferings together ... and turn them into grief? What use is grief to a horse? You see, I'm lost. What use, I should be asking, are questions like these to an overworked psychiatrist in a provincial hospital....The thing is, I'm desperate. You see, I'm wearing that horse's head myself. That's the feeling. All reined up in old language and assumptions, straining to jump clean-hoofed on to a whole track of being I only suspect is there. I can't see it, because my educated, average head is being held at the wrong angle.... The only thing I know for sure is this: a horse's head is finally unknowable to me.[24]

[22] A. Artaud, *The Theatre and its Double*, trans. Victor Corti (London: Calder and Boyars, 1977), 64.

[23] Ibid., 64.

[24] Shaffer, *Equus*, 17–18.

What is at loss here is not the psychiatrist, but real theatre. The 'grief to a horse', out of the reasoning to the natural world, represents the imagination and creativity which is above the everyday activities of human beings. It is something magical that can only happen in dreams and which theatre should be able to express and awaken in us. Through *Equus*, the playwright is bringing back to the audience a theatre which is "an expression of the pre-rational phase in history … founded on the assumption that there are in nature and in the psyche occult, uncontrollable forces."[25] It is a human need to make sense of the value of existence, which often requires going through pain and suffering. Like Pizarro, who chooses to invest all his hope in the resurrection of Atahuallpa, which is seen as madness in the eyes of his people, finally feeling real pain, and through his tears encountered life for the first time.

The 'uncontrollable force' in *Equus* is the need to worship, a spiritual need rooted in all human beings. Since he was a child, Alan has been taught about God and the Bible by his religious mother, but the boy chooses to create his own religion. Alan chooses the horse as his object of worship because he is fascinated by its closeness to life, as "it's the most naked thing you ever saw! … Even the most broken-down old nag has got its *life*!"[26] Alan believes that the life of a horse is inevitably real, full of freedom and dignity. He rejects his mother's God because he cannot live freely if he is to be bound by rules, even though he admires the idea of Jesus' suffering for the sins of the world. This leaves such an impression that this idea is transferred to his own created god, Equus. But if he is to worship his mother's God, he would have to follow all the rules that are set by the Church instead of his own impulse. The ritual will then become meaningless to him as it is to others who participate in religious rituals more out of fear and obligation, like his mother, whom he thinks worships not out of love, but out of the fear that "God's got eyes everywhere."

For Alan, to worship is to feel life, and during his ritual of worship he encounters a sense of liberation, a moment that belongs only to him and his god. The intimacy of this moment of worship in the play is expressed through the resemblance of Alan's secret ritual to sexual intercourse, while he chanted as he rides the horse naked. Alan needs worship as he thirsts for life, a life that is his own. And it is this that differentiates Alan from Dysart, who is ensnared by society. Like Pizarro, Dysart realizes the barrenness of his life, but is only when faced with a passionate worshipper, Alan, that he understands what he is lacking. Unlike Pizarro, who is finally healed of his emptiness and is relieved by the sweetness of death, Dysart is left to struggle alone with the predicament between his realisation and his professional duty. As he cured Alan of his zeal,

[25] G. Steiner, *The Death of Tragedy* (London: Faber and Faber, 1961), 342.

[26] Shaffer, *Equus*, 49.

he lamented in his final monologue that "There is now, in my mouth, this sharp chain. And it never comes out."[27]

The chain in the horse's mouth is one of the first things Alan notices when he sees a horse for the first time. The horse Trojan tells Alan that "[the chain] never comes out. They have me in chains," so it is Alan's belief that the chain represents the sufferings of Equus.[28] Now, it is Dysart's turn to be enchained, to go through sufferings. He knows that by curing Alan of his worship, he has deprived the boy of *life*. Dysart realises in order to live the life that he envies, he must worship life the way Alan does, but being in a profession that *kills lives*, he is bound by society which hindered his relief that could be achieved through worship. Just as modern drama about everyday lives failed to achieve the cathartic effect of classic Tragedies.

THE SACRIFICIAL RITE

In *The Gift of the Gorgon*, Shaffer finally revived Greek tragedy on stage by adding in elements of violence and revenge, and offering a sacrificial victim. The main character Edward Damson, a playwright attempting to create plays resembling the violent Greek tragedy is sacrificed for a new form of Tragedy to be born on the modern stage, achieving cathartic relieve for the audience, central to what makes a Tragedy successful according to Aristotle's *Poetics*.

The Gorgon is a play about the different views on revenge between Edward and his wife Helen. Inside the story between these two-modern people, is the myth of Athena and the hero Perseus, whom Edward uses to represent Helen and himself. And he communicates with his wife through scenes he wrote about Athena and Perseus. Shaffer made use of Greek myths to draw out the main themes of the play—revenge and justice—which are central to Greek Tragedies. Philip Damson, son of Edward, states that "it may not be so good to live in *Greece* too long. I've always imagined people who live here have revenge on the brain."[29] This is echoed by Edward later when he states that he believes in the rightness of Clytemnestra avenging her daughter by killing her husband Agamemnon. Both father and son consider revenge as a quality that is intrinsically Hellenic. This is Shaffer's reason for referring to *The Gift of the Gorgon* as his Greek play, not only because it is set in Greece, or that he has made use of the Greek myths in the play. The play is rather about the ancient Greek idea of revenge, justice, and inevitable destiny.

---

[27] Ibid., 109.

[28] Ibid., 66.

[29] Shaffer, *The Gift of the Gorgon*, 5.

All these myths and rituals, ideas of revenge and justice are used to lead to the most important idea in this play—Theatre. If the horses in *Equus* symbolise the ritualistic element and the sacredness in ancient theatre, Edward Damson, in *The Gorgon*, represents ancient theatre. He thinks that it was Greece which allows him to realise what he is—"a playwright [which is the] world's most indispensable job."[30] Edward worships theatre which he believes is, "the only religion that can never die … an *illuminant*, sacred and indispensable";[31] it is from Greek theatre that Edward has found his belief, a belief in justice which is the core of most religions. But Edward's belief is based on the primitive Greek justice that laws in modern society cannot satisfy, an eye for an eye, where violence has to be cleansed by blood, and revenge is the ritual for this cleansing. Therefore, he believes in the inevitable ending for Agamemnon, who sacrifices his daughter, so his death was justice. Edward's quote from *Hamlet*, "Revenge my foul and most unnatural murder," which he sees as the centre of the play, and his question, "Will you *clean* the world or leave it dirty?" explains that he believes Agamemnon is sacrificed in order to keep the world clean, and Agamemnon's death is "Pure revenge, which means pure justice."[32] For him, theatre is religion, drama is the sacrificial rite, and as a playwright, he is the chief priest whose job is to stir the fire of theatre and make it blaze again, to carry out violent rituals which relieves people of the need for vengeance.

When his wife Helen argues that "any play, for whatever reason, which says "Take the way of blood and then dance afterwards' is evil!" opposing to Edward's idea that "there are such things as unforgivable acts."[33] Edward realised they have different religions, and he announces through Perseus: "I am guardian of its virtue: the sense of right! The justice only men can make! … I am no puppet to be walked by strings of your instruction!"[34] At that very moment, Helen, his personal Athena, turns from being his "Goddess of Restraint" to "Mistress of Control."[35] In his Perseus scene to Helen, the hero unleashed the Furies from Athena's chariot, and he sets free his own obsession with violence and revenge. So Perseus "*marches off stage with a Fury on either side, all stepping together. Athena retires up the ramp, defeated, with bowed head and*

[30] Ibid., 16.
[31] Ibid., 22.
[32] Ibid., 17.
[33] Ibid., 56.
[34] Ibid., 61.
[35] Ibid., 62.

crumpled body."[36] Edward turns away from Helen, seeking his own glory with his Irish play, a revenge tragedy filled with blood and violence.

When the play turns out to be a failure, Edward sees Helen as his betrayer, and eventually helps Helen awaken her own desire for revenge, building her into "the instrument of [his] retribution—and [his] atonement," making her cleanse him with his blood, and so gives to her: "the Sacred Gift of Vengeance,"[37] then he takes his own life. Forcing his wife to finally share his believe, as Helen tells his bastard son Philip:

> **Helen** (fierce) Haven't you understood him yet? Don't you remember what he said? "There are such things as unforgivable acts—beyond the pale of pardon." I said, "No: I'll never believe that!" What did he say then? "I'll make you." Make you! Well, that's what he's done. I believe it now—absolutely. Oh God, I do.[38]

Edward has turned his Athena into one of the Furies with revenge in her blood through his own blood. But his spell on Helen is undone by his son, who reminds Helen of who she is, that she must forgive him. Helen then understands that to defeat her husband, she must forgive instead. Between Edward and Helen, Helen wins the war, but not without compromise. Edward's loss represents the defeat of Greek tragedy in modern theatre, he loses because modern society is different from primitive society, therefore to bring Greek tragedy to modern theatre is problematic. Greek drama is a kind of sacrifice which in primitive society is "an instrument of prevention in the struggle against violence," but judicial system in modern societies has caused us to lose sight of the significance of sacrifice and the role played by sacrificial ritual to the implicit vengeance impulse of the civilized population.[39] Edward sees the need for revenge to bring real justice to the world, but living in a modern society where people suppress their urge for violence, ideas from ancient Greek tragedy fail to have its cathartic power. The failure of his final play not only defeats him in his career, but also his belief in theatre. He gains the knowledge that religion or theatre is not needed anymore.

In *The Gorgon*, Edward is the surrogate victim of the sacrificial rite, through him, the world is made to see the horror of vengeance, by cleansing himself with blood, he is cleansing the world of its violence. His death does not resemble the end of vengeance, but shows that life carries on, as his

[36] Ibid., 63.
[37] Ibid., 84.
[38] Ibid., 86.
[39] Girard, *Violence and the Sacred*, 18.

vengeful blood is passed on to Helen, the goddess of restraint. The murder of a surrogate victim may not be able to prevent violence as it did in ancient times, because the world is brought to a more civilized and more advanced level. The only cure is as Philip puts it, "We must be bigger than our ancestors, or we have no point."[40] Helen too believes, "If you show violence to a violent man --- / You turn into him yourself."[41] So, the ultimate weapon to conquer vengeance is forgiveness, to show that you are not turning into him who has offended you is the greatest revenge. Therefore, Helen's final cry in the play "I forgive you! I forgive you! I forgive! I forgive! I forgive! I forgive! I forgive! I forgive! I forgive!... I *forgive!*!"[42] echo in the heads of the audience, ended with an 'Amen' as they leave the theatre.

In Greek Tragedies, violence and revenge may be considered justice. The reasons might not be understandable to modern, civilized people because there is a judicial system "which serves to deflect the menace of vengeance [and the] decisions of the judiciary are invariably presented as the final word on vengeance."[43] Thus, in our modern society, violence may be limited and revenge is something which people may think about but do not act on. It is for this reason that Edward's Irish play fails, because his audience does not empathize with the violent revenge he ended his play with.

On the other hand, from *The Gorgon*, Shaffer has shown that theatre still has the power to heal. Although Edward wants theatre to be "cleansing or cathartic," "restorative" and which would "reclaim its moral power,"[44] by writing a ritualistic play filled with violence and revenge, he fails to turn his audience "into a congregation, ... experiencing instant moral conversion. [They are] not being transformed or restored to a cleansing primitive virtue" like those of the Greek tragedies in ancient times and "his play shrinks into being just that: a play and nothing more."[45]

Putting Greek tragedy directly on stage creates problems for a modern audience, but through *The Gift of the Gorgon*, Shaffer has created a modern Tragedy which draws heavily on the Greek's and achieves similar effect. The play confronts the audience with their need for vengeance, their propensity to violence and their blood lust, but at the same time they are reminded of who they are. On the other hand, Edward as a representation of ancient theatre, is not

[40] Shaffer, *The Gift of the Gorgon*, 89.
[41] Ibid., 17.
[42] Ibid., 90.
[43] Girard, *Violence and the Sacred*, 16.
[44] Shaffer, *The Gift of the Gorgon*, 64.
[45] Ibid., 66.

being sacrificed to announce the death of tragedy, but rather its renewal. After the failure of his play, Edward claims that "The world doesn't need Theatre anymore. Not just *my* theatre—I'm only the quaint priest of a spent faith, who once tried to stoke a sacred fire that went out long ago."[46] So, by killing the surrogate victim, Shaffer is also killing the depressing idea that the 'sacred fire of theatre went out long ago', bringing about a renewal, a new form of ritualistic tragedy, one that is not exactly a replica of Greek Tragedy, but one that suits modern theatre. Shaffer has successfully created the play that Edward struggles to write, one that is:

> like Athena's shield, hammered and wrought in a celestial smithy: a great shining surface in which you can see all the truth by reflection! The audience assembled before it, and peered into it together, in communion.... It faced them with towering shapes of their most intense and terrible desires. Undeniable pictures, formed of blazing words. They came away astounded. Scared. Exalted. Seeing themselves, perhaps for the first time, and their world—which they'd always thought ordinary—lit with the fire of transformation![47]

CONCLUSION

All three plays studied here are related to ideas of ritual and worship because Shaffer recognizes that drama is essentially religious. To understand the religious significance in drama, we need to recognize that Shaffer's dramas are self-reflexive, they are plays about theatre, and through these plays, Shaffer is experimenting with the essential elements of theatre including the use of masks, ritual, myth, and the sacrificial victim.

Gilbert and Tompkins, explained that "ritual is always efficacious for the community and enacted for a particular audience to preserve the order and meaning of anything from harvests to marriage, birth, and death."[48] Furthermore, Burkman cited anthropologist Kluckhohn that ritual "is an obsessive repetitive activity—often a symbolic dramatization of the fundamental "needs" of the society."[49] The Spring Festival, a ritual from which Greek tragedy is derived, was a celebration of the harvest, and hence, a ritual for the basic necessity of food. Modern society having fulfilled these basic needs, now strives

---

[46] Ibid., 75.

[47] Ibid., 21–22.

[48] H. Gilbert and J. Tompkins, *Post Colonial Drama: Theory, practice, politics* (London: Routledge, 1996), 57.

[49] K. H. Burkman, *The Arrival of Godot: Ritual Patterns in Modern Drama* (London: Fairleigh Dickinson University Press, 1986), 34.

for self-realisation. Artaud argued that "we surely need theatre that wakes us up heart and nerves ... we feel an urgent need for theatre [that] arouses deep echoes within us."[50] So, theatre is needed to fulfill this realisation for society, and this makes theatre a ritual. Shaffer emphasizes the significance of this "need" in theatre through Edward Damson, who lamented that "Theatre was an *illuminant*, sacred and indispensable. What is it now? Rows of seats for people to sit with folded arms. People who have forgotten their needs."[51] MacMurraugh-Kavanagh wrote that for Shaffer, theatre is:

> a place of worship, an arena in which communal needs are channeled into a space where rite and ritual dominate. In the modern context in which 'God is Dead' and where a vacuum exists in worship's place, Shaffer seeks to express the spiritual in the one area where the irrational cannot be displaced—the theatre.[52]

The spiritual quest in Shaffer's plays is the passion for life. Therefore, he creates a ritual to worship life, and during this ritual, audiences are made to feel the emotions they are capable of having but are not released in real life. This ritualistic catharsis can only take place in theatre which is capable of creating a religious experience, in which, "we apprehend a sense of meaning, harmony, and peace in worship and in life. It is a sense composed of more than emotion. It is one that comes from insight, recognition, and acceptance."[53]

Through his theatre, Shaffer reminds his audience of man's need for faith, which our cultural and societal institutions as obstacles to the fulfillment of our deepest human needs are the recurring theme of most of his plays.[54] Finally, through Edward, a playwright and sacrificial victim, theatre and sacrifice coalesce into one. Drama has lost its freedom, restricted as it is by modern theories and the norms and expectation of modern society. Therefore, a sacrifice is needed to regain the power of theatre, so Shaffer offers Edward Damson whose thirst for violence and vengeance represents elements in Tragedy which may seem problematic on the modern stage, by sacrificing him, a new kind of tragedy is born. That is the meaning of tragic action "a cyclic death and rebirth ... centering on a sacrificial death which through lament and discovery becomes a rebirth: the death of the old is the triumph of the new.[55] To conquer the

[50] Artaud, *The Theatre and its Double*, 64.

[51] Shaffer, *The Gift of the Gorgon*, 22.

[52] MacMurraugh-Kavanagh, *Peter Shaffer*, 17.

[53] E. Block, "Drama and Religious Experience, or Why Theater Still Matters," *Logos: A Journal of Catholic Thought and Culture* 8, no. 1 (2005): 83.

[54] Joan F. Dean, "Peter Shaffer's Recurrent Character Type," *Modern Drama* 21, no. 3 (1978): 297–305.

[55] R. Williams, *Modern Tragedy* (Stanford: Stanford University Press, 1966), 44.

Gorgon, a mirror is needed to see her reflection. By placing the problematic elements of Greek tragedy on stage, Shaffer successfully rebirth Tragedy.

SACRED EVERYDAY: THEOLOGICAL INTERPRETATION OF JAMES LEGGE'S "FATHERLAND NARRATIVE"

Lei Ayong
(School of Foreign Languages,
Minjiang University, Fuzhou China 350108)

ABSTRACT

In his travel logs and autobiography, James Legge (1815–1897) narrated carefully his childhood daily life in his "fatherland," and portrayed a religious sentiment blended by the "sublimity of Mount Zion" and the "beauty of the Garden of Eden," which were provoked by the natural landscape of his hometown. Legge's spiritual growth and the establishment of his religious belief were greatly influenced by his early years' experience of the natural landscape of his hometown. The latent sacred imprint on him by his childhood experience of daily life was later intertwined with his long missionary and academic career, and always revealed in one way or another. Legge's praise of nature mingled with strong religious sentiments, which reveals a thought of natural theology that God is universal. Legge's "fatherland narrative" is a romantic biblical expression of restoration to the sacred, which manifests realizing the beautiful vision of "nostalgia for paradise" by returning to the sacred life and denotes a Messianic thought of universal salvation.

**

"Fatherland" is a core concept connoting rich religious sentiments in the Christian tradition. Especially in the Old Testament, "fatherland" plays an important role in the narrative of faith and hope. "Fatherland" denotes special significance for Christian missionaries, both in terms of everyday secular experience and religious and spiritual belief. In 1886, James Legge (1815–1897), former missionary to China and currently professor of Chinese language and literature at the University of Oxford, gave a sermon titled "The Bearing of Our Knowledge of Comparative Religion on Christian Religious" at a Christian conference in Oxford. Legge retrospected his schooling and religious experience in his early years. He said, "In theology I had read much and thought a good deal. In sectarian polity I was a Congregationalist, though even then bringing to Individualism; doctrinally, I was what we used to call a 'moderate Calvinist'. Thanks to the keen air, the granitic soil, and the 'halisome pareitch' of Aberdeenshire, I had a sound and strong constitution; and more than all, I had a mind to work, and a habit of working."[1] This self-description reveals Legge's "ideological background" of his "translation career" as a missionary scholar. In terms of everyday experience, people easily tend to connect "fatherland" with the places where they were born and raised. However, Legge's narrative indicates that for Christians, the faith of "fatherland" is a kind of "deepest spiritual expectation" closely connected with biblical narratives[2]. Whether in Jewish biblical tradition of Judaism or Christian theology, "restoration to fatherland" usually implies redemption, as Mark Brett argues[3].

ZION: LEGGE'S FATHERLAND IMPRESSION

Zion's religious and emotional connotation came from Jerusalem as the site of Jewish national capital and Holy Temple. As the Holy City for Judaism and Christianity, Jerusalem endows Zion with the faith of "fatherland," both in Jewish tradition and Christian culture. This explains why Legge, a devoted Calvinist, compared his hometown to Zion. Legge was born in Huntly, a small town in Aberdeenshire of northeast Scotland. Legge recalled in his later years, "It was my home till I went to England. Of Huntly I have only the most pleasant recollections." In the opening of his autobiography "Notes of My Life," Legge made an affectionate description of his hometown Huntly. He wrote that the "little town gathered in a hollow" is surrounded by hills "covered with heath and fir trees," and sheltered on two sides by Bogie and Deveron rivers. When Legge was a child, whenever someone mentioned the language of the 125th Psalm about "the mountains standing round about Jerusalem," and that of the 40th about Mount Zion, as "beautiful for situation, the joy of the whole Earth," he would always thought of Huntly.[4]

That Huntly's natural landscape provoked Legge's religious sentiments and imagination may be further explained by some accounts of Huntly in 1820s from Legge's contemporary George Gray, a village elder of Huntly. As Gray

* This research was financially supported by the Humanities and Social Science Foundation of Ministry of Education of China (Grant NO. 20YJAZH049), the Social Science Foundation of Fujian Province of China (Grant No. FJ2019B064), and the Social Science Foundation of Minjiang University (Grant No. MYS19024).

[1] James Legge, "The Bearing of Our Knowledge of Comparative Religion on Christian Religions," read at the Christian Conference, November 15, 1886, manuscript, Council for World Mission (hereafter cited as CWM)/London Missionary Society (hereafter cited as LMS)/China/Personal/Box 4, School of Oriental and African Studies, (hereafter cited as SOAS), London, p. 4.

[2] Mark G. Brett, *Decolonizing God: The Bible in the Tides of Empire* (Sheffield: Sheffield Phoenix Press, 2009), 198.

[3] Ibid., 199.

[4] James Legge, *Notes of My Life*, 1897, manuscript, MS. Eng. misc. d. 996, New Bodleian Library, University of Oxford, fol. 1.

recollected, some of the hills in Huntly were "covered with thriving plantations, but others are bare, notably the rugged Binn on the north and Glower-ower-'em on the east. The bareness, however, adds dignity to the hills and picturesqueness to the landscape."[5]

Apparently, the "sublimity" displayed by the mountains "covered with rocks much more difficult and unmanageable" has been quietly implanted into young Legge's mind. What Huntly's natural landscape impressed young Legge had been gradually displayed in his subsequent life. In 1823, eight-year-old Legge was sent to Buckie, a coastal town in northern Banffshire, where he felt the sublimity of the sea for the first time. When Legge stood on a high place, looking at the vast sea and listening to the waves slamming the rock, he was "thrilled through his whole being and the idea of sublimity arose in his soul," immediately followed by the reflection that "This is grand and I understand it, but there is that within me, which is grander and greater than this." Legge said later that the feeling had never left him.[6]

While the journey in Buckie enabled Legge to experience the "sublimity" of nature, a hike in the countryside of Rothiemay during the summer of 1832 made Legge realize for the first time the "beauty" of nature. During the hike, when Legge reached a clearing in the woods, "the loveliness of the sight" took possession of his soul, and he "stood entranced gazing long upon the scene." Legge recalled in his later years, "I have seen other scenes as lovely in other parts of the world, and sublimity greater than that of the sea at Buckie, but the grandeur of that and the beauty of this have not yet ceased frequently to rise before me, and make me thank God that so wonderfully He has formed nature, and endowed man."[7]

The religious sentiments caused by the beauty of nature enabled Legge to develop a habit of hiking from his boyhood. In 1864, when traveling on the West River in Canton, he came to a place called "Abyss of the Flying Water" when he saw the waterfall and stream in the shade with "solace, refreshment, and invigoration" and the flower with rich colour and delicate beauty, what he thought of first was "Him who is the All-wise and Beautiful." Legge said, "The flower, the cascade, the stream, the mountain, with its frowning rocks and

[5] George Gray, *Recollections of Huntly as It Was Seventy Years Ago* (Banff: Banffshire Journal Office, 1892), 17.

[6] James Legge, *Notes of My Life*, 1897, manuscript, MS. Eng. misc. d. 996, New Bodleian Library, University of Oxford, fol. 8.

[7] Ibid., fols. 29–30.

glorious trees, are alike made and constituted by God for men."[8] All of these made Legge think of the verses from Milton's *Paradise Lost*:

> These are thy glorious works, Parent of good,
> Almighty; thine this universal frame,
> Thus wondrous fair; Thyself how wondrous then! [9]

The power of nature aroused Legge's complex religious feelings about the miraculous Creations, which prompted him to have a deep experience of correspondence between Heaven and Earth very early. This kind of experience reached its climax when he visited the Altar of Heaven, "the greatest sight in Peking,"[10] before leaving China in 1873.[11] When Legge stood in front of the magnificent "three triple circular terrace," imagining that "the rulers of China, as the high priests of their people, have for three thousand years at the same season of the year, knelt in worship of the ruler of Heaven and Earth," He "never felt under a more holy awe than when he was there." He "took off his shoes," and treaded on the "holy ground."[12] Before leaving the topmost terrace, Legge "gathered the party" with him "round the central stone," and there they raised the Doxology:

> Praise God from whom all blessings flow,
> Praise Him all creatures here below,
> Praise Him above, ye heavenly host;
> Praise Father, Son and Holy Ghost.[13]

The visit at the Altar of Heaven was, as Legge said himself, an event imbued with "much of a pilgrim spirit,"[14] which reflected a "solemn" sense of sacredness and mission inspired by the pagan altar. This solemn feeling can be

---

[8] James Legge, *Three Weeks on the West River of Canton. Compiled from the Journals of Rev. Dr. Legge, Dr. Palmer and Mr. Tsang Kwei-Hwan* (Hong Kong: De Souza & Co., 1866), 16–17.

[9] John Milton, *Paradise Lost* 5:153–155, cited in Legge, *Three Weeks on the West River of Canton*, 17.

[10] James Legge, "Journey in North China and America," 1873, typescript, CWM/LMS/China/Personal/Box 7, SOAS, London, p. 12.

[11] Further discussion, see: Norman J. Girardot, *The Victorian Translation of China: James Legge's Oriental Pilgrimage* (Berkeley: University of California Press, 2002), 86-89; Lauren F. Pfister, *Striving for "The Whole Duty of Man": James Legge and the Scottish Protestant Encounter with China*, vol. 2 (Frankfurt am Main: Peter Lang, 2004), 243.

[12] James Legge, "Notes of a Tour round the World," 1873, typescript, CWM/LMS/China/Personal/Box 7, SOAS, London, p. 13.

[13] Ibid., 14.

[14] Norman J. Girardot, *The Victorian Translation of China: James Legge's Oriental Pilgrimage* (Berkeley, CA: University of California Press, 2002), 87.

traced back to his religious sentiments to nature in his childhood, a mixed feeling promoted by the sublimity of Mount Zion and the beauty of the Garden of Eden.

HOLY CITY: LEGGE'S SPIRITUAL HOMELAND

Legge's recollections of Huntly's natural landscape are easily reminiscent of the Garden of Eden in the Old Testament. In fact, it is in Huntly that he spent his happy childhood and boyhood, playing in the wilderness after school, climbing trees and looking for bird nests. Legge said, "It was my home till I went to England in 1835. Of Huntly I have only the most pleasant recollections."[15]

Curiously, in his autobiography, articles, letters and diaries, what Legge mentioned his hometown is mainly about the natural scenery, but rarely mentions the human landscapes such as the streets, houses, and residents in the town. This is quite different from the recollections of Huntly by Legge's contemporary and fellow town men George Gray and George MacDonald (1824–1905).[16] In MacDonald's memory, Huntley was not always pleasant-looking. MacDonald wrote, "What might be seen from this window certainly could not be called a very pleasant prospect. A broad street with low houses of cold grey stone, with perhaps the town drummer playing in the distance."[17] Obviously, MacDonald, the "Scottish beloved storyteller"[18] and "Victorian mythmaker,"[19] described his hometown in a "restraint" tone. However, in the recollections of George Gray, a village elder born in a peasant family, the predominance of low thatched houses give the town a squat and unimposing appearance:

> ... the streets were not well kept.... Owning to indifferent drainage, pools and open ditches were to be seen all the year round, covered in summer with green slime.... Ashpits were to be seen even on the principal streets. They were an eyesore to many, though little was thought in general of their insanitary influence. It must be owned that a quaint verse, originally

---

15 James Legge, *Notes of My Life*, 1897, manuscript, MS. Eng. misc. d. 996, New Bodleian Library, University of Oxford, fol. 1.

16 See MacDonald's autobiographical novels *Robert Falconer*, *Alec Forbes of Howglen*, and *Ranald Bannerman's Boyhood*, and Gray, *Recollections of Huntly*.

17 George MacDonald, *Robert Falconer*, vol. 1 (London: Hurst and Blackett, Publishers, 1868), 9. Also see the quotation in Willam Raeper, *George MacDonald* (Tring, Herts, England: Lion Publishing, 1987), 24.

18 Michael R. Phillips, *George MacDonald: Scotland's Beloved Storyteller* (Minneapolis, MN: Bethany House, 1987).

19 Rolland Hein, *George MacDonald: Victorian Mythmaker* (Eugene, OR: Wipf and Stock Publishers, 2014).

applied to another place, might, with slight alteration, be found suitable:

Huntly is a borough too,
A kirk without a steeple,
A midden stance at mony a door,
And very thrifty people.[20]

Gray also mentioned the poor living conditions of Huntly's common people at that time. He wrote, "Household accommodation generally was deficient. To have a but a ben and bed-closet was the highest limit a working man could attain to. Oftener the accommodation was shared by two families. There were no lathed walls and few plastered ceilings. The 'but' end may have had a wooden floor and a sort of grate. There was no floor elsewhere in the 'ben!' Except the hereditary eight-day clock and chest of drawers, the furniture was of the plainest description. There were no carpets and table cloths and every member of the family worked,"[21] and "food and clothing were more simple."[22]

It is found that, different from MacDonald's and Gray's accounts, Legge's recollections focused on Huntly's natural scenery and "ignored" the human and social landscape in the town, which shows his contradictory mentality towards his hometown as a "Holy City" to him. Perhaps this contradiction was brought about by the "grey" side of Huntly. Apparently, in the early 19th century, Huntly, the "spiritual home" of Legge, was not the "Garden of Eden," nor the "Promised Land flowing with milk and honey."

Huntly is situated in the north of Scotland and has harsh natural conditions. Before the mid-19th century, the majority of local people were living in poverty. In Aberdeenshire where Huntly is located, there had been many famines and epidemics in history. In the first half of the 19th century, three great industrial recessions of 1816–1818, 1825, and 1836 occurred successively throughout Scotland, followed by three savage epidemics in 1816-1818, 1827–1828, and 1837–1839. Typhus was the major killer. Between 1831–1832, Scotland experienced a very serious cholera attack, which claimed 10,000 victims.[23]

In such a condition, three other children of Legge's family, two daughters and one son, had died before Legge's birth, and his mother was also taken away due to illness soon after it. At the age of about eight, Legge had been laid down with a severe attack of typhus fever for several weeks, almost killed. He

[20] Gray, *Recollections of Huntly*, 17, 18–19.

[21] Ibid., 44.

[22] Ibid., 30.

[23] Thomas Marin Devine, *Exploring the Scottish Past: Themes in the History of Scottish Society* (East Linton: Tuckwell Press Ltd., 1995), 129–30.

recollected the very hot and almost rainless summer of 1825 when the corn and barley were cut down before they had grown more than half their height. During the great commercial distress of 1825–1826, Legge's family discussed daily livelihoods from day to day, and fortunately his father eventually stood firm, and the trouble passed by.[24]

The great commercial depression gave a death blow to the trade in Huntly.[25] Also due to the economic recession, Scottish Highlanders began to exile from their hometown[26] and flocked into Huntly and the locals' living space was squeezed.[27] The rapid industrialization also produced a large surplus of laborers.[28] Therefore, in order to make a living, a considerable number of local people had to leave their homes to "seek for fortune." In his autobiography, Legge mentioned two such cases: One is that his elder brother George Legge (1802–1861) went to England to seek his fortune after graduating from King's College in Aberdeen. The other is that one of his cousins went to the West India Islands to "earn a living."[29]

But hardships do not always have a negative impact. Hash living environments will always promote an awe of the "law of nature" and may help people to cultivate a simple and tough character and foster a spirit of adventure. In George Gray's recollections, although Huntly people in the early 19th century lived a simple and rough life, they were "unconstrained" and hospitable, and had more brotherly feeling and less exclusiveness. Gray even thought that the people then were "more industrious, frugal, and self-reliant," and it was the industry and frugality that led to their independence.[30] Gray insisted that his narrative was "scrupulous accuracy." But in David S. Robb's view, as a "grass-root" observer, George Gray's recollections show a "personal" and "autobiographical" sense. Rob believes that this kind of narrative feels "faintly equivocal" and even "faux-naïf."[31] Obviously, Rob has some reservations about the

---

24 James Legge, *Notes of My Life*, 1897, manuscript, MS. Eng. misc. d. 996, New Bodleian Library, University of Oxford, fols. 2, 10.

25 Gray, *Recollections of Huntly*, 26.

26 Marjory Harper, *Adventurers and Exiles: The Great Scottish Exodus* (London: Profile Books Ltd., 2004), 45.

27 Gray, *Recollections of Huntly*, 14.

28 Devine, *Exploring the Scottish Past*, 130.

29 James Legge, *Notes of My Life*, 1897, manuscript, MS. Eng. misc. d. 996, New Bodleian Library, University of Oxford, fols. 3, 14. Further discussion, see: Marjory Harper, *Adventurers and Exiles*.

30 Gray, *Recollections of Huntly*, 30, 44.

31 David S. Robb, "Introduction," in *Huntly in Former Days: Two Studies of Huntly's Past* (Woking: Knaphill Print Company, 1998), 10–11.

"objective validity" of Gray's accounts. However, the Scots' "restlessness" revealed by Gray's narrative had been long since well-known[32]. In a certain sense, this kind of "restlessness" can be regarded as a certain expression of "independent spirit" resulted from the pressure of living environment, and tends to further develop into an action of "migration" and "exploration." Marjory Harper points out, "Since the Middle Ages a least, Scots had habitually sought adventure or sanctuary in England and throughout Europe, before they began to turn their eyes westward, initially to Ulster in the seventeenth century, and then by the eighteenth century across the Atlantic to the Americas," and then resulted in "the remarkable nineteenth-century diaspora."[33] But perhaps in the aforementioned sense, Harper believes that despite these cautionary tales, Aberdeen's human exports during the 19th century "were generally driven by ambition rather than despair."[34]

It is understandable that in the heart of Legge, Huntly, like the "Holy City" under "Mount Zion," is not a materially prosperous paradise and by no means a place of exile, but the spiritual home. The harsh and rough wilderness of Huntly brought Legge the majesty of the "God" in the Old Testament. Through the sublimity of nature, God's condescending overlook shows that people are small and humble. For Legge, Huntly is more like the "Holy City" than the "Garden of Eden." Like Jerusalem, Huntly is the birthplace of faith for Legge, where was born William Milne (1785–1822), a Pauline missionary pioneer who Legge had admired greatly since childhood.

EDEN: LEGGE'S SPIRITUAL SALVATION

In the Old Testament, Eden or the Garden of Eden is a paradise on earth, the happy living place of Adam and Eve, the first man and the first woman. In Christian theology, Eden implies the themes of fall and salvation, death and eternality. Legge never used Eden to name his hometown, but when traveling on the West River of Canton, Legge apparently referred to Eden when describing the landscape of "Abyss of the Flying Water." The verses quoted by Legge to portray the scenery are from the fifth volume of Milton's *Paradise Lost*, which depicts Adam and Eve waking up in the Garden of Eden after being tempted by Satan in their dreams. It is in this volume of *Paradise Lost* that we witness the true fall of Satan. Here for the first time in the poem we actually witness the precise moment when Satan falls, either in presuming to set himself up as God on his own mock "Mount of Congregation," or more decisively in

[32] Harper, *Adventurers and Exiles*, 1.

[33] Ibid., 1.

[34] Marjory Harper, "Aberdonians Abroad: Two Centuries of Human Exports from North-eastern Scotland," in *The City and Its Worlds: Aspects of Aberdeen's History since 1794*, ed. Terry Brotherstone & Donald J. Withrington (Glasgow: Cruithne Press, 1996), 81.

denying having been created by God in the first place.[35] From this we can easily see that for Legge there is a special metaphorical meaning of Eden, which contains a potential danger of "Paradise Lost" and a mission of salvation.

On November 5, 1872, Legge gave a speech entitled "The Colony of Hongkong" at the Hong Kong City Hall. Legge recollected that when he arrived in Hong Kong in early May 1843 and saw the ranges of hills embosoming the tranquil waters of the bay, he recalled his "fatherland," and even seemed to feel that he "had found at last the home" for which he had left Scotland. Legge then described, whenever he stood on the top of the hill overlooking the entire Victoria Harbour, he saw a city with "docks and prayas," "imposing terraces" and "magnificent residences" was growing on the ever barren island. Although Legge was charmed with the appearance of the great work created by "human energy and skill," he sometimes fancied "Britannia standing on the Peak, and looking down with an emotion of pride on the great Babylon which her sons have built."[36] On the departure from Hong Kong in 1873, Legge once again mentioned the bustling beauty of Hong Kong under the brilliant night lights, and contrasted it with that in 1843, the year of his arrival -- "When I first looked on the space it was mostly empty, and covered with rocks much more difficult and unmanageable than Scotch hills." Then he asked himself, "What will not the will and force of man, aided by wealth and science, accomplish?"[37]

The inner activities of Legge on his final departure from Hong Kong show that in his early years at Huntly, Legge already had reflections on material and spirit. In his view, wealth and science may change the secular world, but spiritual salvation still has a long way to go. Obviously, when Legge was looking at the landscape of Hong Kong where he had lived for 30 years and was about to leave for hometown, a complex and inexplicable mood caught him. In Jan Morris' accounts, Hong Kong, the boom city once considered the second home by Legge, was "a louche and lascivious city," "a haunt of pirates and racketeers, prostitutes, gamblers and confidence men."[38] Although Legge expressed his excitement over the "Hong Kong's growth" for more than 30 years in his speech at the Hong Kong City Hall in 1872, he apparently saw the increasing dark side of Hong Kong which was generally regarded as the "smuggling

[35] Noam Reisner, *John Milton's Paradise Lost: A Reading Guide* (Edinburgh: Edinburgh University Press Ltd., 2011), 70.

[36] James Legge, "The Colony of Hongkong," *The China Review: or, Notes & Queries on the Far East* 1, no. 3 (November–December 1872): 163, 165.

[37] H. E. Legge, *James Legge: Missionary and Scholar* (London: The Religious Tract Society, 1905), 177.

[38] Michiko Kakutani, "Books of the Times: The Familiar Evils of Hong Kong, Then and Now," *The New York Times*, January 3, 1989. More details, see: Jan Morris, *Hong Kong* (New York: Random House, 1989).

center," a place spawned and "nurtured by the opium trade," and he also realized that some of his views were "visionary and Utopian" in someone's eyes.[39] Therefore, Legge might feel that Hong Kong, the prospering bridge tower under the control of the British Empire, was more and more like the falling "Babylon," rather than the rising "Jerusalem."

These "contradictory and complex" sentiments are also reflected in his travel log during his journey in North China. When bumping on the roads in North China Plain, Legge unconsciously contrasted between the rural scenes of North China and the United Kingdom. He noticed a striking difference: in England and Scotland, the country was "diversified by farm houses" and "dotted by the dwelling-houses, each with its offices and farm-yard and garden perhaps, around it and a clump of trees," and "these give life and picturesqueness to a landscape," while in the country of North China, any place was "squalid-looking."[40]

It can be seen that Legge's impression of his hometown results from a subconscious "double filtering" by history and reality. While unconsciously revealing the superiority of Western civilization, it also reveals some kind of anxiety. Furthermore, for Legge, the "pilgrim" from the kingdom of Christ, the Altar of Heaven presents a mixture of wonderful and strange sentiments towards the pagan "Eden" and the Chosen people's Jerusalem, as Legge described the situation when they left the Altar of Heaven: "Then we left the place in silence, each one, I believe, inwardly praying that the light of nature and tradition may soon give place in China to the light of revelation, Emperor and people believing in Jesus, and calling Him blessed."[41]

As Norman J. Girardot points out, Legge's accounts of the Altar of Heaven suggests "the similarity of these Chinese practices and the ancient Jewish Temple sacrifice."[42] Legge's praise of nature mingled with strong religious sentiments, which actually reveals a thought of natural theology that God is universal. This idea opened a gap in the harsh Calvinist theology Legge received in his early years and was ultimately manifested in his deciphering "the strange Chinese texts of his later years."[43] Through the historical texts pasted up by memory fragments, it can be seen faintly that Legge's faith was closely related

---

[39] James Legge, "The Colony of Hongkong," 168–9.

[40] James Legge, "Journey in North China and America," 1873, typescript, CWM/LMS/China/Personal/Box 7, SOAS, London, p. 25. H. E. Legge, *James Legge: Missionary and Scholar* (London: The Religious Tract Society, 1905), 183–4.

[41] James Legge, "Notes of a Tour round the World," 1873, typescript, CWM/LMS/China/Personal/Box 7, SOAS, London, p. 14.

[42] Norman J. Girardot, *The Victorian Translation of China: James Legge's Oriental Pilgrimage* (Berkeley, CA: University of California Press, 2002), 87.

[43] Ibid., 25.

to his physical and spiritual experience of Huntly's natural landscapes in daily life of his early years, and this hidden childhood branding, later intertwined with his long missionary and academic career, was sometimes revealed in this way or that.

Conclusion

It can be found that the biblical texts lay an intertextual background as a textual link in Legge's "fatherland narrative." Legge's romantic narrative expresses sacred themes in everyday life. By everyday narrative, the presentation of the Bible is no longer a textual phenomenon, but turns to be an event of sacred representation interweaved with the world, the nature, man and things. Legge's "fatherland narrative" is full of primitive, mythological, and biblical images and personal childhood memories, revealing a kind of sacredness. In the process of everyday narrative, the sacred manifests itself in the secular space and promotes the generation of religious affections and religious beliefs, and everyday existence is thus consecrated in the horizon of faith. Mircea Eliade (1907–1986) explained, "What ever the historical context in which he is placed, *homo religiosus* always believes that there is an absolute reality, the sacred, which transcends this world but manifests itself in this world, thereby sanctifying it and making it real." For *homo religiosus*, namely the religious man, "being and the sacred are one."[44] Religious man believes that man has a potentiality to detect something of the existence and nature of God in the evidence of Creation and in the urgings of the human heart,[45] and is able to, as Adam Ferguson (1723–1816) argued, recognize the first intimations of God's will declared "by means of the order established in His works."[46]

As a Calvinist, Legge clearly held a similar view. Calvinism does not deny actually the possibility of natural religion. The opening sentence of the Westminster Confession of 1648, whose teaching was authoritative for Scottish and English Calvinists, acknowledges that "the Light of Nature, and the Works of Creation and Providence do so far manifest the Goodness, Wisdom, and Power of God, as to leave Men unexcusable," and the message is reinforced by biblical texts. From these grounds, Scottish scholar Alexander Broadie further points out that Calvinist theologians inherited from Calvin a concept of *sensus divinitatis*, the idea that much as human beings have unmediated knowledge of the natural world by using their senses, so, even in their fallen state, they have

---

[44] Mircea Eliade, *The Sacred and Profane: The Nature of Religion* (New York: Harcourt, Brace & World, Inc., 1987), 202, 210.

[45] Alexander Broadie, ed., *The Cambridge Companion to the Scottish Enlightenment* (Cambridge: Cambridge University Press, 2003), 32.

[46] Christopher J. Berry, *Social Theory of the Scottish Enlightenment* (Edinburgh: Edinburgh University Press, 1997), 167.

the residue of a religious sense to have an unmediated knowledge of "things divine." From this perspective, the natural world and the Bible, or the "Book of the World" and the "Book of the Word," are equally open to inspection.[47] But we also clearly see in Legge's "fatherland narrative" that the experience of the sacred or the holy, with a sudden burst or arrival of divine sense that man could never be prepared for, has some "tearing" effect on everyday life, as described by William James (1842–1910) and Rudolf Otto (1869–1937)[48].

Furthermore, in the 19th century, how to experience in the "Book of the World" the essence of faith as observed in the "Book of the Word" also began to pose a challenge to the "modern people" in the post-Romantic era, in whose eyes that "science" and "religion" were confrontational and the increases in scientific knowledge and understanding had an increasing impact on Christian belief and were no longer thought to demonstrate the perfection of God's Design ever more clearly and conclusively[49]. Industrialization, scientism and rationalism gradually expelled the sacred from man's spiritual home, and man was lost in secular everyday life. In this sense, "return to fatherland" is a biblical expression of restoration to the sacred. It is easily found that Legge's "fatherland narrative" is permeated with profound "nostalgia for paradise."

As in other cultures, "fatherland" in the Bible connotes a sense of "safe and peaceful dwelling."[50] But for Christians, "fatherland" could not be a land of happiness in "this world" yet, or their worldly hometowns could be no longer their true "fatherland," as the Bible says, "For here have we no continuing city, but we seek one to come" (Heb. 13:14 KJV).[51] Similar sayings are found in the Letter to Diognetus, an anonymous Christian apologetic work written probably in the early 2nd century AD: "Every foreign land is a fatherland to them, and every fatherland is a foreign land.... Their conversation is on the earth, but their citizenship is in heaven." In this sense, Christians could be but pilgrims and strangers in "this world" and their true "citizenship" was "in heaven" (Phil. 3:20 KJV).[52]

"Nostalgia for paradise" implies a "heart of the Sacred" and expresses a desire to return to "the sacred." In Christian imagination, "fatherland" as an expression of "holy land" means a center or heart of the world. Thus, it is easily

---

[47] Broadie, *The Cambridge Companion to the Scottish Enlightenment*, 32–33.

[48] Yai-chow Wong, "On the Sacredness and Ordinariness of Religious Experience," *Logos & Pneuma: Chinese Journal of Theology* 36 (Spring 2008): 196.

[49] Berry, *Social theory of the Scottish Enlightenment*, 167.

[50] E.g. "and they shall be safe in their land" (Ezek. 34:27 KJV).

[51] Luis Gutheinz, ed., *A Foreign Language-Chinese Christian Theological Lexicon of Terms and Persons* (Taipei: Kuangchi Cultural Group, 2005), 377.

[52] Georges Florovsky, *Christianity and Culture* (Belmont, MA: Nordland Publishing Company, 1974), 68–69.

understood that biblical images such as Zion, Holy City, Eden and Heaven constitute the main motifs of Legge's "fatherland narrative." In a sense, Legge's "fatherland narrative" is a biblical expression of Eliade's "nostalgia for paradise." As we have seen, Legge's "fatherland narrative" reveals some nostalgic sentiments, where the intertwining of Scottish migration tradition and Christian missionary's sojourn identity deeply resonates with the historical experience of Jewish diaspora and shows in narrative the power of existence. In the theological sense, what "returning to fatherland" manifests is not only national sentiment, but also to realize the beautiful vision of "nostalgia for paradise" by returning to the sacred life, which denotes a Messianic thought of universal salvation.

FROM QUOTIDIAN TECHNOLOGIES TO UNSPEAKABLE LIMITS: G. K. CHESTERTON AND FABRICE HADJADJ*

Brian Sudlow
(Aston University, UK)

Of the two writers mentioned in the title of this paper I dare say most readers will have heard of G. K. Chesterton and that almost nobody will have heard of Fabrice Hadjadj. Chesterton who died in 1936, thirty-five years before Hadjadj was even born, was perhaps the most influential and certainly the most prolific English Catholic writer and intellectual of the Belle Epoque and the interwar period. His claim to immortality in English Catholic literature rests on his literary and polemical output, from *Heretics* (1905), *Orthodoxy* (1908) and *The Man who was Thursday* (1908), all published before his conversion to Catholicism, to *St Francis of Assisi* (1923), *The Everlasting Man* (1925) and the magisterial *St Thomas Aquinas* (1932). "Chesterton makes one despair," wrote Etienne Gilson, France's preeminent historian of medieval philosophy in the middle of the twentieth century; "I have been studying St. Thomas all my life and I could never have written such a book." From C. S. Lewis to Jorge Luis Borges, from George Orwell to Alfred Hitchcock, and from Irish Republican Michael Collins to Ghandi himself, Chesterton is evoked by many as an inspiration or a provocation. A mere jobbing journalist in his own eyes, Chesterton was described as *fidei defensor* in Pope Pius XI's telegram of condolence to the English people on Chesterton's death, an expression discretely redacted when the text was reproduced in the newspapers. A swift canter through his bibliography reveals him to be a poet, a playwright, a detective novelist, a polemicist, a historian, and through it all, a wit. Others have described him as an anarchist, an idealist, a prophet, a theologian and most recently even a saint; an investigation into the holiness of his life was even conducted by the diocese of Northampton where he died. Its negative outcome has not tempered the devotion of Chesterton's most fervent followers.

It seems unfair then to bring Chesterton together with the relatively unknown Fabrice Hadjadj in this paper, but there are good reasons for doing so. In French Catholic circles, Fabrice Hadjadj (1971–) is one of the most extraordinarily versatile thinkers, writers and artists of the twenty-first century. Hadjadj's oeuvre includes essays, plays, art criticism, works of popular exegesis and original songs, and he is the holder of numerous literary prizes,

* Due to Covid lockdown restrictions in the United Kingdom, the author has been unable to locate and provide precise references for some sources cited or alluded to in this article.

including the 2006 Grand prix catholique de littérature (2006) for *Réussir sa mort. Anti-méthode pour vivre* (2005), and the 2009 Prix de littérature religieuse (2010) for *La Foi des démons ou l'athéisme dépassé* (2009). In 2014–16, he served two years as a consultor to the Vatican's Pontifical Council for the Laity while in 2018 he convened the prestigious Lenten Lectures at the cathedral of Notre Dame in Paris at the invitation of the new archbishop Michel Aupetit, one of his intellectual allies. 2020 arguably has marked a decisive turning in his career with the successful launch of his new novel for adolescents *L'Attrape Malheur* being crowned with the French literary award le *Prix Vendredi*. At the same time Hadjadj has also been awarded the Cardinal Lustiger Prize by the prestigious *Académie française* in recognition of his importance as a writer of religious faith.

This paper is part of a project to explore, understand and evaluate Hadjadj's literary achievements more deeply and to initiate dialogue on their merits.[1] I use the term literary here advisedly. Much of the publicity surrounding Hadjadj in France casts him as an *agrégé de philosophie*, a holder of one of France's most distinguished academic accolades. He was at one time a student of the late Jean-Louis Chrétien whose Neoplatonism has left an imprint on Hadjadj's work and whose relentless work ethic Hadjadj appears to emulate. One of my very first hypotheses about Hadjadj was that he was a philosophical controversialist, an author fond of wrong-footing his readers and wrestling them to the ground in the tradition of the writers of holy violence, like Léon Bloy or Georges Bernanos. Watch any interview with Hadjadj on Youtube and you will find him a master of the Thomistic *sed contra*, the nuanced rebuttal, an interlocutor who constantly resets the sloppy terms of popular or indeed academic debate through definition and distinction. What then do I mean by alluding to his *literary* project?

For Hadjadj, writing is not firstly about polemics because, for him at least, it is not firstly about communication. As he sees it, it is about trying to think something true about the world in a transcendent frame and, at the same time, about trying to craft that truth into verbal form. Thereby we might class him as a writer of *fullness* in the sense elaborated by Charles Taylor in *A Secular Age* and by which Taylor was trying to tease out the characteristics of a worldview open to a common sacred domain (not merely a private sacred as evoked by

[1] See also: Brian Sudlow, "I know why the philosopher sings: exploring the work of Fabrice Hadjadj," *Logos: A Journal of Catholic Thought and Culture* 23, no. 2 (2020): 78–104; "Techno-rationalities and the motherhood trilogy of Fabrice Hadjadj: Beyond the reaches of Kaufmann's médico-religieu," *Modern and Contemporary France* (April 23, 2020), accessed December 1, 2020, https://doi.org/10.1080/09639489.2020.175
2163; "Les limites de la science et de la technologie: Fabrice Hadjadj et l'obsolescence du merveilleux science-fictionnel," *Oeuvres et critiques* 44, no. 2 (2019): 67–85.

Michel Leiris).[2] Furthermore, his vocation as a writer is also crucial to Hadjadj's own self-understanding. As he told me in an interview in February 2019, he sometimes does not know what he thinks about a question until he writes about it. Wherever he goes, his notebook goes with him, and his writing affords him the mental laboratory or, better perhaps, the mental workshop in which concept, affect and script mutually gestate. The craft of writing and the craft of thinking are then, for Hadjadj, intertwined, and would be so even had he never chosen to publish. In Hadjadj's store cupboard, as his personal assistant complained to me with incomprehension, there are countless notebooks filled with poems hardly any of which are published.

The mention of Léon Bloy above brings me to the inspiration for this paper now. When he was a young man, a recent convert from anarchism and atheism to the Catholic faith, Hadjadj revelled in reading Bloy. Bloy was one of the most important figures of the French Catholic literary revival of the Belle Epoque, a novelist, polemicist and prolific diarist. He was a complex, volatile but also saintly character who impressed Jacques and Raissa Maritain sufficiently to shelve their plans for suicide and convert to Catholicism. Bloy's angry denunciations of the tepidity of the Catholic bourgeoisie find a stimulating echo in Hadjadj's first collection of essays entitled *Les violents s'en emparent* (1999)—*The Violent Bear it Away*. Nowadays, however, as Hadjadj explained to me, he would much rather spend his time reading G. K. Chesterton. I was not surprised by this confession, and not only because—in what seemed like a very Chestertonian moment of levity—I had just been squirted with a water pistol by Hadjadj's two-year-old son Moïse. More importantly, it confirmed another long-held intuition of mine: that Hadjadj and Chesterton were natural intellectual stablemates, albeit of different generations.

With this necessarily lengthy introduction, this paper aims to achieve two things. The first is to explore three points of comparison between Chesterton's and Hadjadj's oeuvres: bibliographical range, macro-structural manipulation and literary ethos. In all three areas, my hypothesis is that we will find many points of convergence between Hadjadj and Chesterton. The second part of my argument will test the connections between their shared literary ethos and the problematic of the sacred and the everyday, especially in a context of secular hegemony which insists on their separation or their privatisation. This test, I hope, will bring into sharper relief certain aspects of Hadjadj's literary hinterland, while also deepening our understanding of Chesterton's imaginative debt to France, a debt only poorly acknowledged in the secondary literature.

---

[2] Charles Taylor, *A Secular Age* (Cambridge, MA: Belknap Press, 2007), 6; Michel Leiris, "The Sacred in Everyday Life," in *The College of Sociology* (1937–38), ed. Denis Hollier, *Theory of History of Literature*, vol. 41 (Minneapolis, MN: University of Minnesota Press, 1988), 98–102. Originally published in the collection For a college of sociology, 8 January 1938.

PART 1

The first point of comparison between Chesterton and Hadjadj consists in the sheer range of work that they produce. Chesterton has the advantage here by publishing over a significantly longer period—about thirty-six years in fact—whereas Hadjadj's first significant publication does not appear until 1999 only twenty years ago. The time would not matter so much if they were only reproducing the same kinds of writing for each publication, but both writers consistently defy rigid specialism. In his first ten years as a published writer, from 1900 to 1910, Chesterton brings out two collections of poetry, three major essays, five biographical studies, three novels and one short story collection. I do not count here the numerous newspaper articles that are later compiled and published in single volumes. In a comparable period for Hadjadj from 1999–2009, there are four major essays, four plays, two books of art commentary (one jointly written), one collection of poetry and a range of review or newspaper articles that are uncollected and difficult to trace. While the number of publications is striking, more so in Chesterton's case, my point here is more about the range and variety of output.

Arguably, this is less surprising for Chesterton, a Belle Epoque childless *homme de lettres*, than it is for Hadjadj, a contemporary writer and father of nine children who has held a series of teaching posts. Nevertheless, the parallels remain significant. Both are poets, and while Chesterton excels in fiction, Hadjadj is the more productive and indeed more talented playwright. Chesterton's expressive tendency finds an outlet in his biographical sketches, which are in fact more sketches than biographies. Hadjadj's aesthetic interests have found expression in art commentary, and his study of *L'Agneau mystique*, the famous Ghent altar piece by the Van Eyck brothers, was awarded the *Prix du cercle Montherlant-Académie des Beaux Art* in 2008. A preference for the essay format is very marked in both authors, although Chesterton opts for the philosophical essay, while Hadjadj, for all his reputation as a philosopher, engages often in a kind of theological and exegetical philosophizing.

Their common refusal to be constrained or pigeonholed comes into even greater focus when we consider the attitudes of both writers to the question of genre. Chesterton's chef d'oeuvre in this area is *The Man who was Thursday* (1908), usually classed as a novel but by Chesterton as a *nightmare*. *The Man who was Thursday*, the relentless chase of an anarchist leader by undercover police, is a kind of metaphor for Chesterton's escape from intellectual subjectivism in the dark years of the decadent 1890s; if it is a story, it is one that pushes aside the constraints of plot and subplot, before finally demolishing the realist assumptions that we are led to think underpin it. It is really a modernist literary experiment *avant la lettre* as we say in French—before its time. Arguably, we might also regard Chesterton's biographical sketches as subversions of the genre since they make little pretence of being biographies of any kind. Instead, they tend to be platforms for Chesterton's theorisations of various questions, sometimes even related to the lives of the biography's subject. They are a pot pourri of insight, polemic and argument but very little biography as such.

For all that, Hadjadj's defiance of genre conventions surpasses even Chesterton's. I characterise his manipulation of genre conventions as a form of literary disruption in which parody and creative subversion play strong roles. For example, Hadjadj frequently uses the term 'manuel' or 'anti-manuel' for his works, driven as he is to overturn the techno-logistics of self-help books or the assumptions of techno-scientific design. On a different tack, readers of *Reussir sa mort* (2005) and *Paradis à la porte* (2011), are instructed that they can read the chapters of these books in any order. This, I argue, is not an excuse for Hadjadj to avoid the burden of organising these works more adroitly, but rather a means of undermining the rectilinearity of rationalised thought.

One final and perhaps extreme example might be useful here. In his 2003 mystery play *Passion-Résurrection,* a work designed to be acted in front of a polyptych of the death and resurrection of Christ by the late French artist Arcabas, the order of the scenes is actually controlled by a group of spectators who roll dice as part of a board game that moves the actors randomly between scenes. It is a device inspired by the archaeological discovery of some form of Roman street game scratched on the flagstones of *Gabbatha*, the place where Jesus was condemned to death. In the preface to this work Hadjadj accepts that such a procedure means that the play will rarely be performed in the same order and may appear in varying degrees of completeness. But why not? Why have we ever assumed that a traditional fourth-wall drama could adequately represent the meaning of the events of the incarnation? Furthermore, Hadjadj's involvement of the spectators in the play is a method of dramatizing the complicity—ignorant or otherwise—of humans in the death of Christ, thus dissolving the conventional positioning of readers or spectators as simple consumers of theatre. In other words, while Chesterton's literary techniques involve a disregard for convention and sometimes experimentation with it, Hadjadj's often require a positive deconstruction of genre conventions to achieve his own creative ends.

Now, one might interpret the overturning of convention and the eschewal of specialisation as acts of hubris. These literary gestures seem to belong to a romantic literary instinct, anchored in the supremacy of individual taste over collective norms. The eschewal of specialisation in both authors could be read as a failure to have learned the lessons inscribed in the defeat of Renaissance Man, or the failure of the sapiential tradition before the contemporary informational tsunami. In this light, ambitious literary range appears like creative overreach, and the disruption of conventions like naivety. In short, faced with all the literary inventiveness of Chesteton and Hadjadj, should we perhaps conclude, "Forgive them, reader, for they know not what they do"?

Yet this would be too harsh a judgment for at least two reasons. First, there is about them something of the *reactionary revolution* described by Richard Griffiths in his 1966 study of that name. While neither writer would define themselves in such terms—while neither is simply a polemicist or a wilful irritant against the established order—they stand against the tide, most especially the tide of ambient intellectual and cultural secularism that characterised Belle Epoque England, just as it characterises contemporary France. If these two authors are moderns, they are moderns who are trying to build paths back to the porous self, to use again the language of Charles Taylor, the self that is available to a cosmos full of meaning, rather than one that designs itself in a giddy rage of intersectional rivalry on a canvas where every meaning is held to be the result of random construction. For this reason, I read the disruptive tendencies I have described more as acts of liberation than as instances of mere revolt; liberation from the burdens of scepticism, and liberation from the locked-in syndromes of materialism and idealism that offer the human subject only the freedoms of a meaningless cosmos and the *bellum omnium contra omnes*.

Furthermore, the second reason to reject a harsh reading of Chesterton's and Hadjadj's disruption of conventions is that both are openly and avowedly clowns. This is a moral rather than a performative posture, and an *ethos* rather than a *mythos*. Both authors see humility as a foundational norm of their intellectual endeavours, and it is a humility that frequently breaks into humour and wit. Chesterton's commitment to this posture is inscribed in his 'Ethics of Elfland', a key chapter in his essay *Orthodoxy*, that posits as its fourth conclusion that the proper form of thanks for the purpose of the world is some form of humility and restraint, forever pitched between earnestness and wit. In this last regard, if the former is given expression in his Chesterton's Fr Brown stories, the latter is embodied by so many of his novelistic leads: Innocent Smith of *Manalive* (1911) or Humphrey Pump and Captain Dalroy in his 1914 novel *The Flying Inn*. Chesterton's love of the fool takes on a different texture in St Francis of Assisi where he characterises Francis as one of the jongleurs de Dieu: "The jongleur was properly a joculator or jester; sometimes he was what we should call a juggler."... Chesterton goes on to describe Francis's journey thus:

> Anyhow, there was not a rag of him left that was not ridiculous. Everybody knew that at the best he had made a fool of himself. It was a solid objective fact, like the stones in the road, that he had made a fool of himself. He saw himself as an object, very small and distinct like a fly walking on a clear windowpane; and it was unmistakably a fool. And as he stared at the word "fool" written in luminous letters before him, the word itself began to shine and change.... Of the intrinsic internal essence of the experience, I make no pretence of writing at all. But the external effect of it, for the purpose of this narrative, may be

> expressed by saying that when Francis came forth from his cave of vision, he was wearing the same word "fool" as a feather in his cap; as a crest or even a crown. He would go on being a fool; he would become more and more of a fool; he would be the court fool of the King of Paradise. (Chapter 5, St Francis of Assisi).

This figure of the fool is archetypal for Chesterton. It is found is so many of his works, and it is there, I argue, in his overturning of certain conventions and in his readiness to tumble like the *jongleur de Dieu* from genre to genre.

A similar observation, it seems to me, can be made of Hadjadj and perhaps expressed in even stronger terms. The figure of the clown does not appear in Hadjadj's writings until about 2012 but from that point forward it is frequently given pride of place. In his 2012 essay *Comment parler de Dieu aujourd'hui: anti-manuel d'évangélisation*, he writes the following:

> [The Christian] is a clown because of the disproportion between what he speaks of and what is: his mouth is too small for the infinite and his heart too narrow for a measureless love. He has put on Christ but, like a clown in his oversized costume, he gets lost in it, all tangled up, finds his foot caught in the trouser leg and then—crash!—he is on the ground at the very moment he was just about to start talking of heaven.[3]

The clown resurfaces in Hadjajd's work the following year in his theatrical monologue *Solo pour un clown* and then again in the 2017 work *Être clown en 99 leçons: guide (pas très pratique), essai (raté), récit (peu romanesque)*, yet another example of his cavalier reinvention of genre. In this case, what starts as a guidebook for clowns (who do not know they are clowns), evolves into a reflection on the nature of wonder, and eventually traces the story of a clown who finally turns up outside the Hadjadj residence. In the conclusion, Hadjadj addresses the clown directly:

> Here you are now, clown, before my door with your wife and daughter. You have been ringing the bell for some time. You are even addressing me through the keyhole, calling out the name on the plaque.
>
> Am I only the Ringmaster or am I the White Clown of this story?

[3] Fabrice Hadjadj, *Comment parler de Dieu aujourd'hui* (Paris: Salvator, 2012), 128.

> I will have to stop writing in order to answer the door, to look at you while I conceal my surprise at recognizing you—doubtless before driving you away.[4]

The similarities with the Chestertonian clown are tangible but so too are the differences. Both are fools in the eyes of the world. Yet while Chesterton's clown is somewhat accomplished, Hadjadj's clown is inept beyond measure. Chesterton's clown is benign and entranced; Hadjadj's is bemused and serene. Ultimately, we might see in them the very opposite of the self, as posited by Charles Cooley: *I am what I think you think I am*. Hadjadj's clown, like Chesterton's, might say rather: *I am what I have discovered God knows me to be*. The sense of freedom in such a discovery seems tangible. The subject is no longer a project retrieved from the perceptions of others, but a coming to self-awareness as a creature of God in spite of everything.

PART 2

So, what does this comparison of Chesterton and Hadjadj do for us who are preoccupied in these roundtables by the problematic of the sacred and the everyday? We could fill a whole year's worth of round tables and never come to the end of the debates about the sacred let alone the everyday. Yet their very distinction in the working title for these sessions is suggestive of one of the key issues in their juxtaposition: to many the everyday and the sacred are mutually exclusive. The sacred is, by definition, that which is special, reserved and set aside. It is associated with acts of religion and potentially sacrifice. Indeed, sacrifice means to make sacred, as if the *oblata*, the offerings of the sacrifice, must pass by virtue of some ritual from an unsacred or pre-sacred existence to a sacred one.

Nevertheless, even such general terms raise questions, not only about whether anything *needs* to be made holy, but also whether anything *can* be made holy. We come thereby to the notion of the *everyday*, especially for those who conceptualize it as one of the features of contemporary secular experience. The late Michael Sheringham has shown how the everyday, le *quotidien*, became a point of multiple discourses in the cultural evolution of France in the second half of the twentieth century, thanks to figures such as Henri Lefebvre, Michel de Certeau and Georges Perec.[5] Through such authors, the everyday appears as a kind of alternative aesthetic related to, though distinct from, modernization as a general set of political and sociological processes. For some theorists, it is a way of valorizing individual subjectivity in its battle against the mundanity of ambient spaces, rhythms and objects. De Certeau's *The*

[4] Ibid., 153.

[5] *Everyday Life: Theories and Practices from Surrealism to the Present* (Oxford University Press, 2009).

Practice of Everyday Life even envisages the everyday as a province of resistance. Countering such a view Rita Felski's treatment of the everyday embraces mundanity with greater positivity, most especially in its manifestations through repetition, home and habit.[6] Now, while Felski's analysis remains as resolutely secular in its assumptions as Lefebvre's or Perec's—because unavailable to anything transcendent in the cosmos—her conclusion that "it is time, perhaps, to make peace with the ordinariness of daily life" appears to indicate one fruitful path down which we can pursue our comparison of Chesterton and Hadjadj.[7] For it seems to me that while Chesterton pursues the ordinary as a path towards the sacred, Hadjadj has argued for a path from the sacred back to the ordinary. How then, I ask, do Chesterton and Hadjadj make peace with the ordinariness of daily life?

For Chesterton I take as my primary data the essay collection *Tremendous Trifles* (1909), incidentally and inconsequentially the first Chesterton book I ever read thirty years ago.[8] This collection of pieces first published as newspaper essays, contains many vignettes of everyday life, from 'A piece of chalk', 'The secret of a train', and 'On lying in bed', to 'What I found in my pocket' and 'A tragedy of twopence' [*sic*]. Of all these, 'The secret of a train' arguably provides the best example of Chesterton's recovery of the sacred through the ordinary. Late one night, boarding a train that is hardly lit, he finds himself all alone and smokes his cigar in his silent carriage. When the train then comes to an unexpected halt among the fields beyond the town, Chesterton is suddenly surprised to see the head of the stoker pop through the open window and inform him that there is a dead body being transported on the train. So far, so everyday: trains stop all the time, the dead are sometimes transported by train. But it is the subsequent reaction of Chesterton that typifies a particular response to the intersection of the everyday and the sacred:

> But when the train had started with its unknown burden, I did do one thing, and did it quite instinctively, without stopping to think, or to think more than a flash. I threw away my cigar. Something that is as old as man and has to do with all mourning and ceremonial told me to do it. There was something unnecessarily horrible, it seemed to me, in the idea of there being only two men in that train, and one of them dead and the other smoking a cigar. And as the red and gold of the butt end of it faded like a funeral torch trampled out at some symbolic moment of a procession, I realised how immortal ritual is. I

[6] Rita Felski, "The Invention of Everyday Life," *Cool Moves: a journal of culture/theory/politics* 39 (Winter 1999): 15–31.

[7] Ibid., 31.

[8] G. K. Chesterton, *Tremendous Trifles* (London: Methuen, 1909).

> realised (what is the origin and essence of all ritual) that in the presence of those sacred riddles about which we can say nothing it is more decent merely to do something. And I realised that ritual will always mean throwing away something; *destroying* our corn or wine upon the altar of our gods. (13–14)

In this passage I find at least one Chestertonian route to peace with the everyday. The everyday is not thrown away with the cigar; rather, through this gesture, it is seen as relative to the intangible. What is key is not the privation he imposes on himself, so much as what the privation makes space for, even in the everyday. The privation, therefore, is not simply negation, no more so than stepping back from a painting means you do not want to be near it. It is a matter of perspective—a perspective that brings into view a world of the unseen—but it is also a matter of practice, or ritual as Chesterton classes it. The everyday loses its flatness through such a practice of privation, but like the surface of a body of water that loses its reflectiveness only to reveal its depths.

Hadjadj's route to peace with the everyday begins in an entirely different place, but it seems to me that he ends up back where Chesterton leaves off, valorizing the everyday. His book *Résurrection, mode d'emploi* (2016) was translated unfortunately with the title *The Resurrection: Experience Life in the Risen Christ*. I say unfortunately because the translation loses the intertextual allusion to the infamous *Suicide, mode d'emploi* (1982), the suicide's handbook of how to kill oneself that was a popular guide before the internet took over the role. This work is a good example of Hadjadj's philosophizing from a position that does not *ipso facto* exclude revelation. In fact, in this work, Christian revelation is taken as a given, a datum, on the basis of which Hadjadj proceeds to explore what the encounter of the glorious and the everyday means in a post-resurrection world. He explains his thesis thus in the introduction:

> The apparitions of the Resurrected One have an eminently practical character. They are not hallucinations, fleeing the here and now and dabbling in the beyond. They bring us back to love of neighbor, teach us to see things from on high, i.e. not things that do not belong to the common lot of mortals but the same things from the perspective of the Spirit.... One can flee from Egypt, but this liberation would be the greatest disaster if every one of the Hebrews only left slavery behind to become a little Pharaoh (18).

The book pores over the proximity of the relationship of the resurrected Christ to the material world, as represented in the gospels. For example, the first thing Christ does after his resurrection is carefully to fold his burial cloths. This gesture denotes the kind of immersion in the everyday that Hadjadj finds generally in the hidden life of Christ when he works as a carpenter in an obscure village. Here, Hadjadj makes his peace with the everyday not by establishing its relativity to the intangible, but by establishing how the intangible or the transcendent valorizes the everyday. I quote now from a later chapter in which he has just discussed the abstract character of our own digital culture:

> The meaning of the incarnation implies the meaning of the flesh, openness to the supernatural being not a denaturalization but a return to the sources of nature. One who has not felt the order of things through his hands can only preach empty words about how things should be ordered. He is not realist enough to bear witness to the resurrection (136).

Just as for Chesterton the privation of a certain gesture was not a denial of the everyday but an enriching moment of its relativity, so Hadjadj's argument uses the relation of the sacred to the everyday to exclude those who would use the sacred as an excuse to ignore the everyday. Hadjadj's position is an injunction against those who are so heavenly minded, they are no earthly good. As Hadjadj sees it, beginning with the incarnation and the resurrection as data, is not to invalidate the empirical but to return to its depths.

CONCLUSIONS

The problematic of the sacred and the everyday continues to be contested, but both Hadjadj and Chesterton in their distinct ways try to make the peace that perhaps surpasses understanding. In Chesterton we see a line of discovery that passes from quotidian techniques—technological strata and practices—to the limits of the beyond. I find this deduction entirely typical of his willingness to drive reason hard in shaking lose from the skepticism of Enlightenment thought. Moreover, we know from other sources that this is a style of dialectic that he associated most strongly with the French tradition and one he admired even in its most irreligious practitioners.

In Hadjadj we pass in almost the opposite direction from the intangible—*noli me tangere*—to the tangible where both seem to live in new ways. At the heart of both concerns is a project that Hadjadj himself has captured most eloquently in the following terms:

> That God became human, that he embraces our daily actions and thereby brings them back to their sacred source all seems necessary, not so as to accomplish astonishing exploits but to save even the most elementary actions (74).

I am reminded here of the distinction of the ineffable and the indicible which Hadjadj sets forth in *Comment parler de Dieu aujourd'hui* (2012), not only because the *ineffable* seems to evoke the sacred more clearly, but also because, for some believers, the *indicible* or unspeakable nature of the everyday defines the limits of its ability to embrace the ineffable. And yet, as Hadjadj also explains in *Comment parler de Dieu aujourd'hui*, the unspeakable ultimately calls forth prayer, that most elemental form of human words. In this light, learning to speak about the apparent limits of the everyday may paradoxically lead back to the sacred *ineffable*.

Part IV
The Sacred and the Everyday in Religious Consciousness

Translating Two Minds in the Tradition of One Faith: Considerations of Intercultural Dynamics in the Parallels of John Henry Newman (1801–1890) and Joseph Ma Xiangbo (1840–1939)

Cyril Jerome Law, Jr. 劉偉傑
(University of Saint Joseph, Macau)

Summary

Interculturality is considered a constant given in the development of most major religious movements during the process of propagation coming into contact with diverse tongues, mores, and sentiments. And one of the chief, if not decisive, instruments contributing to this ever dynamic spread and reception of beliefs and cultures is translation. Christianity purports to be an incarnational religion, where the Word made flesh expresses the divine in human terms. Its doctrines are enshrined in a faith tradition that is developed largely through interpretation and translation. This short paper will cut into this sacral literary tradition by paralleling two influential modern Christian thinkers, John Henry Newman from the Anglophone school, and Joseph Ma Xiangbo from the Orient, to see how attempts at translating the ideas and works of people from distinct cultural milieux is both reflective of the necessary developmental nature of Christian teachings in the historical continuum of time and space, and indicative of the intellectual challenges that never cease to accompany the literary effervescence stemming from comparative religious studies.

**

In the *Grammar of Assent*, John Henry Newman writes:

> Every one who thinks on these subjects [about revealed religion] takes a course of his own, though it will also happen to be the course which others take besides himself. The minds of many separately bear them forward in the same direction, and they are confirmed in it by each other.[1]

[1] *An Essay in Aid of a Grammar of Assent* (London: Longmans, Green, and Co., 1870), 409. Emphases added.

Although no evidence suggests that John Henry Newman and Joseph Ma Xiangbo knew each other, a credible case could be made in confirming their congruous thinking by a parallel examination of their works, in light of their journeys of faith instantiated in the diverse ecclesial-social situations across 19th century England and early 20th century China. Hence the image I wish to put before us here may be described as the *Two Minds of One Faith.* Or, in a rather coarse way of putting it, I am trying to portray Ma Xiangbo as the Newman of China, and Newman the Ma Xiangbo of England.

The meeting, reconciliation and eventual harmony of faith and reason is a question of perennial significance in religious studies, but it is also a crucial topic in disciplines such as apologetics and fundamental theology. Comparative literary studies play an equally vivid part in analysing the verbal and written means by which language, as a product of reason and culture, conveys creedal contents. The Christian tradition embraces and expounds the enigma of faith and reason not only on the theoretical plane; it appropriates the notion that both faith and reason are integral partners to the homo credens, the believing man, as well as the *homo dicens*, man capable of speech.

It has always been of interest to me to bring John Henry Newman and Ma Xiangbo into conversation to appreciate how each of them elaborated with unrivalled literary and rhetorical prowess on the relationship between the revelatory nature of Christianity and the capacity of mankind (with its natural endowments of conscience, reason, and freedom of will) to arrive at the certainty of theistic faith. The propagation of their thoguhts and apologetical endeavours necessarily required adaptation of style and register in response to the needs of their audience or correspondents. Much of their best arguments grew out of controversies against, what they saw as, the rationalistic tendencies of 'liberalism' and 'modernism' popular in the religious and political circles of nineteenth century England and early twentieth century Republican China.

I took Newman and Ma to task for parallel study firstly because they profess the same faith, and secondly because of the high regard they each enjoy within their own cultural traditions. Newman's standing in the Christian west is hardly disputable, even if mixed opinions abound. His fame as one of the most masterful Victorian English writers is also rarely contested.[2] One obituary states: "All the resources of a master of English style—except, perhaps, one, description—were at his command: pure diction, clear arrangement, irony, dignity, a copious command of words, combined with a reserve in the use of them—all these qualities went to make up the charm of Newman's style."[3] But what

[2] David J. DeLaura, ed., *Victorian Prose: A Guide to Research* (New York: The Modern Language Association of America, 1973), 160–65.

[3] From the Athenaeum in *The Press on Cardinal Newman*, ed. Michael F. Glancey (private printing, undated), 22.

concerns us most here is the acknowledged theological significance of Newman's idea of the development of belief in the supernatural truths of Christianity that are known primarily through revelation, which, in essence, is a form of communication or self-disclosure of a personal God with a definite and intelligible message.

In the case of Ma Xiangbo, he is a unique specimen of a scholar who combines both the classical Chinese canonical tradition with a mastery of western learning, thanks largely to the scholastic education and Jesuit clerical formation he received at *Collège Saint-Ignace* and at the *Seminary of Zikawei* in Shanghai. His apologetical writings and well-reasoned rhetoric opened the eyes and ears of the Chinese audience to an autochtonous Catholic scholar whose belief in the power of revelation left a considerable impression, mirroring the intellectual stamp of evangelising pioneers like Matteo Ricci. Moreover, owing to his own political aspirations and knowledge in western constitutional theories, Ma is also looked up to as an oft-consulted lay patrician among the modern Chinese literati associated with the nationalistic and democratic movements at the turn of the 20th century. Ma, nicknamed the Cicero of China while alive, is now best remembered as the educator who founded three modern universities in China, namely, Aurora College, Fudan University, Fujen University, and as the mastermind behind the planning of the Chinese Academy of Humanities and Sciences 函夏考文苑. In sum, Newman and Ma can be reckoned as a kind of polymath or *homo universalis* representative of their respective era and culture. Many of Newman and Ma's associates, followers or foes, are themselves highly educated and literate figures of note.

Because of their need to articulate higher and broader truths in the paradoxically universal confine of the global Catholic faith, both Newman and Ma have each enriched the English and Chinese language to encapsulate things, peoples, places, and ideas "foreign" to England and China. Think of the very expression, "the Far East"—it was coined by Newman in his famous sermon, *The Second Spring*, on 13 July in 1852. Newman was referring to the Jesuit missionary St. Francis Xavier (a relic of his arm bone is kept right within the St. Joseph Seminary in Macau where this conference paper is being delivered). Incidentally, Francis Xavier died the same year the other Jesuit Matteo Ricci was born; and it was Ricci's apostolate that brought Ma Xiangbo's ancestors into the Catholic faith in the sixteenth century. It was also Newman who used the term 'Vincentians' the first time in the English language to refer to the Congregation of the Missions, or better known as the Lazarist Fathers in Europe, who took over much of the the missionary work in China after the suppression of the Society of Jesus. And perhaps, to our amusement or surprise, it was also in Newman's writings that we find the first appearance of the noun "inter-relations" (1848) and the adjective "unexciting" (1833) in the English language! Imagine that.

The English translation of the classical patristic Gospel commentary, the 4-volume *Catena Aurea—Commentary on the Four Gospels, Collected out of the Works of the Fathers by St. Thomas Aquinas* (1841), is carried out under Newman's auspices. Newman explains in the Preface to the translated work that, "By a CATENA PATRUM is meant a string or series of passages selected from the writings of various Fathers, and arranged for the elucidation of some portion of Scripture...."[4] Newman saw this as an answer to an urgent need for the Christian Church of his own age. Writing in 1839, he says, "Nothing is more wanted in our Church than a standard Commentary on Scripture."[5] The Englishing of the *Catena* can be seen as Newman's concrete contribution to the fulfilment of that want. Moreover, this work represents a milestone in his ardent promotion of patristic studies among English readers.[6]

In relation to the Catena Aurea, it is interesting to note Newman's personal take on the special character of each of the Gospels, which is succinctly given here:

> Each evangelist presents Jesus "differently." Matthew's description has a "severe subtlety," Mark's a "minuteness and exactness," Luke's a "sort of poetic beauty, and John's "heavenly and mysterious" quality is quite palpable.[7]

In the parallel effort to "present Jesus 'differently'," so that he be better and more widely known among the Chinese, Ma Xiangbo, on the other side of the globe, spent much effort grappling with the question of the Chinese rendition of Scripture. In the *Preface to the Literal Translation of the Saving Gospels* 救世福音對譯序 (1936), he said, "translation is an exchange, that is, to swap one

[4] In *Catena Aurea – Commentary on the Four Gospels, Collected out of the Works of the Fathers by St. Thomas Aquinas*, vol. 1 St. Matthew (London: Baronius Press, 2009, being a reproduction of the 1841 edition published by John Henry Parker, Oxford; and J.G.F. and J. Rivington, London), ix.

[5] *The Letters and Diaries of John Henry Newman*, vol.7 (Oxford: Clarendon Press, 1995), 11.

[6] "[A]t each stage— young Tractarian, middle-aged proponent of doctrinal development, elderly Cardinal— it was to the Alexandrian Fathers that Newman turned to make sure that contemporary growth was rooted in orthodox truth. Yet, he adapted his understanding of those Fathers to each stage of his life....Newman is therefore a key figure in the growth and development of patristic scholarship, particularly in the Anglophone world." In Benjamin John King, *Newman and the Alexandrian Fathers: Shaping Doctrine in Nineteenth-Century England* (Oxford: Oxford University Press, 2012), vii–viii. See also Roderick Strange, *Newman and the Gospel of Christ* (Oxford: Oxford University Press, 1981) for a focused analytic exposition of Newman's Christology largely influenced by the Alexandrian tradition.

[7] Newman's Sermon 508 in BOA A.11.12. (18 October 1840), untitled, 2–3, quoted in *Francis McGrath, John Henry Newman: Universal Revelation* (Tunbridge Wells, Kent: Burns & Oates, 1997), 134.

language for another so as to achieve mutual understanding."[8] Earlier on, he lays down a threefold principle of scriptural translation in *An Initiative Proposal on the Uniformity of Scriptural and Religious Terms* 統一經文芻議 (1929):

> First, one must value simplicity and intelligibility, [so as to aid] a smooth understanding of the meaning and logic [of the text]. Secondly, one must value a sense of solemnity and gravitas (貴莊重), [so that] both those with more refined sensibilities and commoner tastes may equally appreciate [the text]. Thirdly, and most importantly, one must value accuracy and propriety, [so that] there is nothing against the doctrines of the Faith.[9]

Ma Xiangbo produced a sizable scriptural reference tool entitled *A Plain Narrative Commentary of the New Covenant History Combined and Rearranged* 新史合編直講 (1913), in addition to his translation of the four Gospels. In 1901 Ma Xiangbo began to translate Andrea Mastai-Ferretti's *Les Évangélistes unis, traduits et commentés* (original Italian edition in 1818; French edition 1866).[10] The original work, *Les Évangélistes*, is a harmonisation of the four Gospels into a single narrative, preserving portions unique to each Gospel while editing out certain repetitions.

The publication Ma edited is divided into twenty volumes preceded by an exhaustive twenty-page topical index, followed by another twenty pages of liturgical index of scripture passages divided according to the annual cycles of ordinary, sanctoral, communal, and votive Mass lectionary, plus a ten-page explicative table of Chinese transliterations of foreign names, including the titles of biblical books, some patristic works and their authors, all alphabetically arranged. This last table of transliteration of names is a pristine sample of the hard-thought-out fruit of Ma Xiangbo's religious, intellectual, and cultural labour, for he has long been bedevilled by the quest of finding an

[8] Quoted in Ma Xiangbo Ji, *馬相伯集*, ed. by Zhu Waizheng (Shanghai: Fudan University Press, 1996), 586.

[9] Ibid., 504.

[10] Zhang Ruogu, *馬相伯先生年譜 [The Biographical Chronology of Mr Ma Xiangbo]* (Changsha: The Commercial Press, 1939), 204; Fang Hao, "馬相伯先生與聖經" ["Mr Ma Xiangbo and Sacred Scripture"] (1975), in *方豪晚年論文輯 fanghao wannian lunwen ji [A Collection of Fang Hao's Later Writings]* (Taipei: Fujen Catholic University Press, 2010), 139–50 (141). It is not clear what are the sources behind Lu Yongling's "Bibliographical Index to the Life and Work of Ma Xiangbo," in *Ma Xiangbo and the Mind of Modern China 1840–1939* (Armonk, NY: Sharpe, 1996), 285 in putting down 1894 as the first publishing year for Ma's *新史合編直講 [A Plain Narrative of the New Covenant History Combined and Rearranged]*.

acceptable resolution to the discrepancies in the different translations of terminology since the introduction of Christianity to China.[11]

What Ma Xiangbo did in this monumental *Commentary* was he first translated the texts of the proper Gospel passages into classical scholarly Chinese, then he translated the exegetical sections and commentaries using the colloquial language (*bái huà* 白話 [plain speech]) in an easy-to-read style. This presentation of Scripture with a combination of classical and colloquial styles of Chinese writing is Ma's unique attempt at preserving the elegance and respect due to the sacred text while trying to appeal to the popular taste of the general readership at the same time. Ma Xiangbo was responsible for a good number of Chinese Christian and philosophic terms either in the form of transliterations or literal translations, sometimes by incorporating ancient classical Chinese characters with proper pedigree or sometimes by furnishing fresh expressions altogether.

And when a biblical concept does not have a corresponding idea in Chinese, Ma resorts to the venerable practice of a direct transliteration of sounds (such as the untranslated 'Amen', 'Alleluia', and even retaining the transliteration of 'Verbum' of the vulgate Latin as 物爾朋 *wuerpeng* after the properly translated word 聖言, 'the Holy Word'), or an approximation of its meaning.[12] In one of Ma's apologetical works, *The Relationship between Sacred Scripture and Human Community* 聖經與人群之關係, when citing Matthew 5:22, the terms 'raca' and 'gehenna' are given in the Chinese transliterations as 拉加 and 災痕 plus exegetical annotations to the meanings of the word.[13] But in a linguistically complex China, where mutually unintelligible regional dialects abound, Ma Xiangbo thinks the challenge must be overcome by taking the classical approach, that is, to maintain the purity of the language by not mixing colloquial expressions with the received written form. Annotations should be given for the more obscure passages and the sounds of the transliterated names of persons and places must strive for maximal uniformity throughout China. It is interesting to note that in his translations, Ma deliberately chooses to use historical classical Chinese terms or expressions, especially those not later than the time of Christ and the apostolic age (Han Dynasty). Ma's idea is that this

---

[11] This question will be revisited again in the later section on Ma's *Initiative Proposal on the Uniformity of Scriptural and Religious Terms* (1929).

[12] Augustine already intimated this practice in scriptural translation in his *De Doctrina Christiana*: "'In some cases, although they could be translated, the original form is preserved for the sake of its solemn authority [propter sanctiorem auctoritatem]', such as amen and alleluia." Quoted in Uwe Michael Lang, *The Voice of the Church at Prayer: Reflections on Liturgy and Language* (San Francisco, CA: Ignatius Press, 2012), 48.

[13] Li Tiangang, ed., *Ma Xiangbo Juan馬相伯卷* (Beijing: Renmin University Press, 2014), 163.

way would best capture the spirit and meaning of the original.[14] But this translation strategy of Ma, if hypothetically adopted by Newman and applied to his would-be English Bible, would bound to fail because the Proto Germanic form of Old English or Roman Brittonic current at the time of Jesus are not comparable to the sophistication of the ancient Chinese literary culture that belongs to the same cultural and intellectual continuum of subsequent ages down to Ma's time. The sort of language used by the people living on the British Isles at the first stage of the Common Era prior to the arrival of the Germanic tribes is practically foreign to Newman's 19th century Britain.[15] But in Ma Xiangbo's case, his artful choice is not only not anachronistic but quite justifiable because classical literary Chinese has already been in a stable form long before English by comparison. Therefore, for most literate Chinese in early 20th century China, terms and expressions from the 11th century B.C. on are part of the collective, comprehensible native Chinese cultural heritage. Ma Xiangbo's attempt is a combination of his loyalty to the inspired text and a respectful, intelligent preservation of ancient Chinese literary traditions.

Seen together, the significance of the appearance of the English *Catena Aurea* under Newman and Ma Xiangbo's Chinese *Plain Narrative Commentary* is threefold.

First, they constitute part of the Christian Church's consistent and universal need to unlock the hidden meanings of Sacred Scripture through detailed and reasoned analysis. These commentaries are fruits of the Church's long tradition of collective reflections on the revealed words, as well as the crystallisations of the many "theological conversations and controversies" engendered in the Church's doctrinal development.[16]

Second, they helped arouse the attention of their readers in the Anglophone and Chinese world to the core contribution of the Church Fathers, that is, the explication of Sacred Scripture, or, "scriptural hermeneutics."[17] Not only is the *Catena* strictly patristic by nature, Mastai-Ferretti's *Les Évangélistes*, on which Ma's translation is based, is also replete with quotations from the Church Fathers and later authors. And by translating and editing the *Les Évangélistes* and providing it with a bilingual index (Latin-Chinese), Ma Xiangbo became one of the first modern scholars to introduce to the Chinese Catholic

---

[14] *A Preface to the Literal Translation of the Saving Gospels* (1936), quoted in *Ma Xiangbo Ji*, 586. See also Gao Wanyun 高萬雲, "The Contributions to Chinese Rhetoric of Ma Xiangbo 馬相伯對中國修辭學的貢獻," *Rhetoric Learning* 當代修辭學 3 (2010): 80–86.

[15] See Melvyn Bragg, *The Adventure of English: The Biography of a Language* (London: Hodder and Stoughton, 2003), 1.

[16] Uwe Michael Lang, "Newman and the Fathers of the Church," *New Blackfriars* 92, no. 1038 (2011): 144–56 (144).

[17] Ibid., 144.

audience in an organic fashion a whole host of major patristic and pre- and early modern (or Counter-Reformation) writers, such as Athanasius, Baronius, Bede, Bonaventure, Bossuet, Clement, John Chrysostom, Cyril of Jerusalem, Francis de Sales, Gregory of Nazianzen, Jerome, Justin, Leo, Origen, Suarez, and of course, Thomas Aquinas, as well as Protestant authors like Calvin and Luther. This special contribution of Ma's is parallel to Newman's rekindling of the reading of the Fathers among the English by fervently referencing their works in his theological treatises.

Thirdly, these commentaries translation projects, which are practical tools correlated to the liturgical readings by their division into pericopes, represent Newman's and Ma's recognition of, and their determination to cultivate, an attitude towards the study of Sacred Scripture with deeper roots in the liturgical tradition. These works are also indicative of the inchoate development in Newman's and Ma's theological reflections on the data and import of Revelation—*Fides quaerens intellectum*—and they both conscientiously chose the Church Fathers as their orthodox guides.

Vast and multiple pagan regions (in the non-pejorative sense of the dated usage of the term) have been evangelized even before the Bible is translated into the native people's languages, let alone appearing in any approximate written form of divergent non-literary dialects.[18] Newman, in his *Oxford University Sermons*, spells out the *modus operandi* by which ideas incarnate:

> [I]t were idle to expect that the courses of thought marked out in one language should, except in their great outlines and main centres, correspond to those of another. Multitudes of ideas expressed in the one do not even enter into the other, and can only be conveyed by some economy or accommodation, by circumlocutions, phrases, limiting words, figures, or some bold and happy expedient. And sometimes, from the continual demand, foreign words become naturalized.[19]

Thus, it is imperative that we have a realistic, that is, a balanced view of the role that culture and language plays in the process of evangelization, neither exaggerating its capacity as an agent, nor undervaluing its influence on shaping

[18] For example, Mandarin Chinese, or Putonghua, is written as spoken, like English or Italian, but Cantonese is essentially a spoken tongue without the corresponding written characters for all its sounds. Thus, reading out a printed text written in Mandarin with Cantonese pronunciation is an anomaly, but is a generally accepted practice. This awkward phenomenon creates no minor challenge to evangelization and catechizing of non-Mandarin speakers, especially with regard to the auricular comprehension of liturgical readings at Mass.

[19] "The Theory of developments in Religious Doctrine," Sermon 15 in *Fifteen Sermons Preached Before the University of Oxford* (London: Longmans, Green, and Co., 1843), 341–2.

our prevenient state of mind prior to the actualization of Faith in people's hearts.

Each in his unique manner, Newman and Ma are representative of a fresh approach in the exposition of the revelatory foundations of Christian beliefs, while not neglecting their pronounced adherence to the authority of the Roman Catholic Church. In other words, their place and influence in raising the level Catholic apologetical discourse both in the English and Chinese speaking world is what I also wish to highlight. Newman's and Ma's originality consists mainly in the adoption of a more direct personal style of engagement with the social and religious issues of modernity; and by responding to these challenges, they applied and tested Christian principles through multifarious media of communication (journal articles, letters, diaries, memoranda, sermons, speeches, and in the case of Ma Xiangbo, the added use of radio broadcast), and left behind them a vast corpus of apologetical instruments replete with cutting insight.

Newman scholarship in the past century has seen substantial development through multidisciplinary studies. It would be profitable to borrow some of the successful models of/approaches to Newman studies and apply them to the comparatively rich fount of materials associated with Ma Xiangbo, with the hope of according Ma a more prominent academic assessment in worldwide Christian and comparative cultural studies.

Ma is relatively less studied, so by juxtaposing him with Newman, it helps to show not only that churchmen steeped in the western Christian tradition can engage in developed theological discourse, but that people like Ma, a Chinese former Jesuit, who shared remarkable intellectual and spiritual qualities with Newman, can contribute to Christian apologetics and religious literature in breath and in depth.

This parallel study is also, by the nature of the case, a kind of philosophical odyssey into two worlds. It is an imponderable task to try to quantify and measure the ideological differences existing between English and Chinese cultures a century ago, let alone to detect the rise and changes of crossbred sub-cultures born out of the westernization of some parts of China through colonial administration, trade, modern industry, education, and religion across time. This phenomenon has been recently described by some psychologists as the difference in East-West "cognitive profiles."[20] The difference in genre, semantics, and rhetorical use of the English and Chinese language also raises some fascinating questions about the supracultural aspects of a 'universal revelation' and the articulation of faith-responses. A comparison between the two fecund religious

[20] David Robson, "How East and West Think in *Profoundly Different Ways*," January 19, 2017, accessed January 20, 2017, http://www.bbc.com/future/story/20170118-how-east-and-west-think-in-profoundly-different-ways.

minds representative of the Occidental and Oriental cultures should yield a sharpened awareness of the uniqueness and complementarity of the human expressions of the divine.

If I may indulge in using some phenomenological parlance, Newman and Ma each exhibit certain moral traits that could be justifiably styled as *personalist*, which is essentially an existentialist designation for a philosophic personality with a strong consciousness of the primacy of the incommunicable self as the subjective core of will, action, values and affection. But the essential inter-subjective nature of human beings implies authentic openness of self to the other. *Cor ad cor loquitur*—heart speaks to heart. And Newman and Ma's winning personalist influence on their admirers is in no small part due to the sincere and successful application of their literary skills. Newman's oft-quoted words in *The Grammar of Assent* reads beautifully:

> The heart is commonly reached, not through the reason, but through the imagination, by means of direct impressions, by the testimony of facts and events, by history, by description. Persons influence us, voices melt us, looks subdue us, deeds inflame us.[21]

Although I entitled this paper "Translating Two Minds in the Tradition of One Faith," I suppose it would be more accurate to say that, after paralleling Newman the quintessential English Catholic and Ma Xiangbo the underdog Father of Chinese Catholicism, theirs has been more of a case of Two Minds Tanslating One Faith, as they sought to baptize the world redeemed by Christ's precious blood, one with the water of the River Thames, the other, of the Yellow River.

[21] *An Essay in Aid of A Grammar of Assent* (London: Longmans, Green, and Co., 1870), 92–93.

WHAT GOES AROUND COMES AROUND? THE (NON-)EXISTENCE OF (DIVINE) RETRIBUTION IN ANCIENT CHINESE LITERATURE AND THE HEBREW BIBLE

Chin Hei (Andrew) Leong
(University of Saint Joseph, Macau)

INTRODUCTION

In human history, there is not a day in which one cannot find any injustice. And across different cultures, retribution is seen as a way towards justice. A classical study on this topic is the publication of a French sociologist Marcel Mauss' *Essai sur le don* in 1925. According to Mauss' observation, members in an archaic society are forced to reciprocate that which s/he has received.[1] The source of this force are twofold.[2] On the one hand, such norm is established in the process during which a given society has developed to be stabilized.[3] On the other hand, this practice is strongly linked to the perceived "magical, religious, and spiritual force."[4] In short, the principle of retribution operates on both the societal and transcendental levels.

In this paper, I would like to give a preliminary comparison between the development of the idea of the reciprocity of the good and evil that one has done in two great cultures, the one that is visible is the Hebrew Bible and the other that is expressed in Ancient Chinese Literature (pre-Chin).

[1] Marcel Mauss, *The Gift: The Form and Reason for Exchange in Archaic Societies*, trans. W. D. Halls (London: Routledge, 1990), 10–59. Mauss' theory has not remained uncriticized, as in: Alain Testart, "What Is a Gift?," trans. Susan Emanuel and Lorraine Perlman, HAU: *Journal of Ethnographic Theory* 3, no.1 (2013): 249–61 [251-254]. However, the criticism mostly centers on the vagueness of Mauss' articulation of his theory, and points to a necessary refinement of his definition and categorizations. The obligation or expectation of reciprocity in exchange, which is the key notion of Mauss' theory, remains honored by most sociologists. See; e.g., Alain Testart, "Uncertainties of the 'Obligation to Reciprocate': A Critique of Mauss," in *Marcel Mauss: A Centenary Tribute*, ed. Wendy James and N. J. Allen (New York: Berghahn, 1998), 97–110 [103–4] and Neil Coffee, "Reciprocity," *The Encyclopedia of Ancient History* 10 (2013): 5747–8.

[2] 見：李隆獻，《復仇觀的省察與詮釋：先秦兩漢魏晉南北朝隋唐編》，中國思想史研究叢書 8（臺北市：臺大出版中心，2012年，頁3–5.

[3] Mauss, *The Gift*, 105.

[4] Ibid., 13.

Retribution on Societal Level
Lex Talionis

Exodus 21–22 is one of the most famous passages of the Hebrew Bible, because what we commonly call *lex talionis* finds its sources there, even though we know that such principle pre-exists the Hebrew Bible in the Babylonian Code of Hammurabi (ca. 1754 BCE).[5] Below is the most well-known formulation of this principle:

Exod 21:23-25[6]

וְאִם־אָסֹון יִהְיֶה וְנָתַתָּה נֶפֶשׁ תַּחַת נָפֶשׁ׃

עַיִן תַּחַת עַיִן שֵׁן תַּחַת שֵׁן יָד תַּחַת יָד רֶגֶל תַּחַת רָגֶל׃

כְּוִיָּה תַּחַת כְּוִיָּה פֶּצַע תַּחַת פָּצַע חַבּוּרָה תַּחַת חַבּוּרָה׃ ס

But if injury ensues, you shall give life for life, eye for eye, tooth for tooth, hand for hand, foot for foot, burn for burn, wound for wound, stripe for stripe. (NAB)

It should be pointed out that, according to the biblical stipulations, it is always the culprit who would directly suffer the injury (or death) that he first inflicted upon the victim.

The expression "an eye for an eye, a tooth for a tooth," or similar ones, is not found in Ancient Chinese Classics.[7] However, it was no less a practice in Ancient China, perhaps in an even more extreme way:

《孟子・盡心下・七》:
殺人之父，人亦殺其父，

[5] E.g., in Art. 196: "If a man put out the eye of another man, his eye shall be put out"; Art. 200: "If a man knock out the teeth of his equal, his teeth shall be knocked out."

[6] See also: Lev 24:18–20; Deut 19:21.

[7] For a recent study on the topic in early Chinese literary history, see: 李隆獻，《復仇觀的省察與詮釋：先秦兩漢魏晉南北朝隋唐編》，中國思想史研究叢書 8（臺北：臺大出版中心，2012年）。The lack of explicit stipulation of revenge notwithstanding, the duty to do so is implied in a few pre-Chin classics. For example, one reads in 《禮記》 (*The Book of Rites*): 「父母之讎，不與同生；兄弟之讎，不與聚國，朋友之讎，不與聚鄉，族人之讎，不與聚鄰」("one shall not live together with the person who killed his parents [in the same world]; one shall not live with the person who killed his brother in the same kingdom; one shall not live with the person who killed his friend/companion/comrade in the same village; one shall not live with the person who killed one of his own clan in the same neighborhood"). The implication is that, for instance, if one is aware that the person who killed his parents is in the same kingdom that he is, it is the duty for one to find him and annihilate him so that they would not be in the same kingdom.

When a man kills another's father, that other will kill his father;
殺人之兄，人亦殺其兄，
When a man kills another's elder brother, that other will kill his elder brother.
然則非自殺之也，一閒耳。
So he [i.e. the killer] does not himself indeed do the act, but there is only an interval between him [i.e. the killer] and it [i.e. the death of his own father or brother].

(Mencious, *Tsin Sin*, Part II, ch. 7)[8]

This practice of *lex talionis* is different from that in the Hebrew Bible, but similar to what one finds in the Code of Hammurabi. According to the code, when a builder built a house for someone, but it was not built properly and fell and:

> If it kill the son of the owner the son of that builder shall be put to death. (art. 230)

This practice that is witnessed in Mencius and Hammurabi can be called "strict talion." In terms of the operation of the principle, the difference between Mencius and Hammurabi on the one hand and the Hebrew Bible on the other is the focus. In the Bible, the focus is solely on the direct victim of the assault. But here, the focus is on the loss to the living caused by the assault. Thus, if A causes B to lose his father, B's retribution is not on A but A's father, so that A would also lose his father and suffer the same feeling of loss that B has gone through.

The two ways of administering *lex talionis* likewise express two different moralities, particularly concerning vengeance. It is generally accepted among biblical scholars that one of the purposes of introducing *lex talionis* is to control the escalation of blood vengeance.[9] This intention is made explicit elsewhere in the Torah:

Lev 19:18

לֹא־תִקֹּם וְלֹא־תִטֹּר אֶת־בְּנֵי עַמֶּךָ וְאָהַבְתָּ לְרֵעֲךָ כָּמוֹךָ אֲנִי יְהוָה׃

[8] James Legge, trans., *The Chinese Classics*, vol. 2, *The Works of Mencious*, 2nd ed. (Oxford: Clarendon Press, 1895; repr. Taipei: SMC Publising, 1991), 481.

[9] E.g., Cornelis Houtman, *Exodus*, vol. 3: Chapters 20–40, *Historical Commentary on the Old Testament* (Leuven: Peeters, 2000), 167; William H. C. Propp, *Exodus* 19–40: *A New Translation with Introduction and Commentary*, Anchor Yale Bible 2A (New Haven; London: Yale University Press, 2006), 230.

> You shall not take vengeance or bear a grudge against any of your people, but you shall love your neighbor as yourself: I am the Lord. (NRSV)[10]

In comparison, the teaching on vengeance in Ancient Chinese classics is more ambiguous. In *Tao Te Ching*, Lao Tzu exhorts:

> 《道德經・六十三》
> 報怨以德。
>
> Do good to him who has done you an injury.
> (*Tao Te Ching*, 63)[11]

However, in the Analects one reads:

> 《論語・憲問十四・卅四》
> 或曰：以德報怨，何如
> Some one said, 'What do you say concerning the principle that injury should be recompensed with kindness?'
> 子曰：何以報德？以直報怨，以德報德。
> The Master said, 'With what then will you recompense kindness? Recompense injury with justice, and recompense kindness with kindness.' (*Analects, XIV Hsien Wăn*, 34)[12]

The phrase "[r]ecompense injury with justice" is interpreted as to mean "to recompense injury with injury."[13] Thus, according to the conclusion of the famous Chinese historian 瞿同祖 (Qú Tongzu), ancient Chinese society recognized vengeance not only as a right but even as a *sacred* duty.[14]

---

[10] Otherwise specified, the English translation of the Bible is taken from the NRSV.

[11] D. C. Lau, trans., *Tao Te Ching*, Chinese Classics (Hong Kong: Hong Kong University Press, 1989), 93.

[12] James Legge, trans., *The Chinese Classics*, vol. 1, *Confucian Analects, the Great Learning, and the Doctrine of the Mean*, 2nd ed. (Oxford: Clarendon Press, 1895; repr. Taipei: SMC Publising, 1991), 288.

[13] 張燕嬰（譯注），《論語》，新視野中華經典文庫（香港：中華書局，2012），頁287。另見：錢穆，《論語新解》，錢穆作品精萃（臺北：東大圖書，2004），頁410；

[14] 瞿同祖，《中國法律與中國社會》，新版（北京：中華書局，2003年），頁73。另見：周天游，《古代復仇面面觀》（西安：陝西人民出版社，1992年），頁1。

Non (or Further)-Retribution on Societal Level

In Ancient Chinese Society, evil was always expected to be retributed. But how about good? Is good always reciprocated? In one occasion in Ancient Chinese Literature, one finds the assertation that by returning something the author is actually NOT reciprocating, but expecting something more:

> 《詩經．魏風．木瓜》
> 投我以木瓜。
> There was presented to me a papaya,
>
> 報之以瓊琚。
> And I returned for it a beautiful keu-gem;
>
> 匪報也。
> Not as a return for it,
> 永以為好也。
> But that our relationship might be lasting.
> *(Book of Poetry, Odes of Wei, Muh kwa*, 1)[15]

Here the poet reciprocates a precious jade for a papaya. He justifies such an unproportionate return by claiming that it is not reciprocity at all. He does so in order "that [thei]r relationship might be lasting." However, it is also legitimate to interpret the poet as expecting a further return from the giver of papaya, i.e. a lasting relationship (which is precious), by returning a precious stone. Following this logic, the poet not only accept retribution on the societal level, but instead further it.

To my knowledge, there is not any explicit rejection of receiving reciprocated good in the Hebrew Bible.

Automatic Transcendental Retribution

Descriptions of retribution, in ancient texts of both east and west, are not limited to interpersonal relations, but includes mechanisms involving the supernatural realm. It is exhorted that heavenly blessing is obtained by the virtuous, and disasters befall the wicked. For example, the *Book of Proverbs* teaches that:

> Prov 13:21
>
> חַטָּאִים תְּרַדֵּף רָעָה וְאֶת־צַדִּיקִים יְשַׁלֶּם־טוֹב׃
>
> Misfortune pursues sinners, but prosperity rewards the righteous.A more vivid depiction of poetic justice is also found

---

[15] James Legge, trans., *The Chinese Classics*, vol. 4, *The She King or The Book of Poetry*, 2nd ed. (Oxford: Clarendon Press, 1895; repr. Taipei: SMC Publising, 1991), 107.

among the teachings of the sages:
Prov 26:27

כֹּֽרֶה־שַׁ֭חַת בָּ֣הּ יִפֹּ֑ל וְגֹ֥לֵל אֶ֝֗בֶן אֵלָ֥יו תָּשֽׁוּב׃

Whoever digs a pit will fall into it, and a stone will come back on the one who starts it rolling.

For a few Old Testament scholars, prominent among them being Klaus Koch,[16] find in this verse (among others) the evidence that ancient Israelites generally believed "that 'sin' is itself a destructive agency that contains within itself the seeds of the sinner's downfall. The human act, good or bad, and its consequences for the life of the doer, have an internal and intrinsic connection." Thus, Koch rejects the conventional view that "God is portrayed in the Bible as intervening in human affairs to punish sins."[17]

A similar view is found in a teaching which is attributed to Confucius as recorded in the *Doctrine of the Mean*:

《中庸・十七章一節》

子曰：舜其大孝也與，德為聖人，尊為天子，富有四海之內，宗廟饗之，子孫保之。

The Master said, 'How greatly filial was Shun! His virtue was that of a sage; his dignity was the throne; his riches were all within the four seas. He offered his sacrifices in his ancestral temple, and his descendants preserved the sacrifices to himself.' (*Doctrine of the Mean* 17,1)

《中庸・十七章二節》

故大德必得其位，必得其祿，必得其名，必得其壽。

'Therefore, having such great virtue, it could not but be that he should obtain the throne, that he should obtain those riches, that he should obtain his fame, that he should attain to his long life.' (*Doctrine of the Mean* 17,2)

Likewise, according to the discussion between Mencius and his disciple, he advises that princes should not take advantage of the time of peace and prosperity and spend their days in leisure and indolence but rather in diligence in governance. Then he appeals to this principle:

---

[16] Klaus Koch, "Gibt es ein Vergeltungsdogma im Alten Testament," *Zeitschrift für Theologie und Kirche* 52 (1955): 1–42.

[17] John Barton, *Ethics in Ancient Israel* (Oxford: Oxford University Press, 2014), 212–3.

《孟子・公孫丑上第三・四》

禍福無不自己求之者。

Calamity and happiness in all cases are men's own seeking. (Mencius, *Kung-Sun Ch'âu* I, 4)[18]

In both traditions, there are strong assertions on the principle of poetic justice. One may argue that in such articulations the existence of a deity administering justice is implied. In what follows, we shall see that there are still more explicit depictions of divine retribution, or the lack thereof.

DIVINE RETRIBUTION

THEORETICAL COUNSELS

The Deuteronomists, one of the major schools of theology within the Hebrew Bible, strongly believed blessing was administered by God to those who do good:

Deut 28:1–2 (also vv. 3–14):

וְהָיָה אִם־שָׁמוֹעַ תִּשְׁמַע בְּקוֹל יְהוָה אֱלֹהֶיךָ לִשְׁמֹר לַעֲשׂוֹת אֶת־כָּל־מִצְוֺתָיו
אֲשֶׁר אָנֹכִי מְצַוְּךָ הַיּוֹם וּנְתָנְךָ יְהוָה אֱלֹהֶיךָ עֶלְיוֹן עַל כָּל־גּוֹיֵי הָאָרֶץ׃

If you will only obey the Lord your God, by diligently observing all his commandments that I am commanding you today, the Lord your God will set you high above all the nations of the earth;

וּבָאוּ עָלֶיךָ כָּל־הַבְּרָכוֹת הָאֵלֶּה וְהִשִּׂיגֻךָ כִּי תִשְׁמַע בְּקוֹל יְהוָה אֱלֹהֶיךָ׃

all these blessings shall come upon you and overtake you, if you obey the Lord your God.

Likewise, they were convinced that God retributed disaster upon evildoers:

Deut 28:15 (also vv. 16–68):

וְהָיָה אִם־לֹא תִשְׁמַע בְּקוֹל יְהוָה אֱלֹהֶיךָ לִשְׁמֹר לַעֲשׂוֹת אֶת־כָּל־מִצְוֺתָיו
וְחֻקֹּתָיו אֲשֶׁר אָנֹכִי מְצַוְּךָ הַיּוֹם וּבָאוּ עָלֶיךָ כָּל־הַקְּלָלוֹת הָאֵלֶּה וְהִשִּׂיגוּךָ׃

But if you will not obey the Lord your God by diligently observing all his commandments and decrees, which I am commanding you today, then all these curses shall come upon you and overtake you.

[18] Translation taken from: https://ctext.org/dictionary.pl?if=gb&id=1632#s 10029574 [accessed 23 July, 2019].

The Israelites believed that God administered justice, rewarding the good and punishing the evil, according to a certain norm, i.e. the divine commandments and decrees. Similarly, according to the ancient Chinese record the *Shoo King* (or the *Book of Historical Documents*), the political senior advisor Gaoyao (皋陶) admonishes the legendary Yu the Great (大禹) thus:

> 《尚書・虞書・皋陶謨・六》
>
> 天敘有典，勑我五典，五惇哉。
>
> From Heaven are the [social] arrangements with their several duties; to us it is given to enforce those five duties, and then we have the five courses of generous conduct!
>
> 天秩有禮，自我五禮，有庸哉。
>
> From Heaven are the [social] distinctions with their several ceremonies; from us proceed the observances of those five ceremonies, and then do they appear in regular practice!
>
> 同寅協恭，和衷哉！
>
> When [sovereign and ministers] show a common reverence and respect for these, do they not harmonize the moral nature [of the people]?
>
> 天命有德，五服五章哉；天討有罪，五刑五用哉。
>
> Heaven graciously distinguishes the virtuous; —are there not the five habiliments, five decorations of them? Heaven punishes the guilty; —are there not the five punishments to be severally used for that purpose? (*Shoo King, the Book of Yu, the Counsels of Kaou-Yaou*, 6)[19]

Similar to Deuteronomy 28, Kaou-Yaou asserts that heaven administers retribution after mentioning the established norms.

Political Application

The notion of divine retribution is not only used in building a theoretical framework for personal and political ethics, but it is applied in political action to justify a rebellion. In the Hebrew Bible, the beginning of Dynasty of the House of Jehu serves as a good example.

Earlier in the Books of Kings it is recorded that King Ahab of the House of Omri coveted Naboth's vineyard and murdered him (cf. 1 Kings 21). There

[19] James Legge, trans., *The Chinese Classics*, vol. 3, *The Shoo King or The Book of Historical Documents*, 2nd ed. (Oxford: Clarendon Press, 1895; repr. Taipei: SMC Publising, 1991), 73–74.

YHWH, considering that Ahab repented, decided: "Because he has humbled himself, the evil shall not come in his days; in the days of his son the evil shall come to his house" (v. 29b). When Jehu conspired against Joram, son of Ahab, Jehu killed Joram and threw him at the location of Naboth's vineyard, he claimed that the LORD had said to him the following:

> 2 Kgs 9:26a
>
> אִם־לֹ֠א אֶת־דְּמֵ֨י נָב֜וֹת וְאֶת־דְּמֵ֤י בָנָיו֙ רָאִ֣יתִי אֶ֔מֶשׁ נְאֻם־יְהוָ֔ה וְשִׁלַּמְתִּ֥י לְךָ֛
> בַּחֶלְקָ֥ה הַזֹּ֖את נְאֻם־יְהוָ֑ה
>
> For the blood of Naboth and for the blood of his children that I saw yesterday, says the Lord, I swear I will repay you on this very plot of ground.

Similarly, according to the *Shoo King*, when King Tang of the House of Shang dispatched his army to overthrow King Jie of Xia (i.e. the descendants of Yu the Great), he gave a speech to the troop and said the following:

> 《尚書・商書・湯誓・一》
>
> 格爾眾庶，悉聽朕言，非台小子，敢行稱亂，有夏多罪，天命殛之。
>
> Come, ye multitudes of the people, listen all to my words. It is not I, the little child, who dare to undertake [what may seem to be] a rebellious enterprize (sic.); but for the many crimes of the sovereign of Hea (i.e. Xia) Heaven has given the charge to destroy him.
>
> 今爾有眾，汝曰，我后不恤我眾，舍我穡事，而割正夏。予惟聞汝眾言，夏氏有罪，予畏上帝，不敢不正。
>
> Now, ye multitudes, you are saying, 'Our prince does not compassionate us, but is calling us away from our husbandry to attack and punish [the ruler of] Hea.' I have indeed heard [these] words of you all: [but] the sovereign of Hea is an offender, and, [as] I fear God, I dare not but punish him. (*Shoo King, Books of Shang, Speech of Tang*, 1)[20]

In short, according to these texts, heaven was not only thought of as a personal deity, but He commanded earthly political leaders whom He had appointed to execute His will, to punish the evil rulers by overthrowing him. The

[20] Ibid., 173–4.

success of the coup-d'état would then be perceived as the sign that the new ruler had attained the heavenly mandate.

The Denial of Divine Retribution

As mentioned in §2, one way of rejecting divine retribution while safeguarding the notion of poetic justice is to claim that works, either good or evil, completes itself in returning blessings or disasters back to the doer. We have seen that in the earliest extant texts in both traditions, the idea that the good are rewarded and the evil punished (or: one reaps what one sows) is strongly advertised. As both traditions developed, however, such worldview is challenged.

In the Hebrew Bible, the cry against this cosmic injustice is first found in the later part of the prophetic corpus. For example, prophet Jeremiah's life was threatened because of the message that YHWH assigned to him to deliver, then he complained to YHWH in the first (Jer 11:18–12:6) of the five so-called "Confessions of Jeremiah":

> Jer 12:1
>
> מַדּוּעַ דֶּרֶךְ רְשָׁעִים צָלֵחָה שָׁלוּ כָּל־בֹּגְדֵי בָגֶד׃
>
> Why does the way of the wicked prosper? Why are the workers of treachery at ease? (TNK)

The complaints about the reverse of the presupposed mechanism of the good being rewarded and the wicked punished are also voiced out by other biblical figures (e.g., Hab. 1:4, 13b).

As the development of Old Testament traditions unfolded, the biblical sages went further, claiming not only that the mechanism some time works in the opposite way, but that in reality the good and the wicked would ultimate face the same destiny. Job, the just man on whom suffering suddenly befell simply because of a challenge that the accuser posed to God, exclaims:

> Job 9:22
>
> אַחַת הִיא עַל־כֵּן אָמַרְתִּי תָּם וְרָשָׁע הוּא מְכַלֶּה׃
>
> It [i.e. the destiny of mankind] is all one; therefore I say, he [i.e. God] destroys both the blameless and the wicked.
>
> Qohelet laments the same reality:
>
> Eccl 9:2
>
> הַכֹּל כַּאֲשֶׁר לַכֹּל מִקְרֶה אֶחָד לַצַּדִּיק וְלָרָשָׁע לַטּוֹב וְלַטָּהוֹר וְלַטָּמֵא וְלַזֹּבֵחַ
> וְלַאֲשֶׁר אֵינֶנּוּ זֹבֵחַ כַּטּוֹב כַּחֹטֶא הַנִּשְׁבָּע כַּאֲשֶׁר שְׁבוּעָה יָרֵא׃

> Everything is the same for everybody: the same lot for the just and the wicked, for the good, for the clean and the unclean, for the one who offers sacrifice and the one who does not. As it is for the good, so it is for the sinner; as it is for the one who takes an oath, so it is for the one who fears an oath. (NAB)

We observe the same phenomenon in Ancient Chinese Thought. Xunzi, who, like Mencius, also claims himself to be the true heir of Confucius and severely criticized Mencius, presents a completely different view. We can identify the logical development as follows.

Xunzi first limits the power of Heaven to operate only within the norm, namely rewarding the good and punishing the evil:

> 《荀子・天論第十七・一》
>
> 修道而不貳，則天不能禍。
>
> If you conform to the Way and are not of two minds, then Nature cannot bring about calamity. (*Xunzi* 17.1)[21]

Heaven is not capable of treating humankind at will, either rewarding the evil or afflicting the good, which is the complete opposite of how YHWH treated Job. On the contrary, the wellbeing or suffering of the people depends solely on their ruler:

> 《荀子・問堯第三十二・七》
>
> 天下不治……為惡得福，善者有殃
>
> Since the world is not well governed, … [t]hose who behaved wickedly gained riches, whereas those who were good came to ruin. (*Xunzi* 32.7)[22]

One of the important Daoist books, *Liezi*, discusses its view on the relation between human endeavour and destiny by way of a dialogue between the personified Endeavour and Destiny:

> 《列子・力命第六・一》
>
> 力曰：「壽夭、窮達、貴賤、貧富，我力之所能也。」

---

[21] John Knoblock, trans., *Xunzi II*, Library of Chinese Classics: Chinese-English (Changsha: Hunan People's Publishing House, 1999), 533.

[22] Ibid., 995, 997.

> [Endeavour] said, "I can make a man's life long or short, hard or easy, noble or base, and poor or wealthy." (*Liezi* 6.1)[23]

In response, Destiny lists four examples of both the good suffering undeserved afflictions and the wicked enjoying unmerited wellbeing. Then he says,

> 《列子・力命第六・一》
>
> 若是汝力之所能，柰何壽彼而夭此，窮聖而達逆，賤賢而貴愚，貧善而富惡邪？
>
> If you could do it, why did you make one live long but another short? Why did you put the sage in difficulty while allowing the villains to do whatever they pleased? Why did you make the talented base while the stupid noble? And why did you make the kind poor while the wicked rich? (*Liezi* 6.1)[24]

Therefore, Destiny concludes:

> 《列子・力命第六・一》
>
> 自壽自夭，自窮自達，自貴自賤，自富自貧
>
> It just happens that one lives long or dies young, undergoes hardship or attains one's goal at ease, is noble or base, is rich or poor. (*Liezi* 6.1)[25]

In other words, Lieze denies any causal relations between moral character of one's life and what befalls in one's life. The corollary of this position is the rejection of divine retribution.[26]

After an overview on the various positions regarding divine retribution in both traditions, we shall proceed to a preliminary analysis of the different theologies operating underneath them.

---

[23] Liang Xiaopeng, trans., *Lieze*, Library of Chinese Classics (Beijing: Zhonghua Book Company, 2005), 141.

[24] Ibid., 141.

[25] My own translation. Cf. 莊萬壽（譯注），《新譯列子讀本》三版，古籍今注新譯叢書，（臺北市：三民書局，2017年），頁204-205。

[26] 鄭基良，《善惡報應思想與故事》，（新北市：國立空中大學出版中心，2011年），頁27。

Towards a Comparative Theology

In this section, we shall first briefly look at the two major theories of theodicy corresponding to the two (affirmative and negative) positions on divine retribution in both traditions. At the end, a preliminary comparison of the theological developments in the two traditions shall emerge.

Theological Dialectics in the Hebrew Bible

The two positions on divine retribution in the Hebrew Bible reflect two attitudes towards knowing the divine moral order. The affirmation of divine retribution, mostly seen in the Deuteronomistic History and the earlier prophetic writings, has its basis on the knowledge of the moral standard as revealed at Sinai. In comparison, the negation of divine retribution, found in the later part of the prophetic corpus and Sapiential writings, points to the fact that the way of God is ultimately unknowable to humankind (cf. esp., Job 38:1–4). Therefore, in spite of their scepticism about divine retribution, these biblical writers at the end would still exhort their readers thus:

> Eccl 12:13b
>
> אֶת־הָאֱלֹהִים יְרָא וְאֶת־מִצְוֹתָיו שְׁמוֹר כִּי־זֶה כָּל־הָאָדָם׃
>
> Fear God, and keep his commandments; for that is the whole duty of everyone.

Theologies of Heaven in Ancient Chinese Thought

The two positions on whether heavens administer retribution in Ancient Chinese literature begs the question of the Ancient Chinese understanding of Heaven, particularly: whether Heaven was perceived as a personal deity. As we shall see, the development of the different understandings of Heaven correspond to that of the different positions on divine retribution in Ancient Chinese Thought.

In pre-Confucius Chinese Literature, e.g., the *Book of Poetry* and *Shoo-King*, Heaven is not only portrayed as personal,[27] but it plays the roles of: Dominator (or: Ruler), Revealer, Judge, Creator, and Sustainer.[28] This view on Heaven is inherited by Confucius and his followers (except Xunzi).[29] This

[27] 羅光，《中國哲學思想史——先秦篇》，羅光全書冊六，（台北市：臺灣學生，1996年），頁33–35。

[28] 傅佩榮，《儒道天論發微》，（臺北市：聯經，2010年），頁31–34。

[29] 馮友蘭，《中國哲學史（紀念版）》，增訂臺三版，（臺北市：臺灣商務，2015年），頁184。

theological framework is conducive to an understanding of Heaven as the administer of retribution.

On the contrary, Taoism sees Heaven (and Earth) only as part of the physical world, and hence it is neither personal nor transcendental.[30] Xunzi, albeit a Confucian, followed instead the Taoist understanding of Heaven.[31] Stripping off all theological characters from Heaven, this position can no longer see in it a divine arbitrator of justice. Thus, for Xunzi, the duty of imposing moral order lies with the gentleman (or the prince; 君子).[32]

Conclusion

This paper has presented retribution on two levels, societal and transcendental (divine). We have seen that both the Hebrew Bible and Ancient Chinese Literature share similar (opposing) observations. However, there are significant differences between the two traditions in both anthropological and theological senses. The study has shown that it is easy to identify similarities in two traditions on the surface, but it is more important to discern their fundamental differences (i.e. otherness).

[30] 勞思光，《新編中國哲學史（一）》，四版，（臺北市：三民，2014年），頁227。

[31] 胡適，《中國哲學史大綱：古代哲學史》，二版，（臺北市：臺灣商務，2008年），頁336。

[32] 傅佩榮，《儒道天論發微》，頁165。

EXPLORING THE SACRED IN DAILY LIFE THROUGH THE IGNATIAN EXAMINATION OF CONSCIENCE

Stephan Rothlin, SJ
(Macau Ricci Institute)

ABSTRACT

The paper applies the methodology of the Examination of Conscience as proposed by Ignatius Loyola in his Spiritual Exercises in order to explore some nuances of the term "Sacred." The systematic examination of daily experiences is proposed as a practical key which opens the mind to the significance of apparently insignificant issues of daily life. This perspective on taking so carefully the sequence of daily events and making gradually sense out of it naturally confirms the approach to history as developed by the French historians including Braudel and Chaunu who argued that historical developments need to be understood through the analysis of daily life features and statistics.

The focus on poems from different cultural settings which have been chosen to relate to the term of the "Sacred" may be seen through the lens of *The Spiritual Exercises*. Far from observing just an exterior drama or a kind of mental movie the examination of each day highlights the importance of the individual's conscience that helps him or her to recognize the daily events as a gift from God with a sense of gratitude or shame.

Along similar lines the selected poems are a privileged showcase of the Sacred in its daily expression which does not limit itself to the exclusively religious realm. The poems rather highlight the sacredness of the dignity of each individual evident in the apparent nonsense of everyday life. In such a perspective, Sacredness reveals itself ultimately as a partner not as often claimed an opponent of the European Enlightenment. The Sacred, thus, even without its specific religious rituals and symbols, enhances the attempt to convey a unique dignity with its related inalienable human rights.

A PHILOSOPHICAL METHODOLOGY

The paper aims to resonate the critical analysis of the German philosopher Hermann Lübbe (Lübbe 1985) concerning the term religion after the Enlightenment. Lübbe argues that religion and the Enlightenment ("Aufklärung") may have been enemies in the past; however, this is not the case at the present time. Lübbe argues that the freedom of our culture would not be justified and secured without religion. Hence both Science and Religion need to fight against the common cultural and political threats. Religion, according to Lübbe, constitutes one of the key components of modern culture. Along the same lines this essay argues that religion may also play a decisive role in China within the framework of its economic development, despite its indifference and even skepticism to religious influence. How does religion, the Sacred, which appears to be fading from a secular society, take root? This essay proposes a proven method before the dawn of the Enlightenment, a child of the renaissance so to speak namely the so called "General Examination of Conscience" of *The Spiritual Exercises of Saint Ignatius Loyola* (1491–1556). In his book, *The Spiritual Exercises*, Ignatius Loyola focuses on helpful hints from the Bible and from specific meditations to find the will of God. In order to properly discern the will of God the different steps of the Examination of Conscience allow the retreatant to recognize the gifts of God, to become aware of sins in order to get rid of them and then, from the hour of rising to undertake the present examen and "to ask an account of my soul" (Ganss 1992, 38, no. 43). This essay proposes then to take poems from different cultures and contexts in order to seek for resonances in the text for a meaning of the Sacred which is deeply embedded in the daily reality and, in some sense, bringing the daily reality to its completion, as indicated in a daily scrutiny along the lines of Loyola's "General Examination of Conscience."

Ignatius Loyola has outlined the twofold purpose of the Examination of Conscience in the book of *The Spiritual Exercises*: "to purify oneself, and to make a better confession" (Ganss 1992, 35, no. 32): Thoughts (33–37), Words (38–41) and Deeds (42). The section concludes with a five-point summary of the method for making the General Examination of Conscience (no. 43):

1. The First Point is to give thanks to God our Lord for the benefits I have received.
2. The Second is to ask grace to know my sins and rid myself of them.
3. The Third is to ask an account of my soul from the hour of rising to the present examen, hour by hour or period by period; first as to thoughts, then words, then deeds, in the same order as was given for the particular examination.
4. The Fourth is to ask pardon of God our Lord for my faults.
5. The Fifth is to resolve, with his grace, to amend them. Close with an Our Father.

It may be worth underlining that the first point underlines the attitude of gratitude for all the benefits and talents received from "God our Lord." It is certainly one sided to reduce the examination of conscience to an exclusive preoccupation with one's own sins. It seems a simple but quite effective way to explore the Sacred embedded in daily life by inspiring each one to recognize its presence with gratitude, recognizing also her or his own failures and sin with the goal to improve our thoughts, words and deeds.

Recognizing the dynamics of the Examination of Conscience through poems: the example of Gerard Manley Hopkins (1844–1889) and Octavio Paz (1914–1998)

A brief excursion into the world of two poems may highlight the swinging between the act of thanksgiving as suggested in the examination of conscience, the awareness of sin and the resolve, with divine grace. One of Hopkins' most famous poems is "God's Grandeur" which at the beginning of the poem clearly resonates the first point of the Ignatian Examen by focusing on giving thanks to God for the benefits which start and end with the acknowledgement of God's Grandeur. However already the second phrase articulates the precariousness of the Grandeur of God when it states: "[It] gathers to a greatness, like the ooze of oil. Crushed." In the context of the framework of the examen and the poet's spiritual background we may discover a symbolism of the sin which crushes the greatness of God. It articulates also the drama that men and women rarely recognize this greatness and Grandeur: "Why do men then now not reck his rod? Generations have trod, have trod, have trod; and all is seared with trade; bleared, smeared with toil."

How to get out of this world "bleared, smeared with toil"? The key turning point which some describe with the word "inscape" appears in the second part of the poem where it states: "And for all this, nature is never spent; There lives the dearest freshness deep down things." Despite or even in midst of our indifference there is the experience of "dearest freshness" underneath. From a theological perspective the breakthrough comes in recognizing the gift and greatness of God by being wholly overtaken by the Holy Spirit: "Because the Holy Ghost over the bent/World broods with warm breast and with ah! Bright wings."

The life of Gerard Manley Hopkins could be seen superficially as a complete failure as he never quite seemed to succeed in his subsequent assignments as a priest of the Society of Jesus in slum parishes in England. He regarded himself as a failure and his sermons where perceived as stodgy and dull. In 1883 he wrote "I am always jaded, I cannot tell why, and I suffer from recurring fits of nervous prostration." In 1884 he was sent to the University College of Dublin as a professor of classics. His main work was to sit and mark examination papers. It is sometimes suggested that his profound sense of failure and sadness could be related to the dichotomy in his celibate life between the "flesh" implying sensual desires and the "Spirit" which includes his vow of chastity as a constant resolve to reject sensual pleasures. In this context, the poem "God's Grandeur" could be seen as a breakthrough in overcoming this dichotomy: God's Grandeur is so deeply embedded in his creation, that indeed "nature is never spent" no matter how destructive the reality of sin may pretend to be the final word.

The amazing richness of a day with its swinging between greatness and being crushed can be observed in the monumental poem of the Mexican poet Octavio Paz entitled *Piedra de Sol* ("Sun Stone" of the ancient Aztecan culture), which starts also with a broad description of nature, revealed in "horas de luz" ("hours of light"). The walking through nature shifts to the different aspects of promiscuous human love with "corredores sin fin de la memoria" ("endless corridors of memory"), relating to a multiplicity of relationships as the memory sometimes fades remembering "Laura, Melusine, Persephone, Phyllis, Carmen, Maria…." The climax is the description of human love as a battle which is transforming the world. However as the poem meanders through human misery and its perversions, the Sacred is not absent: "Y el grito en la tarde del Viernes" ("And the cry in the late Friday afternoon") is the cry of the abandoned Christ who is crying on the cross. Also surprisingly in midst of different experiences of promiscuous and sometimes perverse human love comes a panegyric for chastity: "Better the chastity/invisible flower/which bounces in deep silence,/ the diamond of the Saints" which let the masks of the world fall down. "Canta la soledad in su corolla…. y en su centro, vibrante transparencia, lo que llamamos Dios, el ser sin nombre,/se contempla en la nada, el ser sin rostro,/emerge de si mismo, sol de soles,/plenitud de presencias y de nombres" ("The solitude sings in its crown…. And in its Center what we call God, vibrant transparency the being without name, emerges out of itself, the sun of the suns, plenitude of presence and names").

The focus on poems from different cultural settings which have been chosen to relate to the term of the "Sacred" is on the description of ordinary and extraordinary events which are daily recurring while somehow capturing the attention of the poet. Far from staging just an exterior drama or a kind of mental movie, the examination of a day highlights the importance of the conscience of the individual which helps him or her to recognize daily events as a gift from God with a sense of gratitude or shame. In the midst of the cries, in the midst of crime surprisingly the meaning of the invisible flower emerges: "chastity," apparently so much at loggerheads with the whole context of the poem which explores also extensively the ups and downs of human love. However, exactly in this context chastity as the symbol of Sacredness is indeed "the difficult diamond of the Saints which filters the desires," puts love and all the hours of human life in front of "the being without name … the sun of the suns."

The poems are a privileged showcase of the Sacred in its daily expressions which does not limit itself to the exclusively religious realm. The poems rather highlight the sacredness of the dignity of each individual in midst of daily experiences. Sacredness reveals itself ultimately as a partner not as often claimed an opponent of the Enlightenment, with its focus on the overriding importance of reason.

The Sacred, thus, even without its specific religious rituals and symbols, enhances the attempt to convey a unique dignity with its related inalienable human rights. Religious rites are not just confined to a separate detached world but deeply penetrate human reality. As in Pierre Teilhard de Chardin's famous remark concerning the "epi-phany" of Jesus Christ, recognized by him as a "dia-phany," the whole of reality is penetrated with the light of Jesus Christ not somewhat imposed from above.

A key point is a proper understanding of the term "chastity" as the whole context disclosed in both poems. Such an understanding of "chastity" does not allow us to restrict the term to a vow of celibacy within a religious form of life. In fact, a narrow reference to religious persons, for example, in the relationship of the medieval theologian Abélard with Héloise is hard to square with such an interpretation, as it indicates the breaking of a vow. Embracing the broad context of Paz's "Sun Stone," evoking its Aztecan origins among a Nahuati-speaking people that founded the Mexican empire, later conquered by Cortes in 1519, would suggest a broader social reading. In that context "chastity," arguably, contrasts with the collective destructive side of the "*Conquista*," which may be perceived as a rape and a destruction of culture. It signifies a fusion with the local culture embraced in an attitude of profound respect and love. In this sense some Saints seem to have succeeded in cutting the diamond which is not extracted violently from the culture in an act of exploitation that ultimately destroys it, but refers to the Sacred embedded in the complexity of daily life which completes humanity, thus revealing daily life as a fully vibrant "Sun Stone."

Final Remark: The Perspective of Conscience

This short exposition of two poems informed by the Ignatian Spiritual Exercises may also help to grasp how the element of conscience comes into play. In view of a fresh definition of "chastity" in the poem of Octavio Paz, discernment may recognize the ability of one's conscience to reach a "chaste" view of creation as God's gift and beauty while also being able to recognize better the reality of sin revealed in Hopkins' image of being "shod" or cut off from the "Sun Stone." The paper aimed to gather some arguments which emphasize how poems may give a sense of the Sacred in daily life and how the Sacred may be perceived as embedded in daily life. Moreover the Ignatian Examen offered a privileged entry door, so to speak, into exploring the amazing richness of life in the face of God and revealing a new dimension of "chastity" in its social and cosmic dimension as the ultimate accomplishment, overcoming different forms of predatory behavior and reconnecting to the pure and respectful love which cannot be separated from the term dignity with its specific connotation of respect of human rights.

REFERENCES

Ganss, G. E. *The Spiritual Exercises of Saint Ignatius*. A Translation and Commentary. 2nd Indian edition. Anand, Gujarat: Gujarat Sahitya Prakash, 1992.

Hopkins, G. M. *The Complete Poems. With Selected Prose*. London: Harper Collins, 1996.

Lübbe, H. *Religion nach der Aufklärung*. Graz; Vienna; Cologne: Styria, 1986.

Paz, O. *Gedichte. Spanisch und deutsch*. Frankfurt a.M: Suhrkamp, 1977.

CPSIA information can be obtained
at www.ICGtesting.com
Printed in the USA
BVHW050941060223
657963BV00009B/627

9 789996 594083